Mani-rimdu, Sherpa Dance-Drama

MANI-RIMDU

Sherpa Dance-Drama

LUTHER G. JERSTAD

University of Washington Press

SEATTLE AND LONDON

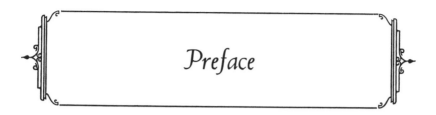

Preface

I FIRST became aware of the Sherpas as a boy through the literature of adventure. The dearth of material on Nepalese, Tibetan, and Sherpa theater aroused my interest, and in 1963 as a member of the American Mount Everest Expedition, I had an opportunity to begin this study of the Sherpas. Grants from the National Geographic Society and the University of Washington Far Eastern and Russian Institute permitted me to return to Nepal during the 1965-66 academic year to complete my research among the Sherpas. Grants from the Explorers Club, and from the Asian Literature Program of the Asia Society, New York, supported final preparation of the manuscript. I wish to express my sincere thanks to the above-mentioned organizations, without whose aid this project could not have been completed.

I also wish to express my appreciation to Turrell V. Wylie, Professor of Asian Languages and Literature, University of Washington, Horace W. Robinson, Director of the University Theatre, University of Oregon, and many others who offered me advice and spent hours reading and correcting this manuscript. In addition, my thanks go to the Abbot of Tengpoche, Nima Tenzing, and numerous Buddhist monks for their assistance. These Sherpas listened patiently to my curious questions and endeavored to answer all queries to the best of their ability.

The material presented in this study was obtained from several sources. Very little concerning Mani-rimdu is contained in books or monographs. The majority of the descriptive information concerning the dances results from my personal experience in the Sherpa villages and monasteries. I have witnessed the festival of Mani-rimdu at both Tengpoche and Thami, and have seen isolated dances from the festival at other monasteries and gombas, performed especially for the purpose of this study. Much of the information contained in this work was obtained from my personal contacts and interviews with Tibetan refugees, Sherpa laymen, the Abbot of Tengpoche, and monks from the Thami and Tengpoche monasteries.

L. G. J.

Portland, Oregon
April, 1969

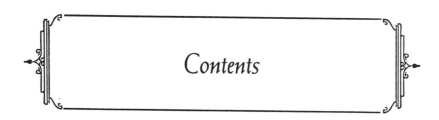

Contents

Illustrations

PHOTOGRAPHS

ix

--⋅◦⊰{ Illustrations }⊱◦⋅--

FIGURES

Introduction

THIS book describes and analyzes a hitherto obscure and almost unknown form of theater among the Sherpas of Nepal. It is a dance-drama known as Mani-rimdu, which is performed within the Buddhist monasteries of this remote hill tribe. The only scholar to investigate this theatrical festival previously was the anthropologist Christoph von Fürer-Haimendorf. His primary concern, however, was with village and social structures within the Sherpa society. He cursorily lists the names of dances, but makes no attempt to analyze them fully, either from a projected religious point of view or from an artistic standpoint. Other writers have briefly mentioned the Sherpa theater, but they were primarily travelers who noted their adventures, and their findings may be admitted only with extreme caution.

I do not explore every aspect of the Mani-rimdu festival. For instance, the musical accompaniment and dance steps are extensions of tantric (mystic) Buddhist forms of worship, and have their origin in Tibetan folk dances and music. Very little is known about them, but when they could be identified, their significance to the dance-drama has been included. The Sherpa religious leaders were unable to clarify the precise meanings of the music or the dance steps; their practice has become so conventionalized and traditionalized that the dancers themselves have little knowledge of their purpose. This study focuses primarily upon the religious and historical message conveyed by the dances of Mani-rimdu. The historical facts concerning the development of this form of theater in Nepal and Tibet are also included. Two of the thirteen acts that comprise the festival of Mani-rimdu are purely humorous, and they are explained and analyzed from the point of view of comedy, and from cultural contexts which further delineate their nature.

The festival of Mani-rimdu is communicated primarily through the medium of dance. Only one act contains dialogue, which is spoken from a brief scenario. The other acts are related to the audience through a highly symbolic language of gesture, costume, and mask, and by reference to the Tibetan Buddhist pantheon.

The Sherpas are Tibetan by culture, religion, ethnic origin, and language. They live in the northeastern section of Nepal along the southern foothills of the Himalayan Mountains. Until recently very little was known of these Buddhist hill people for Nepal was practically sealed off from foreigners until the fifth decade of the twentieth century. Even though few Westerners had been to the Sherpa villages, these highlanders had gained an international reputation. Westerners on mountaineering expeditions to the Himalayan peaks had recognized their sturdy nature, friendliness, and loyalty. Serving as high-altitude porters and cooks and as lowland guides, the Sherpas were written about and praised around hearths and mountain cabins in Europe and America. During the 1920's and 1930's they distinguished themselves with many gallant attempts to scale Mount Everest, and other peaks, with Western mountaineers. The name "Sherpa" occupied the headlines of the world when Sir Edmund Hillary and the Sherpa Tenzing Norgay scaled Mount Everest on the eve of Queen Elizabeth II's coronation in 1953.

The Sherpas and the country of Nepal have more recently become internationally important because of the presence of the Chinese Communists in Tibet. In 1950 Chinese armies invaded the independent country of Tibet with the intention of annexing it to the Chinese empire. British and Indian diplomats declined to support Tibet in the United Nations. The Chinese proceeded to demolish the social structure, religious foundation, ethnic culture, and political institutions of Tibet. The Mahāyāna form of Buddhism, together with 75 per cent of the religious edifices in Tibet, has been destroyed since that time.

Tibet recedes further behind the "bamboo curtain" with each passing day of occupancy. Recent estimates of the Dalai Lama claim that one million people (one-sixth of the Tibetan population) have been pressed into forced labor gangs in China, been exiled from the country, escaped from their homeland, or been executed. If the actions of the Chinese continue at their present rate, Tibet may cease to exist as a distinct cultural and ethnic entity within the next two decades.

The Sherpas of Nepal are one of the few existing remnants of Tibetan culture. They live in the environmental conditions of Tibetans, among mountains, winds, loneliness, and remoteness. The Mahāyāna faith of their ethnic parents thrives vigorously in the Sherpa villages. This is one reason why the Sherpas have become the object of much scholarly investigation in the last decade. The Tibetologist, David Snellgrove, has spent several years studying the nature of Tibetan Buddhism, and for a few months he lived among the Sherpas of Nepal. Fürer-Haimendorf has primarily focused his examinations upon the Sherpas, but he also gathers information about Tibet, for hundreds of Tibetan immigrants reside within the Sherpa communities. In 1964 the Nepalese government, under pressure from the Chinese, declared a twenty-five-mile restricted zone south of the Himalayan crest, into which no Westerner is allowed to travel. The Sherpas themselves are not generally allowed to trade with their Tibetan neighbors, and no expeditions are permitted to scale mountains within the twenty-five-mile restricted area. It is a distinct possibility that these Nepalese hill people will experience further restrictions.

The Sherpas, however, are not studied for the sole purpose of recording a waning Tibetan culture. They are a distinct cultural entity in their own right. In the course of this investigation numerous dissimilarities will be noted between the Tibetans and the Sherpas. The latter have been removed from their ancestral home for over three hundred years, and numerous peculiar traits have manifested themselves in the Sherpa way of life. Their religion and superstitious beliefs have been modified. Their theater has changed appreciably from its progenitor in Tibet. Monastic authorities in Nepal have no voice in political matters, while in Tibet the Dalai Lama was both the spiritual and temporal ruler prior to the Chinese aggression. The Sherpas welcome almost any stranger who happens upon their villages. The Tibetans, on the other hand, traditionally loved isolationism, and expressed misgivings about outsiders.

One of my aims is to elucidate the Buddhist propensity toward drama prior to the Christian era. The Mahāyāna tradition cherished and practiced artistic endeavors, but the Theravāda denounced them. Eventually the two factions totally split asunder, and the Mahāyāna sect began to proselytize in nearby Asian countries. One of the areas in which missionaries sought new converts was Tibet. Indian missionaries carried with them artistic and dramatic principles, as well as strictly religious doctrines. The ultimate result was the founding of a genre of Tibetan theater known as Lha-mo. Animistic rites and Tibetan folklore were incorporated into this new endeavor, which was designed to teach the populace about the acts of Buddhist saints while simultaneously entertaining the audience. One of the ancient forms of folk culture discovered by Buddhist missionaries was a dance-rite, 'Cham, which had its origin in primitive rite and magic. Buddhism altered the form, infused doctrinal codes into it, and couched the result in highly symbolic language. The ensuing form of 'Cham was later altered again when it entered the Khumbu Valley of Nepal. Mani-rimdu is derived from this Tibetan form of theatrical presentation. There are, however, well-defined dissimilarities between Mani-rimdu and the more ritualistic 'Cham.

Chapter I presents the doctrinal foundation of Buddhism

from its beginnings in India through its transfer to Tibet and
Nepal. It examines the principles of that religion which directly
apply to this discussion. The next chapter describes the Sherpas
themselves—their customs, beliefs, villages, environment, and religious institutions that are relevant to the study. A historic over-
view of 'Cham in Tibet, both the animistic and the Buddhist
versions, is included in Chapter III. The fourth chapter deals
specifically with the outdoor theater in which Mani-rimdu is
produced in the Buddhist communities. The festival is a monastic production, and therefore the monastery, the environmental
setting of the monastery, and the aesthetic appreciation of the
dances are included in that chapter. Background material relevant to Mani-rimdu and the description of the first day of the
festival are included in Chapter V. The actual dances—expla-
nations of costumes, characters, religious significance, music,
chanting, and audience participation—are delineated and analyzed in Chapter VI.

Most italicized words are defined or described in the glossary.
Some of these words have been spelled in Sanskrit, and some in
Tibetan. I chose to utilize the language in which certain gods,
concepts, or objects are more universally known to Sherpas and
to Western scholars. *Ḍākinī*, for example, is the Sanskrit appellation for a specific genre of Buddhist demi-goddesses. The
Sherpas use this term as frequently as the Tibetan word
Mkha'-'gro-ma. Where confusion might arise over terms, they
appear in this manner: Skt. *Ḍākinī*, Tib. *Mkha'-'gro-ma*. In a
few instances the Tibetan orthographic spelling is used as well as
the phonetic spelling in order to render the text more readable.
The words then appear as *tor-ma* (phonetic), followed by the
classical spelling (Tib. *gtor-ma*). This method is used to dispel
any misunderstanding or misinterpretation of terms by the
Buddhist or Tibetan scholar. In most cases the English equivalent of a term appears first, and the Tibetan orthographic
rendering follows in parentheses immediately after the word, for
example, the Five Sisters of Long Life (Tib. *Tshe-ring mched-
lnga*). The system of Tibetan spelling used in this study corre-

sponds to that set down by Turrell V. Wylie in "A Standard System of Tibetan Transcription," *Harvard Journal of Asiatic Studies,* XXII (December, 1959), 261-67.

Many quotations from Sherpa Buddhist monks included in this text were stated orally to me in Nepali. If the content of these remarks is erroneous, it is due to my translation and not to the Sherpa informant. Several translations are from Tibetan. They were inscribed on paper by the monk, and later translated by Professor Wylie, or by Rimshi L. Surkhang, both living in Seattle, Washington. My Sherpa companion also orally translated many Tibetan conversations into Nepali or English.

A final note of clarification concerning the spelling of Tengpoche monastery is in order. This name appears on all maps as either "Thyangboche" or "Thangboche." The correct phonetic spelling is Teng-po-che (Tib. Steng-che-dgon). It has been spelled without hyphens in this manuscript as "Tengpoche," in order to aid the reader.

Mani-rimdu, Sherpa Dance-Drama

I. The Religion of the Sherpas

DWELLING HIGH in the southern foothills of the Himalayan Mountains in Nepal is a tribe of Tibetan descendants known as Sherpas. Numbering only about four thousand, the Sherpas speak Tibetan as well as a household language of Tibeto-Burmese origin called Sherpa. Their religion, Buddhism, is derived from Tibet, and most of their cultural ties are with this northern neighbor. Once each year Sherpa lamas[1] present a dramatic dance festival known as Mani-rimdu. It instructs the populace about Buddhism while simultaneously entertaining them. Mani-rimdu is a form of the 'Cham genre of theater from Tibet. This genre consists of festival dances that symbolically eradicate an ancient Tibetan religion called Bon, by depicting the supremacy of Buddhism over that cult.

'Cham, as a genre of drama, is not unique, nor is it indigenous to the Sherpas. James Frazer's *The Golden Bough*,[2] Loomis

[1] The word "lama" is a generic term applied incorrectly to all Buddhist monks in Tibet and Nepal. It is a Tibetan word which means "Superior One" and, strictly speaking, it should be used only for monks considered to be incarnations. See L. Austine Waddell, *The Buddhism of Tibet or Lamaism* (Cambridge: W. Heffner and Sons, 1894), p. 28.

[2] James George Frazer, *The Golden Bough: A Study in Magic and Religion* (New York: Macmillan, 1911).

3

Havemeyer's *The Drama of Savage Peoples,*[3] and other publications have illustrated numerous such tribes and their forms
of dance, drama, ritual, and entertainment. Semantic disputes
have raged over the term "drama" in connection with such rites,
mainly because of ambiguous terminology. It is not the intention here either to affirm or to refute the various concepts of
primitive theater, for merely affixing an appellation does little to
define what occurs within such performances. The aim is to
illustrate one type of festival and to illuminate its main purposes: the renunciation of the ancient religion of Bon; the de-
piction of the displacement of Bon by Buddhism; and the
strengthening of the Sherpas' beliefs in Buddhism.

All cultures have produced, or are still producing, dances and
stories that inform the people about the unseen forces around
them. The Christian church in medieval Europe performed passion, miracle, and mystery plays, complete with angels and saints.
Laymen witnessed the enactment of the Easter story and beheld
Christ rising from the tomb. They heard God direct Abraham
to sacrifice his son Isaac, and they witnessed the good which
came to a man who obeyed the Lord's commands. The tortures
of Hell were vividly painted and audibly reported by actors who
experienced them, and the Devil appeared on stage to enforce
the fears of everlasting damnation. Virtue and Vice were presented in allegorical representations, as religion was preached to
the populace in a visual and entertaining form.

American Indians performed dances in order to understand
and to enter into the unseen forces about them long before
Western man had heard about the New World. Propitiation of
the spirits surrounding these Indians was imperative if life were
to continue. Australian bush tribes sought to constrain spirits
and bring them under the tribe's control through the use of ritual dances and sacrifices. F. M. Cornford[4] and Arthur Haigh[5] re-

[3] Loomis Havemeyer, *The Drama of Savage Peoples* (New Haven: Yale
University Press, 1916).

[4] Francis MacDonald Cornford, *The Origin of Attic Comedy* (Garden
City, N.Y.: Doubleday, 1961).

4

port such primitive dances and rites in pre-fifth-century B.C. Greek culture. In the present day tribal groups in the Philippine Islands perform exorcismic rites to control the forces around them.

One thing is certain in all religious dance or drama rituals: an unseen force pervades life, whether it be a Christian God, a Hindu Brahma, or an Indian totem. It may control life totally or in varying lesser degrees. One of the common methods of dealing with that force was the use of dances, in which an actor assumed the person of the deity or force, paraphrasing the power and explaining it in terms comprehensible to the viewers. All dances of this nature seek to objectify this force, thereby lessening its power. The dance allows man to approach the deity (spiritual, ethereal force) and to worship or praise it on his own terms. By so doing, the primitive man could partially exercise a control over, or at best effect an explanation of, the god. Then he could propitiate it by petition or supplication or sacrifice. "In some primitive cultures," Havemeyer states, "these [dance-drama] rites were of the utmost importance for through them men sought relations with the imaginary environments of ghosts and spirits and attempted to keep them on their side in the struggle for existence."[6]

In the Sherpa culture this struggle is to gain a better incarnation in the next life. The Sherpas, however, cannot be considered primitive. Their basic beliefs lie in the doctrines of Tibetan Buddhism, and the drama serves to portray the dangers of not following the proper path to enlightenment. The main function of Sherpa performances, in religious contexts, is the proselytization of Buddhism over Bon. Since this religion is mentioned frequently in this text, the reader should understand at least the basis of the creed, and perceive how Buddhist dramas came to equate Bonism with all that is evil. Bon is the name

[5] Arthur Elam Haigh, *The Attic Theatre: A Description of the Stage and Theatre of the Athenians and the Dramatic Performances of Athens* (Oxford: The Clarendon Press, 1907).

[6] Havemeyer, *Drama of Savage Peoples*, p. 6.

of the religion, and the terms "Bon-po" and "Bonists" refer to those who practice that cult. "Bonism" is an adjectival noun used synonymously with Bon.

The origin of the word "Bon" is lost in the past, but Helmut Hoffmann states that, "in all probability it once referred to the conjuring of the gods by magic formulas." Hoffmann continues, "The original Bön religion was the national Tibetan form of that old animist-shamanist religion which at one time was widespread not only in Siberia but throughout the whole of Inner Asia, East and West Turkestan, Mongolia, Manchuria, the Tibetan plateaux and even China."[7] Animism holds that souls are attached to all things, either as dwellers or as the driving force of that thing. Various spirits inhabit such natural phenomena as lightning, clouds, water, birds, fish, animals, and trees. Such beliefs have been found in New Zealand, Africa, Haiti, and among the American Indians, besides those areas listed above. Many of these cults are extinct, but a few survive to the present day, one of them in Nepal and Tibet. Many aspects of this religion will be noted in the actual performance of Mani-rimdu in Chapter VI.

Not unlike other animistic religions of the world, which embrace spirits, ghouls, gods, demons, and animals, Bonism is based upon nature worship. In Tibet and Nepal it is a completely nature-rooted and nature-dominated religious idea revolving around the forces and power of the landscape. Its precise form in pre-Buddhist Tibet is difficult to decipher because Bon texts, which are purportedly very old, have a gloss of Buddhism in them. This is, of course, understandable, since no written language existed in Tibet until Buddhism was introduced in the seventh century.[8]

According to Bonists, their religion originated in Shangshung, a country to the west of Tibet which was absorbed into

[7] Helmut Hoffmann, *The Religions of Tibet,* trans. Edward Fitzgerald (New York: Macmillan, 1961), pp. 14-15.
[8] *Ibid.*

6

the Tibetan empire in the eighth century.[9] One of the few
sources of Tibetan history and Bonism predating Buddhism is
an epic poem, the "Kesar Legend." Kesar was the king of a
country called "Ling," near western China, and the narrative
depicts many of the more brutal aspects of Bonism.

Ancient Bonists believed that the world was divided into
three parts: heaven, air, and earth. These three spheres were in-
habited by various spirits, who brought disaster, plagues, and
sickness when they were annoyed by human beings. The following expiatory poem from the Bon-pos was found by B. Laufer:

> The kLu kings are in all streams,
> The gNyan kings are in trees and stones,
> The Masters of the Earth are in the five kinds
>   of earth:
> There, it is said, are the Masters of the Earth,
>   the kLu and the gNyan.
> What kind of company is theirs?
> Scorpions with long stings,
> Ants with notched waists,
> Golden frogs,
> Turquoise-coloured tadpoles,
> Mussel-white butterflies
> These are their company.[10]

Hearth gods, tent gods, field gods, house gods, and man gods
continually plagued Tibetans and gave rise to shamanist priests
who performed purification and expiatory rites in order that life
might continue. In the early Tibetan religion there were many
animal sacrifices, mainly of sheep, monkeys, and dogs, but it is
commonly held that on special occasions larger animals were sacrificed as well.[11] Hoffmann quotes the Bon text "gZermyig" to
illustrate the brutality of Bonism, which probably practiced
human sacrifice.

[9] Charles Bell, *The Religion of Tibet* (Oxford: The Clarendon Press, 1931), p. 17.
[10] Hoffmann, *Religions of Tibet*, pp. 17, 18.
[11] See Waddell, *The Buddhism of Tibet*, pp. 517-18.

In order to bring about the recovery of a sick prince, one of his subjects had to be sacrificed to propitiate the demon:

"The soothsayer seized the man by the feet whilst the Bön-po took his hands. The black Han-dha then cut open the life orifice and tore out the heart. The two, the soothsayer and the Bön-po, then scattered the blood and flesh of the victim to the four corners of heaven."[12]

This fear-inspired religion was deeply imbedded in the Tibetan people. But in India there was a thriving new religion which was to change the course of history in Tibet and Nepal. Buddhism had its origin in a historic personality, Siddhartha Gautama, born of noble parentage, circa 563 B.C., in Lumbini (now known as Rummindei) in southern Nepal. His father was a wealthy landowner and ruler of large estates in the Indian countryside. Gautama is often referred to as Prince Siddhartha, the Śākya Sage, the Tathagatha, Śākyamuni, the Enlightened One, the Lord Buddha, or simply the Buddha. In Sanskrit, "Buddhi" means "intellect" and "Buddha" generally denotes an "enlightened one."

The Buddha lived in an age of great unrest and worldly dissatisfaction. Seeking enlightenment and release from pain and death, he became a disciple of one of the numerous gurus (teachers) and subjected himself to starvation, asceticism, and yogism in his search for truth. His legendary life can be found in the "Jātaka Tales," and in the *Lalitavistara sutra*, immortalized by Edwin Arnold's *The Light of Asia*.[13] Rejecting Indian philosophical and religious systems, the Prince embarked on his own to discover release from life's miseries. He viewed enlightenment as a product of man's own efforts, and he negated the Brahmanical reliance upon supernatural beings. Gods were incapable of aiding man, he believed, for no matter how many sacrifices he offered or how many prayers he chanted, each man grew old and died. Misery, pain, and disease plagued men

[12] Hoffmann, *Religions of Tibet*, p. 22.
[13] Edwin Arnold, *The Light of Asia; or, the Great Renunciation: Being the Life and Teaching of Gautama, Prince of India and Founder of Buddhism* (London: W. Heffner and Sons, 1883).

throughout life. Using the prevalent Indian philosophies of transmigration, karma, and Nirvana, the Śākya Sage set out to find a middle path between extreme hedonism and strict asceticism. He deplored the mystic idea of starvation and hardship as predicating spiritual relevation, for the new enlightenment of Prince Siddhartha was to be in the mind, not in the soul (*atman*). He discarded the idea that sacrifices are necessary to spiritual revelation, and placed all attention upon the individual and his own spirit.

Departing from all teachings and standard philosophies, the Buddha focused his efforts upon the problem of enlightenment. Finally, while resting under a sal tree, he obtained his goal after years of travail. Ananda Coomaraswamy offers a picture of the Buddha's final enlightenment. As he entered the grove of trees, the Buddha said, "Though my skin and my nerves and my bones should waste away and my life blood dry, I will not leave this seat until I have attained supreme enlightenment."[14] A host of demons sought to tempt the Prince, but he remained steadfast. Coomaraswamy continues:

> The Bodhisattva sank into ever deeper and deeper thought. In the first watch of the night he reached the knowledge of Former States of being, in the middle watch he obtained the heavenly eye of Omniscient Vision, and in the third watch he grasped the perfect understanding of the Chain of Causation which is the Origin of Evil, and thus at break of day he attained to Perfect Enlightenment. . . .
>
> Innumerable wonders were manifest at this supreme hour. The earth quaked six times and the whole universe was illuminated by the supernatural splendour of the sixfold rays that proceeded from the body of the seated Buddha. Resentment faded from the hearts of all men, and all lack was supplied, the sick were healed, the chains of hell were loosed, and every creature of whatsoever sort found rest and peace.[15]

Whether one chooses to believe this legendary story or not,

[14] E. A. Burtt (ed.), *Teachings of the Compassionate Buddha* (New York: Mentor Books, 1955), p. 30.
[15] Ananda K. Coomaraswamy, *Buddha and the Gospel of Buddhism* (London: George C. Harrap, 1916), p. 32.

there was a man named Prince Siddhartha who founded a new philosophy among the Indians, and who, after years of searching, claimed to have found the truth while meditating beneath a sal tree.

Confident of his new awareness, the Buddha preached his first sermon, which revealed his insight and established his doctrine. The Four Noble Truths separated his doctrine from all others. The fourth Noble Truth is the Eight-fold Path, which shows men the way out of the maze of suffering and ignorance. Since these tenets will reappear, they are included here for future reference:

1. Now this, monks, is the noble truth of pain: birth is painful, old age is painful, sickness is painful, death is painful, sorrow, lamentation, dejection, and despair are painful. Contact with unpleasant things is painful. . . .

2. Now this, monks, is the noble truth of the cause of pain: the craving, which tends to rebirth, combined with pleasure and lust, finding pleasure here and there; namely, the craving for passion, the craving for existence, the craving for non-existence.

3. Now this, monks, is the noble truth of the cessation of pain, the cessation without a remainder of craving, the abandonment, forsaking, release, nonattachment.

4. Now this, monks, is the noble truth of the way that leads to the cessation of pain: this is the noble Eightfold Way; namely, right views, right intention, right speech, right action, right livelihood, right effort, right mindfulness, right concentration.

This is the noble truth of pain: Thus, monks, among doctrines unheard before, in me sight and knowledge arose, wisdom arose, knowledge arose, light arose.[16]

The Buddha provided the basis for a rational intellectual approach to the problem of release or enlightenment. Unlike Christianity, Buddhism resembles an organic substance, forever in a state of flux and change. The religion of the Buddha does

[16] F. Max Müller (ed.), "Ākankheyya Sutra," *Sacred Books of the East* (Oxford: The Clarendon Press, 1910), XI, 208-9. Also see Coomaraswamy, *Buddha and the Gospel of Buddhism*, p. 35.

not remain constant through the ages, for it is not "delivered" from the hand of an anthropomorphic, supernatural being.

Perhaps the most outstanding aspect of the Buddha's doctrine was the denial of the soul, the theory of *anātman* (non-soul). In this theory all matter is in a state of flux, and nothing proceeds from a single cause. The five elements—earth, water, fire, air, and ether—combine in various associations to produce man, but his composition is only different in outward form from that of a stone or an animal. All phenomena are relationships of the same elements; therefore, to the Buddha, it was absurd to insist that man alone could claim a soul or super-entity. All things are changeable, and as old things decay and disintegrate the elements fashion one more figure anew. This is a complicated process based upon Buddhist logic and karmic connections from past experiences, but it illustrates one of the great differences between the Christian concept of the soul and the Buddhist notion of non-soul. The Christian concept of soul admits of a corporeal entity which has value greater than any other object of the senses. Soul is ego substance, "a noumenal conception of things, i.e., the conception of particulars as having something absolute in them."[17] In Buddhism no particulars exist except in the mind. The Law of Karma, which is the Buddhist term for causation, dictates the destiny of existence. Men cannot change their lives on this earth, because actions in their previous existences have determined the course of the present life. As the bending of a twig affects the entire structure of a tree, so in Buddhism does a small deed permanently affect a man's next incarnation. This is the working out of the Law of Karma. Reality, then, is process and change in which there can be no permanent, personal existence or immortality because existence, which is only a state of being, is controlled by the universal Law of Karma, which constantly changes that state. Therefore, a soul as a super-entity cannot exist. When a man dies, his karma continues with its unalterable destiny into the next incarnation.

[17] D. T. Suzuki, *Outlines of Mahayana Buddhism* (London: Luzac and Company, 1907), p. 42.

11

The body in which the karma is "housed" is only a collection of elements and has no control over the force, for a law of the universe is at work, and it will continue to operate until the virtuous deeds (*bsod-nams*[18]) overcome all evil and the man gains final enlightenment or Nirvana.

This presents another difficult problem in Buddhism, that of the concept of heaven, or final goal, which is known as Nirvana. It is not a material conception of a "City of Gold," or a place where immortality is achieved and men live in eternal bliss. Rather, it is the overcoming of universal forces, a state of consummate enlightenment, for the "Phenomenal existence (*Samsāra*) becomes unconditioned existence: the stilling of the process of transmigration and change."[19] Nirvana places a man out of reach of evil and change, and beyond the grasp of the universal forces. As man does virtuous deeds and heeds the precepts of Buddhism through his numerous reincarnations, his station in religious spheres continually rises until he attains the final goal. Annihilation of thoughts of ego and grasping are the rewards of Nirvana: a man gains compassion for all beings. It represents positive and negative, annihilation and enlightenment, the total understanding of the causes of evil and the path to truth, that is, the Four Noble Truths and the Eight-fold Path.

Following the Buddha's death, circa 483 B.C., disciples recited his teachings at a council. In time, these teachings were reduced to a collection of writings known as the Tripitaka (the Three Baskets): the Vinaya or rules of monastic discipline; the sutras, which are the Buddha's own words and teachings; and the Abhidharma, commentaries akin to Buddhist metaphysics. The master teacher, the Buddha, did not write down what he thought and said. It was left to his followers to record what he

---

[18] *Bsod-nams* is the Sherpa term signifying religious merit. Upon accumulation of sufficient *bsod-nams*, which accrues from meritorious deeds, a man is eligible to enter Nirvana. This concept will be discussed in greater detail in Chapter II.

[19] David Snellgrove, *Buddhist Himalaya: Travels and Studies in Quest of the Origins and Nature of Tibetan Religion* (Oxford: Bruno Cassirer, 1957), p. 31.

pronounced, or what they thought he pronounced, and this gave rise to many divergent interpretations.

During the six centuries following the death of the Śākya Sage, three main movements or schools of Buddhism developed —the Theravāda, the Mahāyāna, and the Yogācāra. Numerous offshoots grew out of these schools, but the bases of the triumvirate have remained virtually unchanged up to contemporary times. All three schools flourish today, sometimes with new infusions, new interpretations, and reformed sects. It is well to keep the movements separate, however, for there are radical differences in some aspects.

The Theravāda school is established in Southeast Asia, Ceylon, and Indonesia. It was thought for centuries that this school was closer to the main original teachings of the Buddha, but recent scholarship has disproved much of that claim. Theravāda is often called Hinayāna, "lesser vehicle," a disparaging term used by Northern Buddhist countries, which follow the Mahāyāna sect, because the Theravāda school speaks of the salvation of the individual. Theravāda believes in the reality of the fundamental elements and in the duality of *samsāra* and Nirvana (the phenomenal existence and the unconditional existence). The terms "Hinayāna," "the Southern School," and "Theravāda" all refer to the same form of Buddhism.

The second main school is the Yogācāra, the "mind only" school. It appeared about the second century, and its greatest exponent was Vasubandhu, who lived in the fifth century. It presumes that nothing exists apart from the mind; the world is unreal as a product of the mind, but real insofar as the mind produces it. Yogācāra influence was felt in Tibet and Nepal to a lesser degree than Mahāyāna.

The third movement, Mahāyāna, had its impetus in a body of literature known as *Prajñāpāramitā*, written about the second century B.C. Also referred to as Mādhyamika, the "middle path," it was expounded and popularized by Nāgārjuna in the second century. Mādhyamika represents the main Buddhist teachings in Tibet and Nepal today, and is popularly called

Mahāyāna, "greater vehicle." This school stresses the doctrine of relativity, believing that no elements are real and that nothing can be predicated of ultimate reality in any sense. Wisdom is the recognition of the fundamental voidness of all phenomenal things.

Hinayāna holds that enlightenment is attainable only by a few monks and that the remainder of humanity must continue through still countless reincarnations, while the Mahāyāna presupposes that all men may gain the final goal of enlightenment. Mahāyāna in Tibet proclaims that under certain circumstances and dangerous short cuts a man may gain enlightenment in one life.[20] The Mahāyāna sect multiplied angelic beings into pantheons of Bodhisattvas (see pages 17-18), and made enlightenment available to a greater number of people. It developed the theory of an eternal compassionate Buddha-mind (Tib. *de-nyid*; Skt. *tatva*) behind the phenomenal world. This made the doctrine more palpable to the masses, because each man became a part of that absolute Buddha-mind. With the aid of a Bodhisattva's mercy, man could terminate the force of karma and take his place as part of that enlightened universal mind. This is the sect that the Sherpas of Nepal follow, and its Bodhisattvas are seen in the dances of Mani-rimdu.

These dances are a form of "tantric" worship or practice,[21] the form to which the monasteries of Khumbu subscribe. Tantrism is a mystical form of Buddhism based upon a class of texts known as tantras. It parallels much of Mahāyāna doctrine, and

[20] Mystics and ascetics who seek salvation by the short path are known as Naljorpas (Yogis). They hold that study is of no use in gaining knowledge; in fact, it is an obstacle. One only knows one's own ideas and visions; the causes which generated those concepts are inaccessible to human beings. It is the yoga concept from India. The ascetic totally removes himself from life and contemplates salvation, thereby bypassing study and good deeds of religion. If he is successful, he achieves Nirvana in one lifetime; if he fails, he must begin in his new incarnation at a lower level of existence. See Alexandra David-Neel, *Magic and Mystery in Tibet* (New York: University Books, 1958), p. 56.

[21] This type of Buddhism is technically known as either *mantrayāna* (the way of spells), or *vajrayāna* (the adamantine way).

likewise had its inception in India. Musical accompaniment of worship is an exclusive tantric convention. The blowing of trumpets, beating of drums, and clashing of cymbals immediately identify the worship as tantric.

Tantrism is a spiritually mystical tradition involving the use of spells and magic formulas and devices. In theory it attempts to establish the inner relationship of natural phenomena: "The parallelism of microcosm and macrocosm; mind and universe; ritual and reality; the world of matter and the world of spirit." The method of accomplishing this becomes a religious precept which requires specially trained and disciplined priests. It requires that one unite the visible, audible, and touchable with the powers of mind, speech, and body in order to realize the final state of completeness and enlightenment.[22] The realization of this goal cannot be expressed in written or oral discourse, for it is an experience of the mind. This creates the necessity for a highly symbolic and denotative form of communication, which only the initiated are capable of comprehending.

Tantric Buddhism in Tibet seeks only one goal, *prajñāpāramitā* (wisdom or knowledge). This is not to say that tantric Mahāyāna doctrine ignores intelligence or judicious study. On the contrary, it believes that through the prudent use of intellect, plus reason, love, and compassion, one attains a union of all one's faculties which results in superior wisdom or *prajñāpāramitā,* beyond the ordinary limits of wisdom (*prajñā*). Tantric Buddhism utilizes texts, paintings, and images to depict sexual union of a Buddha or Bodhisattva with his female counterpart, also known as *prajñā* or *mudrā.* The female represents "wisdom" and the male is symbolic of the "means" of accomplishment. The male is the active element, the female is passive.

Hinduism depicts physical sexual union, not mystical union as in Buddhism. Hinduism employs the *Śakti,* the active female energy which triggers action. Buddhism depicts this union, not as physical, but as an internal psychological process, the unity of

[22] Lama Anagarike Govinda, "Principles of Buddhist Tantrism," *Bulletin of Tibetology,* II, No. 1 (March, 1965), 9.

wisdom (female) and means (male). The Hindu object of such tantric union is to join man to the forces of the universe, but the Buddhist intent is to extricate man from those forces, to free him from the powers which manipulate him. The ultimate result of such union is to activate wisdom in order to attain enlightenment. Existence, to the Buddhists, is "the diversity of *samsāra* [phenomenal existence] and *nirvāna* [unconditioned existence] and enlightenment is their unity . . . the fundamental pattern of existence was conceived as unity in apparent duality."[23] This duality will be noted in some characters in Mani-rimdu dances.

Thubten Tendzin writes that one can speak of a "Tantric spirit . . . in connection with any doctrine or method of which the conscious aim is a transmutation of the human soul in such a way as to enable the true intelligence, the 'mind of Bodhi' to emerge and take command."[24] The tantric spirit seeks to convert whatever is base or polluted, such as ignorance, graspings, or worldly thoughts, into something pure and noble.[25]

Padmasambhava, the founder of Buddhism in Tibet, employed mystical tantric teachings in eighth-century Tibet in order to defeat demons. He utilized spells, magic daggers, and thunderbolts, which were too powerful for the evil spirits to ward off. Through the use of tantric precepts,

> Padma-sambhava succeeded in training up a number of Tibetan lamas who rose to the highest stages of perfection. For his saintliness and masterly expositions, Padma-sambhava is revered by the Tibetans as the Second Buddha. Through the help and guidance of these lamas, the tantric religion became popular all over the country.[26]

The practice of tantric rituals emphasizes the transcending of

[23] Snellgrove, *Buddhist Himalaya*, p. 83.
[24] Thubten Tendzin, "Considerations on Tantric Spirituality," *Bulletin of Tibetology*, II, No. 2 (August, 1965), 25.
[25] *Ibid.*, p. 26.
[26] Nalinaksha Dutt, "Tantric Buddhism," *Bulletin of Tibetology*, I, No. 2 (October, 1964), 13.

the physical world and the attaining of perfect knowledge. Spells of a magical nature are uttered, and musical instruments aid in summoning deities to invoke their magical powers. The monks handle ritual objects, which symbolize supernatural powers of the invited gods and demons. The dances of Mani-rimdu are magical in the tantric sense. They are highly symbolic in costume, ritual objects, movement, and over-all meaning. They are founded in Mahāyāna philosophy, and are tantric in form.

Perhaps the main concept which separates Hinayāna from Mahāyāna is the theory of the Bodhisattva. To the followers of the "greater vehicle" it was not enough to show men the way to enlightenment and final release, for men are prone to stray from the path of truth. A theory was developed in which gods could directly aid men, and the Bodhisattva was the result. He is a being who has gained the release of Nirvana but instead of accepting it, he steps back with compassion in order to aid all other sentient beings in their quest for final release. It is a concept of extreme compassion in which the Bodhisattva, instead of becoming another Buddha, vows to forego his own final liberation from successive rebirths until all other beings in pain and ignorance are able to proceed with him. Through this theory Mahāyāna, and its Bodhisattvas, is a more socially conscious form of Buddhism than Hinayāna, whose emphasis is primarily on the individual, for Mahāyāna embraces all mankind.

The Bodhisattva assumes another incarnation, usually as an abbot of a monastery, to lead and stimulate others. The reincarnate monk is known as a "Rinpoche" (the Great Precious One), that is, one who retains all his knowledge and experience from his former lives. Each Bodhisattva has powers peculiar to him, and his powers border on the supernatural. This renders him not only a living god, but a man of extraordinary wisdom and experience. He is practically infallible in religious precepts. In 1578 the title of Talé (Dalai) was applied to Bsod-nams rgya-mtsho, a Bodhisattva and Dge-lugs-pa lama. In his fifth rebirth, he became not only the ruler of the reformed sect of

17

Buddhism, but also the political king of Tibet.[27] Since then a Bodhisattva has retained the title of Dalai Lama and has enjoyed ecclesiastic and temporal rule of the country. The Dalai Lama is considered to be an incarnation of Avalokiteśvara (Tib. Spyan-ras-gzigs), the Bodhisattva of Mercy. The Abbot of Tengpoche monastery in Nepal is another Bodhisattva, an incarnation of Lama Bundachendzen. (His ascendancy is noted in Chapter II.) Numerous Bodhisattvas appear in the dances of Mani-rimdu (see Chapter VI).

The theory of the Bodhisattva precipitated an entirely new pantheon of gods and goddesses in Northern Buddhist countries that embraced the Mahāyāna doctrines. The theory allowed shamanizing, which the Buddha had rejected. In Tibet and Nepal, however, it aided Buddhism, for the pantheon was expanded to include Bon gods, which Buddhists explained as demons who were converted to the new religion. Consequently, these ancient gods appeared in Buddhist pantheons, where they became fierce defenders of the new faith and were known as "Tutelary Deities." In this manner the old Bon-pos were not confronted with a new religion which cast their gods into the void. Rather, Buddhism utilized their gods' various supernatural powers in a new manner. Many of the Buddhist festivals in Nepal deal with this large pantheon of gods and goddesses. These deities must not be confused with divinely created beings who in turn created the universe, for in Buddhism the universe is the gathering together of forces in a certain form, totally dependent upon natural law. However, much of the Mahāyāna Buddhist literature describes miraculous, divine births for several Bodhisattvas. For the purposes of this brief discussion, such writings should be considered as corruptions of strict Buddhist doctrine.

Buddhist missionaries may have penetrated into Tibet prior to the seventh century, but they apparently failed to gain a foothold among the Tibetans, perhaps because of language barriers.

[27] H. E. Richardson, *A Short History of Tibet* (New York: E. P. Dutton, 1962), p. 41.

Buddhism did not enter Tibet with momentum until the eighth
century, when St. Padmasambhava, an Indian ascetic, arrived
with his manuscripts and missionaries. Tibetan kings desired to
know more about their immediate neighbors to the south, the
Indians, and Padmasambhava had come, at the invitation of
King Khri-srong Lde-btsan, to teach Buddhism.

The new religion, however, met opposition from aristocrats
who cherished Bon practices. The nobility did not oppose
Buddhism as a religion, but as a potential political power which
someday might remove them from control over Tibet. It was
against this opposition that Buddhism utilized its Bodhisattva
theories and supernatural powers. It depicted Padmasambhava
"assimilating the Bön practices into the Mahāyāna creed."[28]
Buddhism gradually overcame aristocratic defiance, and replaced Bon as the state religion. Woodcock explains Buddhism's
victory:

> In the long run, Bön was defeated because Lamaism [Bud-
> dhism] provided all that the old religion could give in the
> way of magic and ecstasy, and in addition offered the consola-
> tory doctrines of Mahāyāna, with its redeeming Bodhisattvas
> willing to sacrifice all hope of eternal peace until the suffering
> of every creature had been brought to an end.
>
> The most important single contribution of Padma-sambhava
> to the development of Buddhism in Tibet was his foundation
> in A.D. 777 of the earliest Tibetan monastery at Samye, and his
> ordination of the first seven Tibetan monks. Up to this time
> Buddhism had still been largely a court religion, its priests
> mainly Indians and Nepālis, isolated linguistically from the
> people. The foundation of Samye was the beginning of a trend
> toward popular Buddhism.[29]

Although the barbarism of the Mohammedan hordes in the
twelfth century brought the demise of Buddhism as an effective
religious force in India and in the Kathmandu Valley of Nepal,

[28] George Woodcock, "The Theocrats of Tibet," *History Today*, XV, No.
2 (February, 1965), 90.
[29] *Ibid.*

19

Tibet remained a stronghold of the religion and continued in its zeal, copying Sanskrit texts, translating them into Tibetan, and composing new ones. During the period between the seventh and seventeenth centuries Tibetan Buddhist missionaries crossed the Himalayan barrier and entered Nepal from the north, to convert the hill people. Living in the rugged mountainous region south of the Himalayas, these people held cultural and social ties with the Tibetans, not with the Indo-Nepalese people of the valleys. Historically, Nepal was the fifty-odd square miles of fertile valley now known as the Kathmandu Valley; the hill tribes had received no attention from Nepalese and Indian sages. Ironically, however, it was in the hill tribes—namely, Sherpas, Mugus, Dolpos, Thakas, and others—that Buddhism ultimately gained a lasting stronghold in Nepal. When speaking of Buddhism in Nepal, one must differentiate between the hill people, whose religion, which came from Tibet, flourishes today, and the valley people, whose Buddhism, which originated in India, virtually died out in the twelfth century.

In Tibet, the pacifistic attitude of Buddhism with its more serene mercy had been opposed by laymen and the nobility, who followed the more overt Bon practices. As was noted earlier, the opposition was based upon political principles, not religious precepts. Bonist politicians used defiance, intrigues, open hostilities, and even assassinations in order to protect their jealously guarded rights. But as time passed the two faiths blended in some aspects, and the mitigational influence of Buddhism gained predominance. Bonism adopted philosophical ideas from Buddhism and "discovered" ancient texts which showed that their concepts resembled those of the Buddhists. Bon deities became friendly and merciful as fierce defenders of the Buddhist faith. Animal sacrifices were replaced by effigies.

The Bon-pos' fears that Buddhism would usurp their political power eventually came to pass when lamas were given temporal rule. In 1642 the fifth Dalai Lama became ruler of Tibet; but formal Bon opposition had ceased. Temporal and spiritual rule of Tibet passed into the hands of one man in the capital city of Lhasa.[30]

The subjugation of Bonism by Buddhism is one of the central themes in Buddhist drama in Tibet. Its purpose is to strengthen the people's faith in Buddhist doctrines, at the expense of Bon. Thus, religion is preached, and laymen learn about the history of their country and the history of Buddhism in Tibet. The origin and background of Tibetan theater are discussed in Chapter III, but a brief analysis of one Tibetan drama is appended here in order to illustrate the proselytizing zeal which is expressed in these Buddhist dramas. This genre of theater differs from Mani-rimdu, for it utilizes written dramas; Mani-rimdu does not use words to convey its meaning.

The play, *Drowazangmo,* is a secular drama of the Lha-mo genre.[31] It depicts evil Bon-pos and saintly Buddhists struggling for supremacy in allegorical conflict as it might be found in an English miracle play of the fifteenth century. It is not only allegorical but supernatural in several aspects. Gods take the form of birds and animals in order to aid the distressed; deities look down from their lofty perches and perceive what humanity is accomplishing. These elements, clearly, are not Buddhist. They represent the carry-over of such notions from Bonism. The plot involves the tribulations of Drowazangmo, a goddess, and her son Prince Kuntulehpa, who are almost destroyed by the evil woman, Queen Hajang. The former represent Buddhism, and the latter figure, the queen, is symbolic of Bon. The play relates the difficulties which Buddhism faced in Tibet as Bonism sought to destroy it.

---

[30] The fourteenth Dalai Lama is now in exile in India, having escaped from Chinese aggression during the turbulent struggles of the 1950's. Tibet today is an occupied country. Its monks and rulers are in exile, have been killed, or were forced to join Chinese labor gangs. For all practical purposes, the religious, cultural, and governmental functions of Tibet as a country have ceased to exist.

[31] For further information, see Luther G. Jerstad, "Buddhist Proselytization in the Tibetan Drama, *Drowazangmo," Western Speech,* XXXI, No. 3 (Summer, 1967), 199-210.

Prior to the formal opening of the play, the narrator says, "If religion is not preached the heart does not understand religious precepts and one will go foolishly to the other doctrine." Religion here means Buddhism, and the "other doctrine" refers to Bonism. The narrator continues:

> There are uniform commands, and similar discourses, and there is need to hear corresponding beseeching. Oh, Jewel in the Lotus Flower . . . Drowazangmo is a being born from the Green Goddess . . . prostrate to the Mother Drolma. . . . These are times of degeneracy. . . . In the Country of Mandrahgang . . . religion's voice did not extend. They did not know how to pronounce the Magic Formula of Six Syllables.[32]

Queen Hajang lives in the country of Mandrahgang, where "religion's voice did not extend." All of the evils which befall the main character, Drowazangmo, relate directly to the fact that she lives in a country where Buddhism is not preached. Drowazangmo is an incarnation of Tārā, Goddess of Mercy, and in the play Mercy and Evil allegorically confront each other. Another thing wrong with Mandrahgang is that the people there did not know how to think of Avalokiteśvara, Bodhisattva of Mercy. Since the Dalai Lama is an incarnation of Avalokiteśvara, there is a direct confrontation between the Buddhism of the Dalai Lama and Bonism. Queen Hajang knows about Buddhism but chooses the way of Bon, and she is featured as a totally brutal person in the play. She seeks to destroy Drowazangmo's two children, who, she fears, will usurp her power in the kingdom. The children represent the new budding religion of Buddhism, which Hajang (Bonism) tries to destroy. The Queen screams:

> I, having the great name of Hajang,
> Will become the enemy of you Drowazangmo.
> Today in the circle of this sun,

[32] Marion H. Duncan (ed. and trans.), "Drowazangmo," *Harvest Festival Dramas of Tibet* (Hong Kong: Orient Publishing Company, 1955), pp. 29-30.

> If I cannot devour you, mother and children three,
> May all the guardian spirits that protect the
> religion of this country seize me.[33]

She invokes the spirits of animism, not the precepts of Buddhism. Drowazangmo, the Buddhist goddess, becomes a second queen to the King of Mandrahgang, and Queen Hajang is jealous of her realm, fearing that she will lose her political power as well as her religious power. Drowazangmo introduces Buddhism to the King, who proclaims it to the entire country. Thus, Buddhism has overcome severe difficulties and triumphed over Bon.

These problems that the drama uses as subject matter are historical facts in Tibet. For example, during the reign of Mes-ag-tshoms (A.D. 704-55) many religious changes took place in favor of Buddhism, but after the King's death certain ministers collaborated and passed a law forbidding the new religion. Monks were banished into exile, and the young King was powerless. The move was political rather than religious, designed to protect the rights of Tibetan aristocrats who worshiped spirits.[34] In the play, Queen Hajang does not oppose Drowazangmo on religious grounds alone, but on political ones as well, for she has no heir to the throne and will lose her power if Drowazangmo's children live to assume leadership. Hajang feigns an illness and directs her priests to perform an exorcismic rite which will result in the children's deaths. The narrator describes her actions: "She made a resting place, spread over it a putrid skin rug, smeared rotten brains on her body, put red ochre upon the left cheek and indigo upon the right cheek, and making zigzag blue and red mucous streaks, she lay down lying like a dead person."[35]

In contrast to Hajang's wild orgiastic exorcism with primitive magic, Drowazangmo's solemn intellectual exhortations of

---

[33] *Ibid.*, p. 44
[34] Hoffmann, *Religions of Tibet*, p. 43.
[35] Duncan (ed. and trans.), "Drowazangmo," p. 51.

Buddhism clearly point out the proselytization in the play:

> In the great state of this world desire is like a dream,
> The great enjoyment of carnal desire is likewise the
>   root of all sin.
> All accumulated works are not enduring.
> Now the great meaning of the future is about to be accomplished.
> When dead there is no contact nor is life for a long time.
> All must meditate on the All Merciful Tutelary Deity.
> The basis of religion is reciting the Six Syllable prayer.
> Abandoning the ten sins one must receive the ten virtues.
> Love and Mercy must never be separated.
> Proceed slowly to the state of merciful non-existence.[36]

Drowazangmo's short speech presents the Buddhist theory of *anātman*, the theory of causality, the essence of the Four Noble Truths, the protection afforded by the Tutelary Deities, the formula of *Om Mani Padme Hum*, the Ten Sins and the Ten Virtues, the Bodhisattva idea of mercy, and the concept of Nirvana.[37]

Buddhism did not totally supplant Bonism in Tibet and Nepal. Bon monasteries flourish today in Nepal, Sikkim, and Ladakh,[38] and there were many in Tibet before the Chinese invasion of 1950, which ended all intercourse between Tibet and the Western world. No one religion totally dominates traditional native practices. Christianity did not rule out Judaism; Hinduism did not destroy Indian animistic religions; and Mo-

---

[36] *Ibid.,* p. 44.

[37] Some of these concepts have been discussed previously in this chapter. *Anātman,* causality, and the theory of karma have been delineated above, as has been the concept of the Four Noble Truths. The Tutelary Deities are the converted Bon demons who serve as defenders of the Buddhist faith. *"Om Mani Padme Hum"* is a magic formula (mantra). Its frequent repetition, Tibetans believe, will assure them a rebirth in the Paradise of the Great Western Bliss, a sort of materialistic concept of Nirvana. It means "Hail Jewel in the Lotus," and it is an invocation addressed to Avalokiteśvara. The Ten Sins and the Ten Virtues are a code of ethics for Tibetans and Sherpas. They are delineated in conjunction with Sherpa ethics in Chapter II. The Bodhisattva concept of mercy and the idea of Nirvana have already been discussed in the body of Chapter I.

[38] David Snellgrove reports on some Bon monasteries in Nepal in his book, *Himalayan Pilgrimage.*

hammedanism did not destroy Hinduism and Buddhism. Rather, the new religious teaching inculcated many of the older practices and dressed them in new doctrines. Such was the case with Buddhism as it sought to usurp the power of Bonism. By using the outward form of Bonism while infusing doctrines of mitigation and mercy, the followers of the Buddha gradually converted most of Central Asia to their religion. One of the many methods of proselytization was the drama, of both the Lha-mo genre as presented above and the 'Cham genre, which will be treated in the discussion of Mani-rimdu in Nepal. What is important to note is that the symbolism of both 'Cham and Lha-mo is calculated to teach and enforce the precepts of Buddhism at the expense of Bonism.

The following chapters present the 'Cham as it is found among the Sherpas in the Khumbu region of Nepal. The Tibetan form of Buddhism is the parent of the Sherpa religion, complete with gods and Bon-po enemies. The struggles of Buddhism in Tibet are the same struggles as those of the Sherpas of Nepal, but with local innovations, deities, and customs added. The 'Cham presents part of that struggle and depicts the workings of Buddhism in theory, doctrine, and practice. It is part of the missionary zeal of Buddhists to offer entertainment and propaganda plus merit for all who participate in and view the enactment of the drama and the dance.

II. The Sherpas

NEPAL, the "Ethnic Turntable of Asia,"[1] lies midway between east and west of the great Himalayan Range. Stretching some 1,250 miles from Afghanistan on the west to Burma on the east, the Himalayas represent the highest frontier in the world, forming the natural boundary between Southern and Central Asia. Nepal covers an area roughly 55,000 square miles between latitude 80° and 88° east and longitude 27° to 30° north. It is 550 miles long and 100 to 150 miles wide,[2] bordered on the north by Tibet, on the east by Sikkim, and on the south and west by India. Nepal is like a fortress whose walls of high mountain ranges were almost impregnable prior to the twentieth century. "She alone among Asiatic Powers has never suffered either the galling triumph of the Moslem or the political and commerical results of Christian (European) expansion."[3]

The first historical reference to Nepal appears in the second

[1] Toni Hagen, *Nepal: The Kingdom in the Himalayas* (Berne, Switzerland: Kummerly and Frey, 1961), p. 35.

[2] For the physical geography of Nepal, see O. H. K. Spate, *India and Pakistan: A General and Regional Geography* (New York: E. P. Dutton, 1954), pp. 405-19. Also see Hagen, *Nepal.*

[3] Spate, *India and Pakistan,* p. 406.

26

century B.C. as "Naipalikam,"[4] part of the Indian subcontinent. Nepal was the name given to what is today the Kathmandu Valley. In past ages, geologically speaking, the valley was covered by a large lake. Tradition relates that Mañjuśrī, Mahāyāna Bodhisattva of Transcendental Wisdom, slashed a passage through the Mahābhārat Hills south of the valley draining the lake and made possible a Buddhist center of population there.[5] Needless to say, the early history of Nepal is steeped in mythology and legends. Some "ancient" texts claim that Buddhists lived in Nepal long before Gautama was born twenty-five hundred years ago. Separating history from fiction has been a major problem for scholars of Nepalese history.[6]

A land of extraordinary topographical changes, Nepal's features range from the malaria-infested jungles of the southern Terai area to the highest mountain in the world, 29,028-foot Mount Everest, in northeastern Nepal. The capital city, Kathmandu, lies about midway between the northern and southern boundaries, and slightly east of central Nepal, at an elevation of 4,435 feet. Roughly two-thirds of Nepal is mountainous; consequently, layer upon layer of terraced hills comprise half of the

[4] Gopal Singh Nepali, *The Newars: An Ethno-Sociological Study of a Himalayan Community* (Bombay: United Asia Publications, 1965), p. 10.

[5] "Swyambu Puran," quoted in Kuladharma Ratna, *Buddhism and Nepal* (Kathmandu, Nepal: Dharmodaya Sabha, 1958), p. 3.

[6] For information on Nepalese history, the reader should consult: Francis Hamilton Buchanan, *An Account of the Kingdom of Nepal, and of the Territories Annexed to this Domain by the House of Gurkha* (Edinburgh: Archibald Constable, 1819); Henry Ambrose Oldfield, *Sketches for Nipal* [*sic*] . . . (London: W. H. Allen, 1880); Luciano Petech, *Medieval History of Nepal* (Rome: Instituto Italiano Per Il Medio Estremo Oriente, 1958); Guiseppe Tucci, *Preliminary Report on Two Scientific Expeditions in Nepal: Materials for the Study of Nepalese History and Culture* (Rome: Instituto Italiano Per Il Medio Estremo Oriente, 1956); D. R. Regmi, *Ancient Nepal* (Calcutta: K. L. Mukhopadhyay, 1960); D. R. Regmi, *Modern Nepal: Rise and Growth in the Eighteenth Century* (Calcutta: K. L. Mukhopadhyay, 1961): and Daniel Wright (ed.), *History of Nepal,* trans. Mumski Shew Shunker Singh and Pandit Sri Gunanand (Calcutta: Susil Gupta, 1958). The accuracy of the last three should be verified constantly.

cultivatable land. Valley dwellers are mainly of Indo-Aryan stock, whose languages are derived from Sanskrit. The northern hill people are generally of Mongolian descent and speak languages of Tibeto-Burmese origin, a branch of the Sino-Tibetan family of languages. Ethnic groups from ancient Nepal are Newārs, Tamangs, Gurungs, Magars, Sunwārs, Rais, Limbus, Buras, and Thakuris, a high Hindu caste to which the royal house belongs. Those of strictly Tibetan origin are Bhotiyas (Tibetans) and Sherpas.[7] Ethnic groups are frequently mixtures of Mongoloid and Indo-Nepalese (Caucasian) blood. Nepali, an Indo-Aryan language which resembles Hindi, is the official language of the country. With the exception of the residents of a few areas, mainly remote hill tribes, all Nepalese people speak Nepali, whether they are of Tibetan or Indo-Nepalese origin. Nearly all ethnic groups speak a tribal language as well, that is, Sherpas speak Sherpa, Newārs speak Newāri, Gurungs speak Gurung, and so forth. These are household languages by means of which culture is propagated in the tribe's respective villages. The Newāri community of Bhadgāon just east of Kathmandu tenaciously clings to its tribal dialect. Approximately 80 per cent of the villagers cannot speak Nepali. On the other hand, a large number of Sherpas, because of their trading sojourns into the Kathmandu Valley, Tibet, and India, speak Tibetan, Sherpa, Nepali, and Hindi. A few may even speak Newāri, Gurung, or Sikkimese, depending upon where their markets lie. My Sherpa companion, who has never attended school, speaks nine languages and dialects, including English. Truly, Nepal is an amalgamation of diverse languages and ethnic origins loosely united by a constitutional monarchy in Kathmandu.

The northern part of Nepal is separated from Tibet by the highest mountains on earth: Everest, Lhotse, Makalu, Cho Oyu, Ānnapurna, Dhāulagiri, Manaslu, Gosainthan, and Kangchenjunga. The last two are considered to be in Tibet and Sikkim, respectively, but they also border on Nepal. Just south of the

[7] Hagen, *Nepal*, p. 61.

Himalayan chain in northeastern Nepal are three large river valleys, the Khumbu, Solu, and Pharak gorges, which form the homeland of most of the Sherpas in Nepal. The Solu and Pharak valleys lie south and east of the main Sherpa settlements in Khumbu. Sherpas of the Solu and Pharak valleys are not as strictly Tibetan in their costumes and culture as their valley neighbors to the north and west. Hindu elements and mixed blood have slightly changed the character of the southern Sherpas. Their agriculture is more closely akin to the Nepalese valleys to the south, and only a few carry on the extensive trade which the Sherpas of Khumbu have developed and maintained. The most westerly settlements of Sherpas are to be found north of Kathmandu in the Helmu area.[8]

The Khumbu Valley lies at the southern foot of the Everest-Lhotse massif. Located approximately 80 air miles east-northeast from Kathmandu, and 150 miles by foot from the capital, the valley averages 14,000 feet in elevation. The area was popularly known as Solu-Khumbu to mountaineering expeditions, but the more proper term for the home of the high-mountain Sherpas dealt with here should be Khumbu.[9] Reference to Sherpas hereafter means the Sherpas of Khumbu unless otherwise stated. The two Mani-rimdu festivals of concern here are held in monasteries in Khumbu—Thami and Tengpoche.

The generic term "Sherpa" is derived from two Tibetan words, "'Shar" meaning east, and "'pa," a suffix meaning "one from." Thus Shar-pa means easterner,[10] and the word "Sherpa" now denotes a tribe of Tibetans living in northeastern Nepal. The origin of the label "easterner" for Sherpas who live south of Tibet is uncertain, though their ancestors may have come from eastern Tibet. The term "Sherpa" has come to be used popularly also as meaning a native Nepalese mountain climber.

[8] Toni Hagen, G. O. Dyhrenfurth, Christoph von Fürer-Haimendorf, and Erwin Schneider, *Mount Everest: Formation, Population, and Exploration of the Everest Region,* trans. E. Noel Bowman (London: Oxford University Press, 1963), pp. 125-26.

[9] *Ibid.,* p. 125.

[10] *Ibid.,* p. 124.

Sherpas are used as high-altitude porters on mountaineering expeditions because of their stamina and strength. They are members of the tribe of Sherpas, and their name derives from that fact, not from special expedition terminology.

The main villages of Khumbu are Namche Bazar, Khumjung, Thami, Pangboche, and Phorche. Chaunrikharka is another main village in the area, but it actually is in the Pharak Valley. They are situated 15 to 30 miles south of Mount Everest in high valleys with ridges and peaks rising above them to heights of 21,000 feet. They are connected by trails, and a person can walk from any one village to any of the others mentioned above in a day's journey. No motor roads have pierced Khumbu's sanctuary, nor is there a road within 140 miles of the nearest Sherpa village. Sir Edmund Hillary built an airfield south of Khumbu at the tiny village of Lukhla. Constructed to receive material for schoolhouse construction in Khumbu, the airport has no facility for passenger service except in cases of emergency. Only single-engine aircraft can operate on the short runway at the high elevation of 9,000 feet.

Facilities for communications are practically nonexistent in Khumbu. A few personal radios owned by wealthy Sherpas and a Nepalese Army short-wave set at Namche Bazar constitute the contact with the outside world. Since Sherpa is a tribal language with no written form, and since few Sherpas outside monasteries read Tibetan or Nepali, newspapers are unavailable. Most news is carried orally by traders who frequent the Sherpa villages. A mail runner delivers letters and newspapers from Kathmandu to Khumbu about a dozen times per year. No telegraph or telephone lines exist, and no Khumbu people hear news of their area on the government radio station, Radio Nepal. For a great majority of Sherpas, the world centers about the Buddhist monasteries, from which learning is dispensed to the people. However, Sherpas are very curious, and they will quiz a foreign visitor for hours about his country, his customs, and the news from the outside world.

Mongoloid by race, the Sherpas resemble American Indians in many respects. Their physical stature ranges from four feet, ten inches in height for a small Sherpa to five feet, eight inches for a tall one. Their complexion is light brown, and their hair is black. Like other Mongoloid peoples, Sherpas have scant body hair, and their eyes are somewhat almond-shaped.

Historically unaware of their past, Sherpas have difficulty in pinpointing exact historical dates. They seldom differentiate between a thing which happened thirty years ago and one which occurred three hundred years ago. It is uncertain when they migrated to Khumbu from Tibet, but by Asian standards it is a recent event, certainly after the time of Columbus' discovery of America. Since Sherpas are ethnically and racially "Tibetan," they must have been exposed to Buddhism prior to their migration to Khumbu. No records, however, reveal the existence of Buddhism in Khumbu prior to the seventeenth century. This suggests that Sherpas brought Buddhism with them when they emigrated from their homeland.

The reason Sherpas chose to live south of the Himalayas is not clear, but they probably moved to escape religious persecution. During the seventeenth century there was chaos and conflict within the Buddhist religion in Tibet. The Yellow Hat Dge-lugs-pa fought, conquered, and oppressed the Red Hat Karma-pa and Rnying-ma-pa sects. The Dge-lugs-pa conducted this campaign in order to gain ascendancy over other sects and become the official state Buddhist sect. Not choosing to abide by such a forced acceptance of different dogma, some Tibetans left their villages and founded new enclaves where freedom from religious persecution could be assured. It is probably owing to this religious dispute that Tibetans from the eastern sections of the country emigrated southward across the Himalayas and eventually settled in Khumbu, where they became known as "Sherpas," that is, "easterners."

Most Sherpas believe that their ancestors entered Nepal west of the Rowaling Himalayas in central Nepal and then moved eastward gradually. They settled first in Solu, where they ousted an earlier Kirānti population.[11] The Kirāntis were an ancient ruling class in Nepal, dating to pre-Christian times. From Solu the Sherpas migrated north into Khumbu, where they have lived ever since. Another legend claims that the Sherpas moved directly to Khumbu from Tibet across Nangpa-la, a famous pass on the main trade route between Tibet and Nepal. The population which now inhabits Khumbu has resided there for at least three hundred years. This seems to indicate that the seventeenth-century date for their migration is accurate. Previous to that date there are no monastic records to shed light on the question. All cultural ties of the Sherpas are with Tibet, and their religion and language emanate from the same source.

An energetic people leading a vigorous and lusty life, the Sherpas have a tradition of independence. They have never known foreign rule, overlords, or colonial powers, either Eastern or Western. For this reason the Sherpas have never feared strangers, except in business dealings, and it has made them an extremely friendly people with a conspicuously nonsuspicious nature. The political power struggles within the Kathmandu Valley which prevailed for centuries never affected the Sherpas' lives or economy. They traded freely wherever they could find markets. A stranger in a Sherpa community is welcomed at almost every home. An ill or injured foreigner is cared for without regard to pay or recognition. Their religion preaches such practices of tolerance and helpfulness, but, more than that, the Sherpas themselves insist upon them as a way of life.

The concept of art forms apart from religion has never been fostered in Khumbu. Life in a Sherpa community depends upon long hours of toil in order to provide day-to-day existence. The luxury of leisure time affects only a few wealthy traders and monks. There is little time to relax, but when Sherpas find the opportunity they squat about the open fire in the home telling stories over glasses of *chang* (rice beer) and *rakshi* (whiskey).

[11] *Ibid.*, p. 143.

Seven days a week from sunup to sundown the Sherpas work in their fields or tend their herds, and diversional activities therefore play little part in their lives. Pure entertainment is rare. However, after the evening meal and a few glasses of spirits, Sherpas often sing and dance to the accompaniment of stringed instruments or hand clapping. The songs reflect ancient legends and heroes, generally associated in some way with religion, but these informal activities are not a worshipful activity or an act of obeisance. Lamas are considered to be a repository for songs and legends, which they teach to the populace. If a song fest is to take place, a monk may be invited to provide additional material. There are also several laymen who know large numbers of songs, which they have usually learned from a lama either in Tibet or in Khumbu. A monk may take part in folk dancing, but strictly as another person in attendance, not as a leader or as a monastic check upon entertainment activities.

What sculpture and painting is found in Khumbu is of a religious nature, for use in the monasteries and gombas,[12] or in a Sherpa's home for his private worship. Many families maintain private chapels for their own worship, and these rooms in the home are adorned with religious objects, paintings, and images. Sculptured objects are primarily made of brass, but a few are carved from wood and stone as well. They are representations of the Buddha or Bodhisattvas from the Mahāyāna pantheon. The most common icon found in Khumbu is Guru Rinpoche, the name given to Padmasambhava, founder of Buddhism in Tibet. He may be seen in many different forms, each of which reminds Buddhists of one or another of his particular powers. These images do not house spirits of the deities but are reminders of the true way Bodhisattvas teach their followers. It is not sacrilegious to keep images in closets or on dusty shelves, but generally they

[12] The gomba is a temple in which most religious rituals are performed. Each village as well as each monastery contains a gomba. It is a generic term analogous to "church," "chapel," or "cathedral" in the West. Therefore, the term "monastic gombas" refers to a gomba, or chapel, in a monastic setting as opposed to a village setting.

are cared for with much attention and are placed upon the home altar.

The use of icons and images symbolizes the abilities of Bodhisattvas and other deities to ward off evil and to protect the followers of the Buddha. Mani-rimdu dances visually instruct Sherpas in the methodology of the peculiar power which a saint possesses. One dance, related in Chapter III, portrays the power of the Buddha as he magically deters evil demons from destroying a human corpse. The dance designates Buddhism not only as a religion which preaches the way to enlightenment, but as a force which protects the individual after his earthly death. The use of these two art forms, dance and sculpture, serves to symbolize the unseen forces, both virtuous and evil. The saint represented in a Sherpa's icon becomes a visual manifestation during Mani-rimdu. Actors impersonate saints and display their powers through the entertaining medium of dance. The dances are animated exhibitions of the power exemplified by a particular deity in a particular iconographic creation.

Religious paintings on canvas or silk, called *thang-kas*, are the only art of that medium found in Khumbu. Comparable to Christian religious paintings, they depict gods in the various pantheons, or they characterize famous actions performed by the gods. Scenes from the life of the Buddha and depictions of the fierce defenders of Buddhism in Tibet are popular subject matter for many of the *thang-kas*. These paintings, like the icons mentioned above, do not signify that a god is physically present because his picture hangs on a wall. Conversely, the *thang-ka* is a reminder of the spirit of that deity, and of the precepts of religion. A private chapel will usually display images, frescoes, and *thang-kas* of the Buddha, Guru Rinpoche, Tārā (Goddess of Mercy), Tutelary Deities, and the particular deity which a family holds sacred.

In Khumbu one man does all the paintings for Sherpas and gombas, although many *thang-kas* have come from Tibet. The artist, Kapa Kalden, now living in Khumjung, earns his living by painting new *thang-kas* from Buddhist scriptures. He is paid

34

for his work, earns religious merit by his activity, and is held in high regard by other Sherpas for his knowledge of scriptures. When he dies, his son will carry on the tradition.

In addition to *thang-kas* and icons, there is another reminder to Sherpas of their Buddhist faith, the "mani" walls which line the trails of Khumbu. Formulas of magical quality are chiseled on stone slabs and then erected in walls along the trails and in circular fashion around entire monasteries and some gombas. The most famous such formula, *Om Mani Padme Hum* ("Hail Jewel in the Lotus"), is another reminder of the Buddha and the precepts of Buddhism.[13] If a man passes the mani wall with "right mindfulness," one of the eight-fold methods which lead to the cessation of pain, he acquires merit whether he is walking the trail carrying a burden or simply for pleasure.

It is obvious that art and religion are inseparable in Khumbu, and that religious art pervades all aspects of Sherpa life. A work of art is not usually admired on purely aesthetic grounds. Art is a form of teaching, and the only dissemination of artistic knowledge is accompanied by instructions as to proper methods of contemplating that art. Village government exercises no control over the practice or participation in art activities, nor does it desire such control. Elements of religion are deferred to the lamas, and things political are reserved for village governments.

The more sophisticated forms of art as we know them in the West—that is, abstract painting, slice-of-life drama, or musical compositions for their own sake—are absent from Sherpa culture. The difficulty of survival and the long hours of eking out a living in Khumbu, coupled with the lack of literacy among the common people, have definitely limited artistic development among the lay Sherpas. One cannot disclaim artistic achievement or ability among them, however, for they enjoy participating in the dance and attempting to paint with crude tools. They treasure their folk dances and monastic dramatic presentations.

---

[13] There is a tradition in Buddhist oral teaching that repetition itself is a good thing and that one acquires merit through its practice whether one understands the chant or not.

Not until their life is eased of its physical burden, however, will the plebeian Sherpas have the time or the opportunity to develop latent artistic skills.

The family is the basic social unit of the Sherpas, just as it is in most Asian societies. Although Sherpa culture is subdivided into clans, of which there are eighteen in Khumbu, these clans do not constitute a caste structure. Caste systems, such as those found in Hindu India and to a lesser degree in Hindu Nepal, are a method of retaining political and social power by the priestly Brahmin caste. Social station is designated by birth according to the nature of defiling work and tasks which a caste member is destined to perform. In India and Nepal a rigid method designates social classes and thereby restrains individuals within that caste.

The Sherpas have no such inclinations in their society. A given clan worships specific deities and holds social gatherings, but it displays no feelings of supremacy over any other clan. The only people within the Sherpa culture who have a social stigma attached to them which could be considered as deprecatory are the Khamendus, an inferior class of Khambas. Khambas originally migrated from the province of Kham in eastern Tibet, but today a Khamba refers to any member of Sherpa society who has resided in Khumbu for less than one generation. The blemish against a Khamba is not severe, for he is free to marry whom he chooses without castigation of either party. He may become a village elder; and a Khamba is the reincarnate Abbot of the Tengpoche monastery. The stigma seems to have arisen over cleanliness of body and a more profligate moral code involving cheating, drinking, and stealing. Most of the Khambas who have migrated to Khumbu from Tibet came penniless, and perhaps the Sherpas have a justifiable claim against their lack of honesty. This stigma, however, involves very few men; the remainder enter society relatively freely. Today Khambas and Sherpas intermingle socially and religiously, but a Khamendu may not drink from the same cup as a Sherpa, and he cannot become a monk.

36

Buddhists regard ironmongers, metalworkers, and butchers as basically evil persons, because Buddhism forbids tampering with minerals and killing. Low-caste Hindus were therefore imported from the valleys to fulfill these tasks, and their lot was an unhappy one. The Sherpa attitudes toward these low-caste Hindus who resided in their midst were the same as those of the Hindus. Recently, however, the Nepalese government passed legislation forbidding the deprivation of a man's civil rights on the basis of caste distinction. The Sherpas immediately admitted the low-caste Hindus to their homes and shared the same cup with them. It appears that Sherpas treated these people in the manner to which they were accustomed, and were not acting out of personal prejudice.

Foreign aid projects have never found their way to the Khumbu valleys. As a social entity, the Sherpas have remained virtually unmolested by Western or Eastern influence, and have been practically ignored by the Nepalese government. The only sign of officialdom in Khumbu is an army check post at Namche Bazar, which inspects passports, trekking permits, and traders who venture that far north. Since Tibet was sealed off by the Chinese in 1951, the Namche Bazar check post has the power to halt all traders going to Tibet without the proper documents. Twenty years ago Sherpas and Tibetans freely exchanged wool, rice, salt, barley, textiles, and livestock across the Himalayas. Today, however, only a handful of Sherpas are allowed to cross the frontier. No Tibetans are allowed to leave their country unless they are on specific business for the Chinese Communists. These severe restrictions have begun to change the economy and freedom which the Sherpas have traditionally enjoyed. The check-post officials in Namche Bazar in no way interfere with village government, except to intern criminals and hasten them to Kathmandu for proper legal action, but that duty is one which the Sherpas would rather not handle anyway.

Perhaps one-third to one-half of the negotiable currency the Sherpas earned during a year came from mountaineering expeditions, which hired Sherpas as porters and climbers. These expeditions employed as many as five hundred at various times during a year. Owing to Chinese political pressure upon the Nepalese government, the entire range of Himalayas in Nepal has been closed to expeditions since 1964. This curtailment of porterage earnings and employment of young men has caused a minor emigration from Khumbu, especially of Sherpa climbers. The ultimate effects of the loss of manpower coupled with the loss of income will in time alter the Sherpas' way of life. Many of the young men have found homes in Kathmandu and Darjeeling, where they can obtain employment and find the excitement to which they were accustomed while associated with expeditions. My Sherpa companion has left Nepal to work in Paris, and more will leave the country shortly.

Theater, drama, and the arts are not now taught in Khumbu schools. In time, however, education will affect the Sherpas' lives, and the arts might become part of the curriculum. Even though the following comments concerning education are unrelated to theater per se, they do illustrate the Sherpas' attitudes toward new theories, discoveries, and knowledge.

The only active schools in Khumbu have been built by Sir Edmund Hillary since 1961. Hillary is a New Zealander who first scaled Everest with Tenzing Norgay in 1953. Immensely impressed with Sherpas on his many visits to Khumbu, Hillary returned in 1960 and asked the people of Khumjung what they would wish if there were one thing he could grant them. Their answer was, "We would like our children to go to school, Sahib." In 1961 that wish became a fact. With backing from American firms, Hillary returned to construct a school at Khumjung; he then received a letter from the people of Thami saying, "We Thami people are requesting your honour to open a school at Thami just like the one in Khumjung. Though our children have eyes but still they are blind."[14] Hillary has now constructed schools in Khumjung, Thami, Pangboche, Teng-

[14] Edmund Hillary, *Schoolhouse in the Clouds* (Garden City, N.Y.: Doubleday, 1964), pp. 2, 3.

38

boche, Chaunrikharka, and Junbesi, staffed them with educated Sherpa teachers, and provided books for the students, all without cost to the Sherpas. Almost every child in these villages attends school, and the parents and townspeople landscape and beautify the grounds and paint and repair the buildings with great pride. The Nepalese government charges duty on all building materials, funds, books, and repairs which Hillary brings into the country, and does not support the system of education in Khumbu in any way. In time the effects of education will be felt in Khumbu, but this instruction is still in its infant stages.

Agrarians and traders, the Sherpas support an adequate economy. One of the main foodstuffs, potatoes, is grown at elevations up to fifteen thousand feet in Khumbu. Imported from Darjeeling, India, probably from the gardens of British governors, the potato has given the Sherpas a stable commodity. A barley flour known as *rtsam-pa* provides the other main food for Sherpas. Yaks are in abundance throughout Khumbu, serving as beasts of burden for trading excursions and providing a source of milk, cheese, meat, and hair for weaving. The Sherpas also derive income from the sale of yak calves, either in Tibet or in Solu or Pharak. Although Sherpas disdain killing, they feel no urge to refrain from eating meat once it has been killed, and so yaks also provide meat for the Sherpa diet. Tibetan peoples have always been traders, and the Sherpas have not lost their zest for that occupation. Farmers who till the fields rely upon the traders, either with yak or human carriers, to transport their goods to distant markets. Trading sojourns take the men away from Khumbu for as long as nine months during the year. This fact makes Sherpa festival times even more joyous, for families try to unite during the period for the main ceremonies. It is a time for visiting old friends and for enjoying one's own family before the next journey. The Mani-rimdu festival occurs after the potato harvest is in, and just prior to the traders' departure with goods for the southern markets in Nepal and India.

It is obvious that Sherpa culture is permeated by the Buddhist religion. The precise date of Buddhism's entry into Khumbu is uncertain. Snellgrove's impression is that it was inaugurated approximately three hundred years ago,[15] while Fürer-Haimendorf thinks four hundred years is nearer to the truth.[16] Since no written language exists among the Sherpas, and monastic records in Tibetan hint at the above dates, such evidence will have to suffice. Three gombas were established early in Khumbu history: Kerok, Pangboche, and Thami. There are no records of gombas established prior to these, so we must assume that they were the earliest, and they have been in existence no longer than three hundred years. Serving as village gombas, but not as monastic establishments, these early centers of religion provided hermitages for the faithful who wished to meditate in solitude. Such caves and dwellings can readily be found today near the villages of Thami, Pangboche, and Dingboche.

Gombas are built upon preselected sites:

> . . . The site is usually commanding and picturesque. . . . It should have a free outlook to the east and catch the first rays of the rising sun; and it should be built in the long axis of the hill; and it is desirable to have a lake in front, even though it be several miles distant. . . . A waterfall . . . is of very good omen, and if one is visible in the neighborhood, the entrance is made in that direction. . . .[17]

In Khumbu, generally, the main door faces east even though it does not catch the first rays of the rising sun. These early morning rays are blocked by the gigantic peaks which surround Sherpa habitations.

Not only do gombas in Khumbu heed the traditions of site placement as stated above, but they claim supernatural, magical

[15] David Snellgrove, *Buddhist Himalaya: Travels and Studies in Quest of the Origins and Nature of Tibetan Religion* (Oxford: Bruno Cassirer, 1957), p. 213.
[16] Christoph von Fürer-Haimendorf, *The Sherpas of Nepal: Buddhist Highlanders* (London: John Murray, 1964), p. 129.
[17] L. Austine Waddell, *The Buddhism of Tibet or Lamaism* (Cambridge: W. Heffner and Sons, 1894), pp. 255-57.

selection of the exact spot. Charles Stonor relates the legend of Pangboche's founding as follows:

> Long ago, many centuries back, San Dorje [Sanga Rdo-rje, Tib. gsang-ba rdo-rje, a reincarnation of Padmasambhava, known as Guru Rinpoche to Sherpas] . . . for reasons now forgotten, quarreled with his people and was hounded out in fear of his life. He took refuge first of all in the forest where Thyangboche [Tengpoche] monastery now stands, and where his footprints, and the prints of his dog's food bowl, can be seen to this day on a rock in the temple porch. Still his people pursued him, and he was again chased away to flee for his life. So, taking one great jump, he flew to Pangboche, where legend says he lived as a hermit for the rest of his life. . . . The temple is built over the rock on which he was accustomed to sit. A small panel opens under the shrine, through which I was shown the imprint of his body in the stone. . . .[18]

Fürer-Haimendorf continues with the legend:

> The people of Pangboche point to many landmarks as the product of Lama Sanga Dorje's miraculous feats. Thus they believe that the groves of old juniper trees to both sides of the gomba sprang from the hairs the saint cut from his head and scattered to the left and right of the site chosen for the temple. There is also a roof like projection of rock, which he is believed to have pulled out of the mountain side to obtain shelter when he first arrived at Pangboche.[19]

The truly organized spine of Sherpa communities is the religious center, either the village gomba or the monastic enclave. The founding of monastic institutions in Khumbu is a relatively recent event, for neither of the monasteries is more than one hundred years old. Thami and Tengpoche are the monasteries of the Khumbu region, and the village gombas look to them for spiritual guidance. Each monastery, as well as most villages, has a main temple. The monastery is complemented by surrounding religious grounds, shrines, and homes for the monks. Desirable monastery sites are isolated from the world, in

---

[18] Charles Stonor, *The Sherpa and the Snowman* (London: Hollis and Carter, 1955), p. 119.
[19] Fürer-Haimendorf, *Sherpas of Nepal*, p. 128.

order to be free from temptations. Tengpoche is located on a 13,000-foot ridge four hours' walk north of Namche Bazar, and two hours' journey south of Pangboche, approximately 20 miles south of Mount Everest. Above Tengpoche rise ridges and peaks up to 22,500 feet, with deep gorges below it. The Thami monastery and gomba are carved out of a hillside at an elevation of 14,500 feet, 500 feet above the village of Thami, two days' journey from the Tibetan border.

All Sherpas pay homage to Guru Rinpoche, whose incarnation, Sanga Rdo-rje, selected the precise sites for gombas and monasteries alike. Lama Sanga Rdo-rje was the sixth reincarnation of his line of Rong-phu lamas when he visited Khumbu. His father was Lama Bundachendzen, a very learned Tibetan monk, who, tradition relates, also visited Khumbu many times. Rdo-rje's line of succession still rules Rong-phu monastery in Tibet, and Sherpa monasteries and gombas look to Rong-phu for spiritual guidance. It was the twelfth incarnation of Rdo-rje's line at Rong-phu who eventually recognized[20] Lama Gulu,

[20] A Rinpoche, or reincarnate Bodhisattva, is generally discovered during the first five years of his life. The former saint, prior to his death, utters pronouncements of where he will be reborn. After the man's death, a search is instituted in that area. The child who is the reincarnation will display certain characteristics, that is, long ear lobes and fingers, marks of a tiger skin on his legs, long eyes and eyebrows which curve upward on the outside, the sign of a conch shell in the palm of his hand, and so on. He may speak at an early age, and generally display signs of unusual intelligence. All his former knowledge is believed to be retained. The young candidate may pick out his former ritual objects or eating bowl from among several supplied for the test. He is then declared the new incarnation and sent off for more education until he is deemed ready for reassertion of his former position. He is regarded as a child, and he must mature before he assumes his new role in the religious world.

Lama Gulu was an adult before he was so recognized. He was an Abbot and probably had done meritorious work through which he was noticed by the Rong-phu Abbot. Since Gulu was the first incarnation of Bundachendzen in several hundred years, the Rong-phu lamas probably were not seeking a child because of the great time lapse, and missed Gulu as a child.

For further reading into this interesting and unparalleled system of locating reincarnate saints, the reader should consult: Charles Bell, *The Religion of Tibet* (Oxford: Clarendon Press, 1931), chap. xii, and Thubten

Abbot of Tengpoche in the 1920's, as a reincarnation of Lama Bundachendzen and, hence, the Rong-phu Abbot's spiritual father. Lama Bundachendzen was a greater Bodhisattva than the Rdo-rje line, and the Abbot of Tengpoche, Lama Gulu, should therefore have received higher stature. However, the reincarnate Bundachendzen was the first incarnation for several hundred years, and the image of Sanga Rdo-rje's line of successors was held in greater repute.[21] Even though the Abbot of Tengpoche is a more towering figure in religious spheres, the Rongphu lamas are considered to be more erudite. Incarnate lamas retain all knowledge from former lives, and since Lama Bundachendzen's successor did not appear for several centuries, the Rong-phu lamas attained ascendancy of knowledge over the Tengpoche abbots. To this day the Rong-phu monastery retains a leadership role over that of Tengpoche.

Besides choosing the site for the Pangboche gomba, Lama Sanga Rdo-rje also selected the site for the Tengpoche monastery, where Mani-rimdu is performed. Snellgrove quotes the following from the biography of the tenth incarnation of Dzarong-phu:

> Aspiring with devotion to the company of the victorious repository of wisdom, the Father Padmasambhava, he triumphed over all attachment to the reality of this world, and flying in a southwesterly direction, he left the imprint of his foot upon a rock. Then flying further, he descended on the great rock on Tengpo-che in Khumbu and there too he left his mark. . . . This is the place where they have recently built a new monastery. Having gained power over the five elements in such a way, he was known as Sanga Dorje, the second Urgyen (Padmasambhava). At that time he had many brilliant pupils both in Shar-Khumbu and in Rong-phu.[22]

Jigme Norbu, *Tibet Is My Country: As Told to Heinrich Harrer* (London: Rupert Hart-Davis, 1960). The latter author is an elder brother of the Dalai Lama. Himself a reincarnate Bodhisattva, Norbu relates the events leading to his discovery, as well as that of his Dalai Lama brother.

[21] Fürer-Haimendorf, *Sherpas of Nepal,* pp. 131-32.

[22] Snellgrove, *Buddhist Himalaya,* pp. 213-14.

43

Lama Sanga Rdo-rje's death, as his life, was accompanied by miraculous events. "His body was not cremated," writes Fürer-Haimendorf, "but evaporated in the form of a rainbow, and only his eyes, tongue and heart remained."[23] The Pangboche lamas enshrined these remains of the great saint in their gomba, where they remain cherished possessions today.

From what is known as fact, it can be established that Tengpoche monastery was founded by Lama Gulu, held to be an incarnation of Lama Bundachendzen, in 1923. The Thami monastery, whose site was also selected by Lama Sanga Rdo-rje, was built in 1920. It is not necessary to include the legendary founding of other gombas and monasteries here. The purpose of describing these few is to illustrate the difficulty of separating fact from myth in Sherpa history.

A distinction between village gombas and the monasteries of Tengpoche and Thami must be borne in mind. The monasteries operate and exist independently of all villages, while village gombas exist only within the framework of the town as a whole, even though they are not controlled by the government. Hereafter statements about the Thami and Tengpoche gombas refer to gombas within a monastic setting. All other gombas mentioned are village gombas, which may have only a part-time lama and depend upon lay assistance to carry out rituals. The monastic gombas, however, never rely upon laymen except for some major menial task, such as rebuilding or repairing the gomba itself. Mani-rimdu festivals take place only within the framework of a monastic setting such as is found at Thami and Tengpoche. Monasteries at Junbesi and Jiwong, south of Khumbu, produce Mani-rimdu also, but this discussion is limited to the Khumbu Mani-rimdu.

Enjoying virtual monopolistic control of the arts in Khumbu, the monasteries of Tengpoche and Thami likewise regulate the production of Mani-rimdu in their respective monastic centers. (The physical execution of that control will be dealt with in a

[23] Hagen *et al.*, *Mount Everest*, p. 169.

44

subsequent chapter.) Village governments, which consist of a town council plus various appointed officials to regulate commerce and conservation, have no power in the formation of monastic policies. Mani-rimdu and other arts are in no way controlled by village government, for drama is a religious affair. During festivals donations of food, clothing, and cash are accepted for the monastery, but the monks dictate the right to produce or not to produce the dances regardless of whether donations are received.

The majority of lamas in Khumbu belong to the Rnying-ma-pa sect of Buddhism from Tibet. An old, unreformed sect, the Rnying-ma-pa dates to the eighth century when it was founded by Padmasambhava. The other sect to which some lamas claim devotion is the semireformed sect of the Sa-skya-pa, founded in the eleventh century.[24] Khumbu monasteries are an amalgamation of these two sects, the distinction being that Rnying-ma-pa doctrine rules over Sa-skya-pa precepts. Lamas support themselves in their choice of monastic life, receiving nothing from village governments. They may come from wealthy families and lend money for interest, or they may own cattle or grow crops for their livelihood. Their homes on the monastery grounds are individually owned, and a monk may sell or rent his home as he desires. Lamas receive only firewood and a small amount of food and money donated to the monastery by devout laymen. Village lamas—those who regulate village gombas and are dissociated from monasteries—may be married, but those of monastic order are strictly celibate. The monks who reside in the monasteries are the actors who perform in the Sherpa theater.

A few religious beliefs and deities of the Sherpas are peculiar to them, and an understanding of them will help to clarify Mani-rimdu itself. Neither purely entertainment nor strictly religious ritual, Mani-rimdu lies somewhere between those two extremes. Through worship and ritual Mani-rimdu reminds the faithful of the precepts of Buddhism and its victory over Bon,

[24] Helmut Hoffmann, *The Religions of Tibet,* trans. Edward Fitzgerald (New York: Macmillan, 1961), p. 135.

but the festival also contains two satirical, buffooning acts that are primarily entertainment. There is no contradiction in entertainment and religion appearing side by side in the same festival. Permeating all of Sherpa life, religion is such an integral part of existence that it cannot adequately be separated from pure frolic, and the Sherpas make no attempt to do so. The Sherpas approach life in a lusty, straightforward manner, and the Buddhist religion in Khumbu merely proclaims guidelines for the acts of moral conduct. If a man adheres diligently to these precepts, he will find it easier to gain a more favorable incarnation in the next life.

Condemnation of moral acts and sanctimonious judgments upon individuals by religious leaders are incompatible with Buddhist tolerance in Khumbu. For example, a monk may break his vow of celibacy, leave the monastery, and marry a Buddhist nun. The consequence of that act disengages the monk from his monastic order, but he is welcome at all festivities, and he may hold a respected place in the village social structure. If he so chooses he may become a village lama, and he may petition for a government position within the village structure. The wrong deed which he committed is not judged by his superiors on this earth, for the high lamas know that his retribution (karma) will be worked out in his next incarnation. His act of forsaking his monastic vows affects only his karma, not his character, personality, or friends on this earth. Sherpas vigorously enjoy life, and they do not concern themselves with others' religious misdeeds so long as they do not harm another individual. Whether a man chooses to become a respected religious hermit or a street vagabond, he is not judged by his fellow men.

This attitude of extreme tolerance of one's fellow man infects ritual fellowship of religion, and it renders that festival or ritual all the more enjoyable. This concept of being able to gain religious merit while enjoying the festival immensely, even to the point of inebriation, marks a peculiarity of Khumbu life. The theory originates in the concept of *bsod-nams*. Sherpas believe that all of life's acts and thoughts are recorded on a mysterious ledger. Each "act of virtue . . . [*dge-ba*] adds to an individual's store of *sönam* [*bsod-nams*], whereas every morally negative action or sin . . . [*sdig-pa*] decreases this store."[25]

The concept works as follows:

Throughout a man's or woman's life, good and bad deeds make their marks on a person's record sheet, and this process is imagined as the action of two anthropomorphic beings, believed to be born with every individual and sitting invisibly on his right and left shoulder. The former known as "lhen-cig-kye-wai-lha" is the person's genius who marks every deed of virtue with a white mark, while the latter known as "lhen-dig-kye-wai-dre" is his evil genius, who strives to lead a man along a downward path and marks every sin with a black sign.[26]

(This moral recording is a function of Gshin-rje Chos-rgyal, one of the characters who appears in the dance of the *Chos-skyongs* in Chapter VI.) With the mechanical totaling up of virtuous and evil deeds, the Sherpa's next incarnation is determined. This idea of *bsod-nams* is a mechanical, easily explainable concept of karma for the lay Sherpa. It eliminates the baffling metaphysical elements which might serve to confuse an illiterate Buddhist. If a man has accumulated plentiful stores of *bsod-nams,* he may be able to enter a paradise above the six spheres, which is known to the Sherpas as "Devachen." The Bodhisattva concept would then reincarnate this virtuous man as a Rinpoche (incarnate) Lama, and he would retain all of his previous knowledge in order to aid other sentient beings in their quest for enlightenment. The theory of *bsod-nams,* then, is an automatic regulator of moral codes. If a man wishes to work diligently, he will follow his Abbot's teachings, but if he chooses merely to retain the status quo in his next incarnation, he can disregard minor virtuous acts and go his own way. This does not "offend" any personal deity, nor does it bring disgrace upon him unless he commits a civil offense, such as murder or thievery. He then steps outside the jurisdiction of the church and is handled by civil authorities.

[25] Fürer-Haimendorf, *Sherpas of Nepal,* p. 272.
[26] Hagen *et al., Mount Everest,* p. 177.

Circumambulating mani walls, construction of mani walls, turning of prayer wheels, performing good deeds for one's fellow men—that is, giving food and clothing to the poor, donating money and food to lamas, and speaking well of one's fellow man —all add *bsod-nams* to a Sherpa's ledger. Partaking in religious and ritual exercises likewise adds to a man's store of *bsod-nams*, as does performing good deeds in relation to animals. Another of the methods of gaining merit is to abandon the ten sins and to receive the ten virtues:

> The ten sins are: taking life; taking what is not given; adultery; lies; slander; anger; senseless talk; covetousness; evil heart; and heresy. The ten virtues are: not taking life; not to take what is not given; to observe purity of morals; to speak the truth; to speak gently, politely; not to break a promise; not to slander; not to covet another's property; not to do mischief or think of doing injury to others; and to regard the purest doctrine.[27]

Acts which cause no harm to others and are mutually agreed upon by participating parties, as in sexual relations, are morally neutral. A monk sins if he indulges in sexual intercourse because he has broken his vow of celibacy, not because he offends a moral principle of the deities. The Sherpas' great respect for individual dignity and independence is illustrated by their concept of moral codes. Sin and enjoyment cannot be synonymous terms when speaking of *bsod-nams,* that is, enjoyment does not lead to sin. The condition of a man's heart causes sin and evil deeds to be committed, and it is not the deed itself which results in sin. During the performance of Mani-rimdu it is not uncommon to witness spectators who have imbibed great quantities of spirits, even to the point of inebriation. If these individuals are not causing others discomfort or preventing one from hearing the chants, they do not lose merit. They are attending the ritual, and if they have done so in good faith, they are supporting religion, which transfers merit to their ledger. This creates the air

---

[27] Marion H. Duncan (ed. and trans.), *Harvest Festival Dramas of Tibet* (Hong Kong: Orient Publishing Company, 1955), p. 41.

of a county fair, since no one can see the condition of the human heart. The lamas do not sit in judgment, and the laymen believe that merely listening to the chants gains meritorious marks for their karma.

Guru Rinpoche is the patron saint of Khumbu, and he is looked upon as a religious saint as well as a historical hero. Each clan of Sherpas worships a specific deity, usually one associated with an area or a mountain in Khumbu. The great protector of Khumbu is the country god Khumbu yul-lha, located on maps as the 19,294 peak, Khumbila, near Khumjung. One aspect of the Yeti (popularly, Abominable Snowman) legend is that the god Khumbu yul-lha sends forth an emanation of the Yeti when he intends harm to anyone. To see a Yeti is a bad omen to Sherpas who believe this version, and the viewer must diligently strive to accumulate merit to offset the omen.[28] Certain clans worship Mount Everest, to which they pray during Mani-rimdu. Fürer-Haimendorf lists a few of the clans and their respective deities:

Pari-lha-tsen karbu, associated with a mountain in Khumbu, worshipped by the Paldorje clan.
Tonak-lha-tsen karbu, associated with an area north of Gokyo, and Long-gyo, associated with a dried-up lake close to Gokyo, worshipped by the Thakto clan.
Tawoche-lha-tsen, associated with the mountain Tawoche above Pangboche, worshipped by the Nawa clan.
Loudze-lha-tsen, associated with the mountain Loudze (Lhotse) near Mt. Everest, worshipped by the Chusherwa clan.
Arkamtse-lha-tsen karbu, associated with a locality above Tangnak, worshipped by the Sherwa clan.
Chiawitsa-kyung karbu, associated with a locality above Maralung, worshipped by the Chiawa clan.
Karte Gyelbu (King of Karte), associated with the village of Karte in Tibet, worshipped by the Mende clan.[29]

These clan deities are inferior to Khumbu yul-lha, the principal locality god of all of Khumbu. Mountain gods are defenders of the faith, and, since they are active gods rather than contempla-

[28] Snellgrove, *Buddhist Himalaya*, p. 294.
[29] Fürer Haimendorf, *Sherpas of Nepal*, pp. 22-23.

tive ones, they undoubtedly were converted to Buddhism from Bonism. The goddess who resides on Mount Everest and the defenders who live on Khumbila will be discussed further in Chapter VI in conjunction with the performance of Mani-rimdu.

Although Mani-rimdu alone is the main dramatic presentation that offers one full day of dance-dramas, other festivals which the Sherpas of Khumbu perform should be mentioned. These festivals present only a few isolated dances, which are generally akin to the Mani-rimdu dances.

One such festival, known as Gdung-rje, is strictly a village temple celebration, usually held in June or July, involving practically all villagers who share one gomba.[30] Lasting eight days, the Gdung-rje festival marks the end of family unity, as herders depart for higher yak pastures with their herds following the celebration. It is the highlight of festive occasions for the Sherpas, and it possibly celebrates the anniversary of the birth of their patron saint, Lama Sanga Rdo-rje (Guru Rinpoche), despite the fact that different villages adhere to slightly different dates.[31] "The religious function of . . . [Gdung-rje] as seen by the Sherpas is the control and destruction of those evil forces which threaten the bodily and spiritual well-being of the community."[32] Fürer-Haimendorf describes the dance which occurs on the sixth day of Gdung-rje:

> As soon as the gemaka [a type of guard] had taken his stand at the gate, two boys dressed in white and representing rurang or skeletons came out of the temple and danced about in the courtyard crowded with spectators. They were soon joined by other dancers wearing demon masks. Their dancing was the untutored jumping about of amateurs, in no way comparable to the skilful and disciplined dancing of the lamas of monasteries. Though built into a ritual context, and no doubt inspired by the dances which the Khumjung people see in the monasteries

[30] *Ibid.*, p. 185.

[31] It could also be the celebration of the Buddha's birth and death, which occurs on the fifteenth of the fourth Tibetan month. This comes in June and July after a "leap" year.

[32] Fürer-Haimendorf, *Sherpas of Nepal*, p. 207.

of Tengpoche and Thami, those dances at the . . . [Gdung-rje] were clearly intended to amuse the spectators, and there was a good deal of horse-play incompatible with the character of a ritual dance. As at the Mani-rimdu at Thami, there also appeared a dancer, wearing a mask of a very old man and supporting himself on a stick. This figure, representing extreme old age, was greeted with a burst of laughter. Even small boys took part in the fun, donning masks much too large for their size, and hopping about in the temple courtyard.

The dancing lasted only about twenty minutes, and when it had come to an end the lamas had completed their recitation. . . .[33]

All Khumbu monastic dances are of twenty-minute duration. The reason why is unknown, but they are rehearsed to accommodate that period of time. The Gdung-rje is a village festival which must use lay assistance to carry out the ritual. At Mani-rimdu no laymen are permitted to participate in the actual ritual and dances.

There are two different forms of New Year's celebrations (February or March by the Western calendar) in Khumbu: one by the villagers and one by the monasteries. Lo-gsar (New Year) is a village celebration by families who prepare feasts and parties for their clan, friends, and neighbors. Long hours are spent in the preparation of food and drink, and equally long hours are spent in entertaining from one home to another to celebrate the occasion. It is a time of dancing and joyous relaxation from early morning until late evening. Monasteries, however, perform ancient rites, which include a few dances, to expel the old year. The Khumbu celebrations, which are derived from the elaborate New Year's festivals in Tibet, are much more subdued than the original.[34] Families come to the monasteries in smaller numbers than is usual during Mani-rimdu, possibly because the New Year's dances are more ritualistic than the for-

[33] *Ibid.*, p. 202.
[34] Marion H. Duncan, *Customs and Superstitions of Tibetans* (London: The Mitre Press, 1964), pp. 143-65. Also see Waddell, *The Buddhism of Tibet*, pp. 513-35. Also see Chapter III of this study for examples of Tibetan New Year's dances.

51

mer. Known as Dgu-gtor 'cham and Smon-lam-'cham, these dances are specifically prayers to the gods to control and exorcise the evil spirits. More animistic and more primitive than Mani-rimdu, the New Year's dances contain a great deal of magical and supernatural endeavors by protective deities. Much of these dances is lost on the populace, and they are not well attended. The highlight of New Year's in Khumbu is the gathering of the clan for more human celebrations.

Another of the festivals at monasteries is the Mong-doh, which marks the termination of the old year. It takes place in January, according to the Western calendar. The two dances of Mong-doh are directed toward the destruction of evil. A skull placed on a pole forms the central image of the festival. Dancers symbolically kill the devil whose head is displayed, and following that act the monks carry the image to a pyre where the final destruction of evil occurs. The region has been made safe from evil by the ritual, and good luck and a fine harvest are virtually assured for the coming year. The victorious monks return to the gomba, and the relieved people return to their villages to begin the preparation of food for their New Year's celebration, which is now safe from harm.

There are fewer monastic rituals which involve the populace in Khumbu than in Tibet. Sherpa society includes fewer monks than does Tibetan society, and religion permeates the Sherpas' private lives. Sherpas are generally less superstitious than their Tibetan brothers, and perhaps this accounts for the fact that there are fewer exorcismic rites in Khumbu than in Tibet. Religion is as strong in Khumbu as in Tibet, but the Sherpas seem to be more independent than their northern neighbors. Perhaps Bonism was not as strongly entrenched in Khumbu as it was in Tibet, and the Sherpas therefore do not feel the need for numerous rites to expel the old gods. In Tibet, monastic communities control the government, while in Khumbu religion and government are completely separate entities. This fact undoubtedly has forced Khumbu lamas to be more realistic in their approach to laymen. No punishments are meted out to laymen who appear to offend the gods, and monks are subject to civil law in Khumbu as are any other citizens. Inhabitants of the monasteries dwell in partial seclusion from the world and practice their religion in solitude.

Buddhism is, however, a socially conscious idea, which attempts to indoctrinate and lead the people in religious spheres. Village civil authorities pay great attention to lamas in matters of religion, but pay no more heed to them in politics than they would to another educated citizen of Khumbu. In short, religion must be vital and honest if it is to survive in a culture such as the Sherpas have developed. It cannot coerce or unduly victimize people in a power struggle. The Sherpas fully realize that their lamas are human, capable of errors of judgment, and susceptible to human frailties and crimes of passion. Still, a reincarnate abbot retains all knowledge from former lives. He is revered as a learned man, and he is a towering source of religious wisdom and truth. In times of despondency or mourning a Sherpa visits his lama, but when in need of legal assistance over a land dispute he will confer with the village headman. This blunt separation of powers in society allows the great zest of life in Sherpa communities to be manifested in a village affair, or in a monastic festival such as Mani-rimdu, with equal enthusiasm.

III. Origin, Background, and Development of Mani-rimdu

THE ORIGIN of Mani-rimdu is not chronicled in any Buddhist writings. Its inception in Tibet is obscure because no literary or artistic histories were recorded in that country. The background must be assembled like a jigsaw puzzle, piecing together numerous allusions to theater and art from Indian, Tibetan, Nepalese, and Western sources into a meaningful whole. It is necessary, therefore, to inspect briefly the beginnings of art in general, and drama in particular, within the framework of early Buddhism, in order to formulate some hypotheses about the inception of Mani-rimdu.

According to one legend, Indian theater had its nascence direct from the hand of Brahma. He commanded that the first dramatic presentation be given in celebration of the victory of good over evil. It was to be presented to the gods for their enjoyment. Mortals also desired the secrets of this new diversion, and Brahma confided all his knowledge of it to the sage Bharata. The resulting treatise became known as the *Bharata Natya Sastra,* the canon of dance and dramaturgy.[1] A similar legend states:

Brahma sat in meditation and from the four Vedas he ex-

[1] Faubion Bowers, *Theatre in the East: A Survey of Asian Dance and Drama* (New York: Grove Press, 1956) , p. 5.

tracted the four elements of speech, song, mime, and sentiment
and so created Natyaveda [Natya Sastra], the holy book of dramaturgy. He said to Indra, "Let this book be passed to those of
the Gods who are skillful, learned, free from stage fright and
given to hard work."

Indra bowed with folded hands and replied, "The Gods are
neither able to receive nor maintain it, nor are they fit to understand and make use of it. Only the sages who know the mystery
of the Vedas and have meditated are capable of putting Natyaveda into practice." So Brahma taught the art of dramaturgy to
Bharata Muni, the great sage, who taught it to his hundred
sons. Thus the celestial Natyaveda was brought from heaven to
earth for the benefit of the people.[2]

This apocryphal creation of theater direct from the hand of an
anthropomorphic god is similar to a Japanese legend,[3] and not
unlike a Tibetan fable which will be noted later.

Apart from mythologic sources, it is known that dramas existed in India prior to the Christian era. The earliest extant
drama is a fragmentary Buddhist work entitled "Cāriputrapra-
karana," written by a Buddhist named Aśvaghosha.[4] "He is not
only a Buddhist poet," writes Ananda Coomaraswamy, "but one
of the greatest of the Sanskrit poets, and the chief forerunner
of Kalidāsa."[5] The author of several Buddhist works, Aśvaghosha
is regarded as the father of Mahāyāna. He lived in the first century, and his writings follow an already firmly established practice. A. B. Keith surmises that Aśvaghosha gleaned his ideology
and style from the *Natya Sastra* because he "follows a train of
tradition in the dialogue from Vedic sources, and the character
traits in the drama are spelled out specifically in the *Natya
Sastra*."[6] If Keith's position is true, then the first dramas in India

[2] Balwant Gargi, *Theatre in India* (New York: Theatre Arts Books,
1962), pp. 4-5.
[3] Faubion Bowers, *Japanese Theatre* (New York: Hill and Wang, 1952),
p. 3.
[4] Arthur Berriedale Keith, *The Sanskrit Drama in Its Origin, Development, Theory and Practice* (London: Oxford University Press, 1924), p. 43.
[5] Ananda K. Coomaraswamy, *Buddha and the Gospel of Buddhism* (London: George C. Harrap, 1916), p. 303.
[6] Keith, *Sanskrit Drama*, p. 84.

would have appeared before the Christian era. It is believed that Buddhists evolved a propensity for the drama shortly after the Buddha's demise in 483 B.C., but no texts of dramas earlier than Aśvaghosha's are extant.

In order to understand the remarkable origin and survival of drama in early Buddhism, it is necessary to examine briefly Theravāda principles concerning artistic activities. (One must distinguish here between Theravāda, the early strict school of Buddhism, and the later school of Mahāyāna, which encouraged art.) Tracing the evolution of Buddhist drama is puzzling, because even though Theravāda Buddhism disclaimed art, monks within the fold experimented with forms of expression including poetry, sculpture, and drama. Outside influences—dramas of non-Buddhist origin—served as models from which monks obtained their inspiration. Theravāda not only had to suppress desires for art within its own ranks, but also to guard its monks and laymen from the evils which it felt were inherent in drama.

The *Mahavāgga* and *Khuddakapātha* sutras pronounced the strict rules of conduct which Theravāda demanded of its followers. Of these, the last five apply only to the clergy:

1. Refrain from killing living things;
2. from taking what is not given;
3. from unchastity;
4. from falsehood;
5. from intoxicants;
6. from eating at unseasonable times;
7. from seeing displays, dancing, singing, and music;
8. from the use of garlands, scents, and unguents;
9. from the use of a high or a big bed;
10. from receiving gold and silver.[7]

The monk was to abandon worldly spectacles. The "displays"

[7] F. Max Müller (ed.), "Mahāvagga Sutra," *Sacred Books of the East* (Oxford: The Clarendon Press, 1910), p. 211; and L. Austine Waddell, *The Buddhism of Tibet or Lamaism* (Cambridge: W. Heffner and Sons, 1894), p. 134.

above are translated as "shows" elsewhere.[8] The *Sigalovida* sutra contains a code of ethics for the layman specifically, which warns him against the dangers inherent in the dance and drama.[9]

Theravāda allowed paintings of landscapes and carvings of humans and animals. It did not permit sculpture which sought emotional expression, for the goal of Theravāda was intellectual contemplation, devoid of emotion. E. R. Saratchandra states, "The solitary existence of the monk was enriched, as far as his material existence was concerned, with all that human skill could achieve in the realm of decorative art and . . . mural painting."[10]

This injunction on emotive arts in the visual form stemmed from the Buddha himself. He did not think of himself as a god, only as a man who discovered the way to enlightenment through human efforts. He considered the images and icons that Indian religions used in their worship to be barbarian and perfidious. For that reason early Buddhist art depicted the presence of the Buddha symbolized by the empty throne for enlightenment, the wheel for the first sermon, and the stupa mound, an architectural form emblematic of his Nirvana.[11]

Despite religious condemnation, monks sought to express their impressions of the Buddha in wooden images. The great missionary, Ashoka, in the third century B.C. developed a cult of relics, an early indication of the growing worship of the Buddha.[12] The earliest extant statues of the Buddha, which date from the second century, are in the Ghandāra caves near Bombay, India. Images are believed to have been carved in the first century, however, and one legend claims that sandalwood icons

[8] Edward J. Thomas, *The History of Buddhist Thought* (New York: Barnes and Noble, 1951), p. 25.

[9] E. R. Saratchandra, *The Sinhalese Folk Play and the Modern Stage* (Colombo, Ceylon: The Daily News Press Lake House, 1953), p. 9.

[10] *Ibid.*

[11] Benjamin Rowland, Jr., *The Evolution of the Buddha Image* (Tokyo: Book Craft, 1963), p. 6.

[12] *Ibid.*

were in existence during the Buddha's lifetime.[13] These early statues depicted the Buddha as a supernatural being, and the various poses captured in the icons depicted the Buddha's numerous powers. Images and icons are an indication of the growing artistic aspirations of the early Buddhist followers, who desired more self-expression than was permissible in mural paintings and landscapes.

Coinciding with the growth of spatial arts, drama motivated further artistic endeavors by the early Buddhists, despite ethical codes which contrived to destroy the impulse. In basic agreement with Keith's supposition that drama existed in India prior to the Christian era, a Buddhist sutra claims early manifestations of the drama. The *Lalitavistara* sutra (biography of the Buddha) claims that the Buddha included knowledge of the drama among his other accomplishments. It also states that Bimbisāra, a contemporary of the Buddha, had a play performed in honor of a pair of Nāga kings.[14] According to the *Mahāvānsa* sutra, "Bimbisāra and Prince Siddhartha were friends, and likewise friends were the fathers of both."[15] Bimbisāra and the Nāga kings are historical personages who resided in the northern plains of India during the sixth century B.C. If Prince Siddhartha and Bimbisāra were, indeed, friends, it is likely that the Buddha would have had some knowledge of the drama.

Another sutra, supposedly written prior to Aśvaghosha's time, further substantiates the proposal that drama was in evidence in early India, and that Buddhists were involved in its practice. The *Avadāna* claims that an actress named Kuvalayā gained merit as a result of associating herself with the performance of a Buddhist play, in which the director played the part of the Buddha.[16] These statements give credence to Keith's postulation that Aśvaghosha followed an already established tradition as he wrote his play.

[13] *Ibid.*
[14] Keith, *Sanskrit Drama*, p. 43.
[15] Thomas, *History of Buddhist Thought*, p. 7.
[16] Sylvain Lévi, *Le Théâtre Indien* (Paris: Champion Press, 1890), p. 320.

Buddhists who yearned for artistic expression were opposed by the strict dicta of Theravāda. As monks experimented with their imaginative creations, the ecclesiastic order tenaciously castigated them as guilty of conduct unbecoming a monk. Exactly when and where ideological battles were waged over the arts, in particular, is unknown. However, several Buddhist councils were convened to discuss differences of opinions. The first of these was summoned by Kāśyapa near the end of the fifth century B.C., in order to deliberate certain laxities in the conduct of ecclesiastics. One such laxity involved rules of conduct, and may have been directed, among other things, against the monks who viewed and were entertained by dramas.

Theravāda cherished its rules of conduct and maintained its right to dictate them. Certain monks sought to mitigate those regulations, and, consequently, offshoots from the mainstream of Buddhism developed. Some eventually matured into new schools of the faith. The differing interpretations of doctrine and rules were the main cause of the trials of Buddhism; the arts were only a minute segment of these disputes, but it is that segment which is of concern here.

In the first century the Mahāyāna school gradually emerged as an organized force. The term "Mahāyāna" will be used hereafter to signify that Buddhist ideology which encouraged the arts. Although technically the term did not appear until the first century, for convenience and clarity it is used here in spiritual opposition to Theravāda and its denunciation of drama. As a result of Mahāyāna's impetus, according to Keith, "the objection of the sacred canon to monks engaging in the amusement of watching . . . shows, whatever their nature, was gradually overcome. . . ."[17]

Mahāyāna proselytized and spread its sphere of influence while Hinayāna (Theravāda) sought only the realm of monks. Mahāyāna was proliferated by zealous missionaries, but Hinayāna contented itself with its conservative doctrines. Hinayāna

[17] Keith, *Sanskrit Drama*, p. 43.

59

discouraged drama, while Mahāyāna utilized art and drama as instruments of instruction. The common bond between the two schools was permanently sundered. Because of Hinayāna's disinterest in art, the remaining references to Buddhism refer specifically to Mahāyāna Buddhism unless otherwise noted.

Mahāyāna, as stated above, utilized art as a teaching device. When it began using drama as such is not known, but Aśvaghosa's play reflects that intent. Keith writes: "Ashvagosa had the ability to turn tales into an instrument for propaganda in support of the Buddhist faith. The play *Cāriputraprakanana* depicts the Buddha converting Cāriputra and delivering a polemic against the Indian theory of the existence of a permanent self."[18] The story from the *Avadāna* sutra may have reflected that instructional inclination as well.

As Buddhist missionaries emigrated from India to nearby countries of Asia, they carried with them the notions about drama to which they had become accustomed. The enjoyment of drama as a form of pleasure was now legitimate to Buddhists. With the repeated performance of plays, a tradition was established regarding methods of production and the edification to be received therefrom. Monks related dance movements, drama forms, pageantry, and aesthetic principles to new cultures as they traveled on their missions of proselytization. Thus drama was transported from India to Tibet, where it was known as the Lha-mo genre.

Before analyzing the Tibetan drama which fostered Mani-rimdu, a final distinction between 'Cham and Lha-mo must be observed. Akin to Western dramas, Lha-mo uses characterization, dialogue, suspense, plot, and conclusions. It communicates a legend or enacts historical events. The inner sentiments of a human being are depicted through a man's apprehensions and ecstasies. He may be an incarnation of a deity, but he takes the form of a human being, and he is perceived by the spectators in

[18] *Ibid.*, p. 81.

human pathos. Dialogue in Lha-mo is written in poetic style, with each verse consisting of seven, nine, or eleven syllables.[19]

The analysis of *Drowazangmo* in Chapter I depicts a Lha-mo form of Tibetan drama. The origin of this genre lies in the Buddhist drama examined earlier in this chapter. It, like classical Sanskrit drama, admits no tragedy, and its chief characters are generally Indian nobility or Brahmins. The *Natya Sastra* is the basis for this type of theatrical presentation. Drowazangmo's parents were both Brahmins, and the play illustrates the passage of Buddhism from India to Tibet, where it converts or destroys Bon deities.

Scripts of Lha-mo exist as literature, and they are used in the study of history in monastery schools in Khumbu. The dates of composition and the authors are unknown. The Sherpas never act out Lha-mo as it is produced in Tibet. Chinese writers refer to Lha-mo as the Tibetan opera, and they are sometimes labeled as sacred dramas or mystery plays by Westerners.

'Cham is an indigenous form of dance-drama from Tibet which was altered to befit Buddhist doctrine. The Mani-rimdu dances of Khumbu are a direct heir of the 'Cham. Unlike Lha-mo, which utilizes ecclesiastic and lay actors either exclusively or interchangeably, depending upon the circumstances of production, both Mani-rimdu and 'Cham permit only monks to portray the acts. 'Cham does not use a plot which is discharged through dialogue, nor do written texts of 'Cham exist. Allegorical masked figures depict deified personages in struggles of a religious nature. The legends it presents are excerpted from Tibetan history and the history of Buddhism in Tibet. The background of 'Cham in Tibet must be examined before we approach the question of Mani-rimdu. We will note some important differences between the Sherpa and the Tibetan forms of drama, which were encouraged by Mahāyāna Buddhism.

The question of 'Cham's embryonic evolution will probably

[19] Chang K'ung, "On Tibetan Poetry," *Central Asiatic Journal*, II, No. 2 (1956), 129.

never be answered. It is inconceivable that Lha-mo could have provided the inception for 'Cham. The former has its foundation in the *Natya Sastra* and a tradition of Sanskrit literature. From what is known of 'Cham, it developed from a primitive Tibetan devil-dance. If Lha-mo developed into 'Cham, the former would have had to become so corrupted in Tibet that it eliminated dialogue, poetry, characterizations, and plot. The Indian sages who imported Buddhist texts to Tibet were scholars from Indian universities. It is improbable that they would have allowed a tradition they valued to be altered so radically. It is my theory that Lha-mo retained the major portion of its characteristics, and that 'Cham blossomed from an indigenous form of dance-drama in Tibet.

Exactly how 'Cham originated is impossible to discern. At the dawn of written history, 'Cham, or dances resembling it, were already in existence. Mention was made in Chapter I of primitive tribal dances which sought the exorcism or propitiation of demon spirits. Such rites, specifically Bon rites in Tibet, provide the only possible explanation of 'Cham's inception. Tibetan Buddhist texts ignore allusions to this genre in theory, origin, or principle.

Buddhism was a dynamic, hydra-like religion which absorbed cults wherever it encountered them. It absorbed a cult of astrology in Burma, and the latter's Gods of the Nine Planets became the Buddha and his eight disciples.[20] An original harvest festival in Burma became a Buddhist festival, probably under the influence of Ashoka.[21] The mountain god, Sonam Deviyo, guardian of the peak Samantakuta in Ceylon, was proclaimed a Bodhisattva,[22] comparable to Khumbu yul-lha in Khumbu. In China another amalgamation of primitive cults and Buddhism emerged. Through dance, Chinese monks depicted the tortures,

[20] Maung Htin Aung, *Folk Elements in Burmese Buddhism* (London: Oxford University Press, 1962), p. 3.
[21] *Ibid.,* p. 125.
[22] Saratchandra, *Sinhalese Folk Play,* p. 5.

burning fires, and freezing snows which awaited men who strayed from the Buddhist path in ignorance and blindness.

Buddhism absorbed numerous other primitive cults and rites which it subverted to its own uses. Spirits of the aboriginal cults were encouraged to meditate upon the hope and redemption preached by the Buddha.[23] As was stated earlier in conjunction with Bon deities, Buddhism converted primitive deities into protective gods of Buddhist pantheons. The outward form of the aboriginal cult was maintained, but the doctrinal foundation was altered. The culture of the literati came in contact with the culture of the folk and effected a new form of drama. This curious relationship which emerged between Buddhism and primitive cultures resulted in the 'Cham as a distinct genre of theater. In the ability of Buddhism to compromise its strict beliefs with those of cults which it encountered, and in its aptitude for absorbing elements of these cults, lies the derivation of this form of drama.

Tibetan Buddhists did not develop a distinct form or systemized design for the production of 'Cham. Rather, each gomba or monastery produced dances in whatever manner it chose. Since Mani-rimdu in Khumbu is probably an amalgam of these various forms of Tibetan 'Cham, an examination of a few Tibetan models and a review of the founding of Tibetan dance is delineated below.

Many Tibetans attribute the origin of their dance to the ascetic, St. Grub-thob Thang-thong, the famous bridge builder of the fifteenth century.[24] One tradition relates that the Tibetans, who were constructing a bridge over the Brahmaputra River, were beset by demons who destroyed their accomplished work each night. Vexed, they sent for the Indian sage Drub-thob Thang-thong, who was versed in spells and who possessed great

[23] Karl Ludwig Reichelt, *Truth and Tradition in Chinese Buddhism: A Study of Chinese Buddhism*, ed. H. T. Hidgkin; trans. Kathrina Van Wagenen Bugge (4th rev. ed.; Shanghai: Commercial Press, 1934), p. 90.

[24] Tsung-lien Shen and Shen-chi Liu, *Tibet and the Tibetans* (Stanford, Calif.: Stanford University Press, 1953), p. 167.

strength. He suggested that the Tibetans institute a dance to attract the mountain demons' attention. They did so, and while the spirits were being entertained, the Tibetans hastily completed their project. Possessing no power to destroy a completed bridge, the evil ones were foiled.[25] Dancing, then, is performed in the saint's honor for the propitiation of those same spirits. It is interesting to note that this story does not speak of defeating demons, only diverting their attention by entertaining dances.

David MacDonald reported a similar legend which he heard at Drepung monastery in Tibet. A vindictive mountain demon lived in the hills behind the monastery. Bound to his rocky perch except for one day during the year, the demon rushed to do harm to the monastic inhabitants on that day. To prevent this, the lamas annually produced a dance on the day of the demon's release. Enthralled while witnessing these dances, the demon forgot all his evil designs.[26] The concept of dance as entertainment is clearly present in these two legends.

Waddell writes that 'Cham "originally appears to have been a devil-dancing cult for exorcising malignant demons and human enemies, associated with human sacrifice and, probably, cannibalism."[27] J. W. Chambers speaks of a ceremony which he witnessed near Peking called "'devil-dances." He claims that their origin can be traced to Tibet and that they were "undoubtedly a relic of the old Mystery Plays of that most mysterious country in the heart of the Himalayan Mountains."[28]

Quite rightly, André Migot states that the term "devil-dances" is an incorrect appellation, disparaging and offensive to Tibetans.[29] However, Migot refers to the present day, and it is common knowledge that devil-dancing and death cults did exist

[25] Marion H. Duncan, *Customs and Superstitions of Tibetans* (London: The Mitre Press, 1964), p. 134.

[26] David MacDonald, *The Land of the Lama* (London: Seely, Service, 1929), p. 212.

[27] Waddell, *Buddhism of Tibet*, p. 516.

[28] J. Wheaton Chambers, "Devil Dancers of the Black Temple," *Travel,* XXXII, No. 5 (March, 1919), 11.

[29] André Migot, "Notes sur le Théâtre Tibétain," *Revue d'Historie du Théâtre,* X, No. 1 (1958), 9.

in Central Asia prior to the entry of Buddhism. "'During the
Buddhist era," Waddell declares, "the devil-dance . . . was given
a Buddhist dress." Continuing with the origin of 'Cham, Waddell writes:

> The unsophisticated Tibetans still call their mystery-play the
> "Dance of the Red-Tiger Devil" [sTag-dmar-cham], a deity of
> the Bön or pre-Buddhist religion of Tibet. The original motive
> of the dances appears to have been to expel the old year with
> its demons of ill-luck, and to propitiate with human sacrifice
> and probably cannibalism the war-god and the guardian spirits,
> most of whom are demonified kings and heroes, in order to
> secure good luck and triumph over enemies in the incoming
> year.[30]

As was noted earlier, pre-Buddhist Tibetan culture and religion were barbarous and cruel by present-day Western standards. Some legends claim that Tibetans are descended from
man-eating ancestry. One tale described them as the offspring of
an alliance of a monkey with a female giant, Rākshari, a man-de-
vouring demon from Hindu mythology.[31] Birds, animals, and demons are represented in 'Cham dances, sometimes symbolically
devouring man. Many of the demon and animal deities symbolize extremely primitive and brutal aspects of the Tibetan past
Today sacrificial effigies are utilized rather than actual animals
or humans, but the vestiges of ancient practices are plainly dis-
cernible in Tibet and in Mani-rimdu in Khumbu.

The concept of mercy accompanied the introduction of
Buddhism into Tibet in the seventh century. Human sacrifice
was condemned, and an effigy of humans was substituted. Traditionally, the Tibetans attribute this substitution to Padmasambhava. It was he who "retained pagan festivals, but altered them
to fit the progress of Buddhism." Waddell continues:

> So, incorporating this ancient and highly popular festival
> [Dance of the Red-Tiger Devil] within their [the Buddhist]
> system, they replaced the human victims by anthropomorphic

[30] Waddell, *Buddhism of Tibet*, p. 516.
[31] Berthold Laufer, *Oriental Theatricals* (Chicago: Field Museum of
Natural History, Department of Anthropology, Guide, Part I, 1923), p. 52.

effigies of dough, into which were inserted models of the larger organs, and also fluid red pigment to represent blood. . . . It [the dance] is made to give the lay spectators a very realistic idea of the dreadful devils from whom the lamas deliver them, and they are familiarized with the appearance of these demons.[32]

In one such dance an effigy of a human is dissected. The scene depicts a historical analogy of the destruction of the evil forces of Bon.

> Shortly after Buddhism had been introduced and stressed in Tibet, King Ral-pa-can, a purveyor of the new doctrine, was assassinated by two pro-Bön ministers in 838. Glang-dar-ma, brother of Ral-pa-can, then ascended the throne and began to persecute the new religion because it threatened his political power. He was assassinated in turn in the fourth year of his reign by Lama Dpal-gyi rdo-rje [Lha-lung Dpal-gyi rdo-rje] who, according to tradition, killed Glang-dar-ma out of compassion to prevent him from accumulating even more evil *karma*.[33]

David MacDonald describes this dance, which he witnessed at Ten-chog-ling monastery during the New Year's festivities in 1920. A corpse (effigy) was brought into the courtyard, and ghouls in masks danced around it. A dancer representing Lha-lung Dpal-gyi rdo-rje led a group of black-hatted dancers who symbolically destroyed the corpse, which represented Glang-dar-ma.

> Each group of lamas, fiends and demons, dances in turn until the entry of Chho-gyal [Gshin-rje Chos-rgyal][34] the bull-headed King of Religion, with his attendant body-guard of terrifying

[32] Waddell, *Buddhism of Tibet*, pp. 518-19.

[33] Helmut Hoffmann, *The Religions of Tibet*, trans. Edward Fitzgerald (New York: Macmillan, 1961), p. 82.

[34] Gshin-rje Chos-rgyal is Yama, Lord of the Dead. He is a form of Shiva, and a wrathful aspect of Avalokiteśvara, frequently represented as a blue buffalo-headed deity. See W. Y. Evans-Wentz (ed.), *The Tibetan Book of the Dead: Or the After-Death Experiences on the Bardo Plane, According to Lama Kazi Dawa-Samdup's English Rendering* (New York: Oxford University Press, 1960), p. 167.

demons. Chho-gyal stabs the lay figure with his magic dagger in each of the limbs and in the heart. Next, taking a sword, he dismembers the body and cuts off the head. Laying open the trunk, he extracts the inner organs, after which his followers rush in and tear the limbs and body to fragments. These are eaten and thrown to the spectators. They represent amulets against disease and misfortune. They then burn the figure of a man, announcing that evil has been destroyed.[35]

Sven Hedin describes another such dance which has its basis of action and doctrine in Bonism:

> Another masked figure, Argham, came out with a bowl of goat's blood which he poured on the steps during the dance. . . . Undoubtedly this ceremony is a relic of the time when the original Bön religion prevailed in Tibet. . . . Buddhism has retained the superstition which in pre-Buddhist times found expression in wild fanatical devil dances, rites, and sacrifices. The object of the ceremony was to exorcise, banish, or propitiate the powerful demons which reign everywhere, in the air, on the earth, and in the water, and whose only function is to plague, torture, and persecute the children of men.[36]

E. F. Knight relates another brutal dance in which demons tore a human image apart with their claws: "The image had red paste for blood, which oozed out during the operation."[37]

Not all of the dances depict Bon brutality as vividly as those described above. The purpose of the dance in Buddhist concepts is to propitiate the demons which Buddhism retained from primitive cults, and to teach the populace about them and the method of overcoming the evil forces. If one trusts in the precepts of Buddhism, its sacred doctrines and magic are depicted as being powerful enough to protect the individual against the onslaught of demons. In one dance the demons attempt to de-

[35] MacDonald, *Land of the Lama,* p. 217.
[36] Sven Hedin, *Trans-Himalaya: Discoveries and Adventures in Tibet,* Vol. I (New York: Macmillan, 1909).
[37] E. F. Knight, *Where Three Empires Meet: A Narrative of Recent Travel in Kashmir, Western Tibet, Gilgit, and the Adjoining Countries* (London: Longmans, Green, 1897), p. 222.

stroy an effigy of man. They are prevented from doing so by lamas with magic spells and gestures. The people are shown that Buddhism can destroy its enemies, as in the case of Glang-dar-ma, and that it also can protect them from evil.

Knight relates one such protective dance in Hemis monastery in Ladakh, which was also observed by MacDonald in Ten-chog-ling monastery near Gyantse in Tibet.[38] An effigy of a corpse, which represents man after death, is beset by *rus-krang* (skeleton dancers). The corpse, however, is protected by a magic triangle[39] inscribed around it, which the *rus-krang* cannot penetrate. The magic of the triangle deters them and deflects their swords, and they are unable to stab the body. Eventually the demons are subdued by a dancer impersonating the Buddha, and the issue is settled.

These "devil-dances," which primarily occur immediately prior to the Tibetan New Year's Day in February, are very serious occasions for Tibetan lamas and laity alike. "There is no mildness or sympathy in the business of coercing demons," Marion Duncan writes, "for life and property are involved and not pleasure. The crowd at the New Year festival is sad and serious, although belief in the efficacy of the exorcism lightens the somberness of the occasion."[40] W. W. Rockhill also states that, "These [dances] are not given for the amusement of the peo-

[38] *Ibid.*, p. 215, and MacDonald, *Land of the Lama*, p. 219.
[39] The magic triangle probably represents the three "essence" mantras of Tibetan Buddhism. Mantras are short prayers to deities, in the form of spells and magical formulas. These three symbolize the three protectors of Buddhism, and the mantra which accompanies each:
  1. Spyan-ras-gzigs (Skt. Avalokiteśvara). He is the seer with keen eyes. His mantra is *Om mani padme hum* ("Hail Jewel in the Lotus").
  2. Jampalyang (Skt. Manjughosh). He is the God of Mystic Wisdom. His mantra is *Om wagi shori mum* ("Hail to the Lord of Speech").
  3. Chakdor (Skt. Vajrapani). He is the wielder of the thunderbolt (*rdo-rje*). His mantra is *Om vajra pani hum* ("Hail to the Holder of the *Rdo-rje*").
See Evans-Wentz (ed.), *Tibetan Book of the Dead*, p. 134.
[40] Marion H. Duncan, "The Tibetan Drama," *China Journal*, XVII, No. 3 (September, 1932), 110.

ple."[41] Gods perform in these festivals, not humans, for when a man dons a mask, he becomes that deity. "They [the Asians] believe that gods do dance, and that when one [human] dances," Edna Emroch writes, "it is the expression of that god within [him]."[42]

All is not an air of gloomy recognition of demons in 'Cham, however, for an element of humor intrudes on the last day of the festivals. Related to religion, but not to exorcismic rites, the humorous dances exist for pure entertainment, and they are enjoyed by the lamas as well as the laity. Lha-mo recognized the audience and the need to entertain them. 'Cham in its origin was purely exorcismic, and no audience was required. Under Buddhist influence, however, entertainment value was added to 'Cham performances. Just how the transfer was accomplished is unknown, but the impetus for humor and entertainment was generated in India. This impetus distinguishes 'Cham as a form of theatrical entertainment.

The comic dances in Tibetan 'Cham furnish an example of the change which had taken place from exorcismic rites to the development of 'Cham. An art form was utilized by the Buddhists, who made still another change in the indigenous 'Cham dances which they encountered in Tibet. They turned the dances from utilitarian purification rites into a creative process which exists primarily for its own sake and for the benefit of the audience.

In Tibet, comic dances follow the serious exorcismic performances on a separate day. Monasteries retained the right to include any forms of humor they chose, or to utilize none. Rockhill reports one monastery in which the only element of humor was in the form of a monk who impersonated the Dalai Lama

[41] William Woodville Rockhill, *The Land of the Lamas: Notes of a Journey Through China, Mongolia, and Tibet* (New York: The Century Company, 1891), p. 247.

[42] Edna Emroch, "Dance of the Orient: A General Survey of the Philosophy and Art of the Dance in the East," *American Dancer*, X (January, 1937), 24.

69

while a layman, who smeared his face with black and white to represent a devil, insulted and mocked the Bodhisattva in humorous fashion.[43] One humorous dance from Tibet is examined here to provide a basis of comparison between Tibetan and Khumbu versions. According to Knight, the dance is

> a sort of harlequinade, full of coarse and often obscene buffoonery, which hugely pleased the audience, and was received with peals of laughter even to the onlooking lamas. Clowns came on and proceeded to burlesque the preceding sacred mysteries. A comic school was one of the chief features of this part of the performance. The schoolmaster was a fatuous old pantaloon. The bare armed and bare-legged boys who represented the scholars wore large masks of moon-shaped, grinning faces. They fought among each other, they chafed their old pedagogue, pinched him from behind and ran away, threw things at him, stole his hat and writing materials, and played all manner of tricks on him; while he tottered after them on his stick trembling with rage, and unable to catch them. . . . Last of all, the schoolmaster prostrated himself with comical action before the bowls of consecrated corn and the images of the gods, and proceeded to ape the worship of the lamas. His scholars, imitating him, prostrated themselves in a row beside him, and engaged in mock prayer and ridiculous gestures and antics at the expense of their own religion. Thus, with an orgie of indecency and blasphemous caricature of all that these people are supposed to hold sacred, the festival ended at dusk.[44]

MacDonald and Duncan provide other descriptions of comic dances during the New Year's Festival in Tibet.[45]

Lha-mo and 'Cham, then, have their religious bases in pre-Christian India. 'Cham is an indigenous form of drama from Tibet and North Central Asia, which originally was a devil-dancing cult of Tibet. Lha-mo was transferred from India to Tibet in essentially its original form, and it thrives today as a

---

[43] William Woodville Rockhill, "Tibet: A Geographical, Ethnographical, and Historic Sketch, Derived from Chinese Sources," *Journal of the Royal Asiatic Society of Great Britain and Ireland*, No. 4 (1891), p. 212.

[44] Knight, *Where Three Empires Meet*, pp. 222-23.

[45] MacDonald, *Land of the Lama*, p. 218; Duncan, *Customs and Superstitions of Tibetans*, pp. 159-60.

distinct theatrical genre in Tibet. The two genres share the same doctrinal basis, but Buddhism maintained the outward form of aboriginal 'Cham and inflicted a veneer of new doctrines upon it. It is the latter form, as it is manifested in Khumbu, with which the balance of this book is concerned. Generally speaking, there is no dialogue, poetry, plot, or characterization in Mani-rimdu, and in this manner it strictly resembles the Tibetan 'Cham. In Khumbu, Lha-mo exists only in the form of historical and literary documents. The texts are studied, but never produced as dramas as they are in Tibet.

Exactly how Mani-rimdu was established in Khumbu remains a mystery. Monasteries are relatively recent in Khumbu, and since Mani-rimdu is strictly a monastic performance, it too is a recent development. Sherpa lamas do not distinguish between 'Cham in Tibet and Mani-rimdu. They claim that "it" was never produced properly in Tibet, but that "they present it properly in Khumbu." This infers that the Khumbu lamas believe that they are in possession of the true form of 'Cham, which they know only as Mani-rimdu. They impart the notion that Mani-rimdu, as an entity, was "always" produced, meaning as far back as Buddhism is traceable in Tibet. The ancient Kerok gomba in Khumbu performs dance ritual, but the Abbot of Tengpoche dismisses those performances as wholly unorthodox. They are primitive and are probably akin to Tibetan New Year's dances. One lama informed me that he had witnessed Mani-rimdu in several Tibetan monasteries. What this undoubtedly reflects is that the 'Cham dances have a long history in Tibet. As no records exist to trace the origin of the Khumbu festival, one must assume that the Sherpa lamas chose what they believed to be the essence of 'Cham dances, infused local doctrines and deities into the performance, and placed an entirely new title upon it.

According to Khumbu lamas, their Mani-rimdu had its origin in Rong-phu, north of Mount Everest. The Rong-phu lamas, they state, learned it originally from monasteries in central Tibet. It was in Rong-phu that Khumbu lamas were instructed in the proper manner of presentation, and they believe that theirs is now the accurate presentation.

It is likely that Lama Gulu provided the inspiration for the production of Mani-rimdu. Fürer-Haimendorf states that in Gulu's lifetime the celebration was "on a grand scale,"[46] which would suggest that the festival originated prior to 1930. Some Tengpoche lamas claim that the dances have been in existence only since 1938. The Thami monastery presented its first Mani-rimdu dances in 1940, and only in 1950 did it present the "proper" dances in their order, and with the correct masks and costumes. This indicates that a final authority on Mani-rimdu exists, probably in an oral tradition. The Abbot of Tengpoche claims that final authoritative right to himself, for even though the dances were originally learned at Rong-phu, monks from there now travel to Khumbu for correct instruction. The Rong-phu monastery was severely damaged by invading Chinese troops in the 1950's, and many lamas were forced to leave or become laborers for the invaders. It may be true that since that time the Abbot of Tengpoche has become an authority on Mani-rimdu by default.

Why more 'Cham dances were not performed in Khumbu before the early decades of the twentieth century is not clear. It is probable that Buddhism in Khumbu was ill-formed and removed from Tibetan models until Lama Gulu was recognized as a reincarnate Bodhisattva in 1923. Gulu founded monastic establishments which had been absent from the Khumbu scene. 'Cham dances, of the large festival type, appeared only in monastic settings in Tibet. Local gombas had neither the manpower necessary to stage such large festivals, nor the wealth needed to purchase masks, costumes, and properties which the dances required. Lamas of village gombas did not possess the knowledge of the "mysteries" for which the scholarly monks of monasteries were noted. The qualifications of knowledge, manpower, and skill therefore probably rendered the dance festivals impossible

[46] Christoph von Fürer-Haimendorf, *The Sherpas of Nepal: Buddhist Highlanders* (London: John Murray, 1964), p. 212.

for local gombas, and since these were the only gombas which existed in Khumbu prior to Lama Gulu's time, it is likely that the sacred dances were one element which was considered too cumbrous for their capabilities.

Mani-rimdu requires many dancers for its production. The monasteries of Tibet regularly housed up to four thousand monks and maintained a substantial manpower reserve upon which to draw for extended dance festivals. Regarding the three- and four-day dance festivals as too ambitious for the score of monks available to them, the Khumbu lamas decreased the number of dances to encompass only one day. In this manner, the number of dancers required was reduced to what the budding new monasteries could accommodate. The essence of the 'Cham dances was upheld, and the presentation could be accomplished by skillful lamas.

Much emphasis is laid upon skillful dancing in Khumbu, and the spectators are well aware of the most accomplished of the performers, both aesthetically and physically. This leads one to assume that Mani-rimdu is more an entertainment for the audience than is true of the Tibetan models, in which only the comic dances are entertaining. In Tibet the mystery dances are not performed on the same day as the comic dances. In Khumbu, on the other hand, two comic presentations are interspersed with the sacred dances. The reason could be the absence of large numbers of dancers to perform an extra day, but that is only a part of the reason. As will be noted later, a comic actor appears during a consecration ceremony the day before the dances begin at Mani-rimdu. It is a serious religious ceremony, but the comic character is present for the benefit of the spectators. He helps the populace visualize long life and fulfills his role as a form of instruction, but he is also entertaining.

A light air of gaiety prevails among the spectators at Mani-rimdu, and no one in the audience actually believes that a god is before them in person. They seem to feel the spirit of the deity in the abstract, that is, an impersonation. No one in Khumbu audiences cowers in fear or shrieks with terror at the gods, as

Duncan reported in Tibetan festivals.[47] What this amounts to is a different attitude on the part of the Khumbu audience toward the 'Cham. The Sherpa lamas have utilized an established form of dancing, incorporated from indigenous devil-dancing in Tibet, but they have further altered it to include local touches and sentiments which their particular audience will accept.

Khumbu lamas have the responsibility in religious matters to ward off evil. The Sherpas freely admit that they do not understand the doctrines or the rites, but they are content and secure in the belief that the lamas have the knowledge, ability, and desire to protect them. This is one factor that has reduced the need for superstitious assumptions among the Sherpas, for the demons are the lamas' concern. The Sherpas no longer regard most of the evil deities as being real, but rather see them as mere manifestations of that evil, which a demon represents. They are encouraged by monastic authorities to recognize the evil within themselves, and the demonology, then, becomes a visual manifestation of the power and source of that evil, not the actual malignant demon who physically harms human beings. It is evident that a people partially emancipated from the belief in living ogres would not deem it necessary to view those devils being destroyed. The dances of Mani-rimdu reflect these beliefs, and for that reason humor is mixed with sacred dances in an entertaining, artful enactment.

The Khumbu lamas use the drama as a technique of instruction in exactly the same manner that Aśvaghosha did in the first century. Aśvaghosha's instructional precepts were altered in Tibet to include indigenous demons in the Buddhist pantheon. The difference between the Khumbu type of instruction through dance and the Tibetan system is that the Sherpas' lamas minister to a people who do not give credence to the belief in most Tibetan demons. The dances in Khumbu depict the manifestations mentioned above, but with an admonition for each person to search his heart for signs of their presence. Tibetan

[47] Duncan, *Customs and Superstitions of Tibetans,* p. 132.

74

demons do appear in Mani-rimdu, but there is practically no emphasis upon coercing them. Again, the dynamism of Buddhism has maintained the outward form of a rite and transposed indigenous values upon it to reflect the circumstances in which it is produced.

IV. The Physical Setting
of Mani-rimdu

ANI-RIMDU can be more fully appreciated by viewing it in its environmental context. The sensuous quality of the scenery which is encountered in Khumbu cannot be ignored. It is an emotional inundation to one from the West, and a moving sight even to the Sherpas, who praise its majestic appearance and the whiteness of the snow mountains. Sherpas, too, are awed by their surroundings, even though the scenery is an everyday experience to them. The huge mountains and deep valleys reduce man and his realm to minuteness. This diminution is not only a physical lessening of men to the Sherpa, but a spiritually humbling experience as well. It causes him to look with awe upon the environment which towers around him. One feels the locality, senses its immensity and aloofness, as perceptibly as one sees it visually. The environment pervades the senses, for it seems that it does not belong to man. It is a world of rock and ice superimposed upon the world of men. While a Sherpa climber struggles against blizzards and hurricanes, his fellow villagers may be digging potatoes a mere five miles away. Sherpas live on the "eaves of the roof of the world." They live on the fringe of the inhabitable. Danger and security, grief and joy, terrifying awe and unbelievable beauty unite in a form of life unique in the world.

Surrounded by such titanic natural splendors as one finds in Khumbu, the Sherpas need not be frequently reminded that life is transitory, and that man is an insignificant pebble on the sands of the universe. Sherpa Buddhists believe that only when man fully realizes just how inconsequential material graspings are, will his spirit fly freely toward the truth of life. Only then can he meditate upon enlightenment and universal understanding. If man is to survive in such an awe-inspiring region, and retain any mental equilibrium, he must know that his physical existence can be destroyed at any given moment. Life is not only transitory, but very unstable in this high mountain area. The concepts most important to the Sherpa do not involve corporeality. He is more concerned with the state of his religious merit (karma) than with his physical existence. The Khumbu citizen realizes that he submits to his environment and copes with it in human struggle. He has no vainglorious notion of conquering it. The very scenery of Khumbu enforces his realization that such attempts would result in failure. This, however, does not suggest resignation or disintegrative fatalism on the part of the Sherpas, for they enjoy their lives and their environment. His homeland forces the man of Khumbu to appraise his ambitions and aspirations realistically.

A foreign visitor may find the Khumbu terrain formidable and alien, but not stark or unattractive. It is green and lush during all but the winter months. There are abundant rivers and forests, and the Sherpas do not wantonly destroy their natural resources. They regulate their forest products through a remarkable method of timber conservation, and they maintain clean water systems by Asian standards. Their houses are whitewashed, and their schools are landscaped to blend into the scenery and not to detract from its natural beauty. To ancient inhabitants it may have been the home of gods and demons, but to present-day Sherpas it is the home of men who have adjusted to its difficulties. The people of Khumbu do not live in fear of nature; rather they coexist with it and all its living creatures. In Buddhist concepts, Khumbu, no matter how challenging it may

77

be, is only an inconsequential segment of hundreds of other worlds. But it is the Sherpas' world. They enjoy it, and they preserve it for their future generations.

The Sherpas, like all other human beings, are individuals. Some are extremely virtuous and friendly, while a few are scoundrels who do not hesitate to steal or cheat in business transactions. A few totally reject outsiders, and some never attend any village celebration or religious meetings. The great majority, however, are happy and peaceful Buddhists who believe in their religion and are very proud of it.

The majority of Sherpas take pride in their communities, but they do not believe that their environment is any more difficult or overwhelming than others. Most accept their role and placement in life, not in terms of resignation, but in terms of a challenge. Sherpas possess the remarkable ability to know themselves. They strive for things within their scope, and do not worry about those phenomena which lie outside their understanding and grasp. Their knowledge of man and his relationship with the unseen world is derived through only one system of religious philosophy, certainly, but their searchings and questions find answers. They understand causation, birth, and degeneration through Buddhist precepts. The world appears as as entity to them, reasoned and concluded in terms of Buddhist philosophy. The Sherpas find peace of mind and order in their society, no matter how overwhelming their environment may be.

The Sherpas' freedom from political oppression, their peace of mind, their right to choose whatever trade they wish, and their innate sense of enjoyment of their home environment result in a truly happy and contented people. It is because of the spirit of the Sherpas and the breathtaking scenery which surrounds them that the dance-dramas of Mani-rimdu are so uniquely impressive to one from the West. One must share, or at least understand or appreciate, their vigorous extramundane existence truly to enjoy their dance-drama in its remarkable setting. The people of Khumbu rejoice in life. They are happy and pleasant, respectful of a peacemaker, and scornful of a man of violence. When they take time out from their duties and gather for a festival such as Mani-rimdu, the result is the uninhibited outpouring of all that is good in a simple people who know that their physical existence is unimportant in universal values of Buddhism.

Dramatic productions in Khumbu are not performed in buildings which are designed specifically for theatrical presentations. There are only three types of edifices in the Sherpa communities: private homes, schools, and religious structures. No other public buildings—such as hotels, stores, or warehouses—exist. Those who wish to present shows must convert existing buildings or outdoor arenas into makeshift theaters. The gomba is the only religious structure of any size, but its interior is encumbered by support pillars which are so closely spaced that they prevent elaborate physical motion by the actor or dancer. The Mani-rimdu dancers require a relatively open space about thirty feet square. Even if presentations were held in the gomba, there would be room for no more than thirty or forty spectators. Three to five hundred people regularly attend this theatrical festival, and this rules out the gomba as a theater.

Sherpa homes are much smaller than the gombas, and are not even remotely capable of accommodating a dramatic production. Consequently, Mani-rimdu must be staged outdoors. Since it is strictly a monastic production, the acting and spectator areas are located adjacent to the monastery gomba, within the compound. The monasteries of Thami and Tengpoche have stone courtyards which are capable of seating spectators, dignitaries, and ecclesiastic authorities. The center of the courtyard is large enough to permit acting and dancing in a special acting area, generally removed from the audience. The nearby gomba and monastic buildings serve as dressing rooms for the actors, and monks' homes become public dwellings, providing housing and cooking facilities for the Sherpas attending Mani-rimdu. The descriptions of these two monasteries and their courtyards aid in understanding this open-air theater.[1]

Thami monastery (elevation 14,500 feet) is located on the long axis of an east-west mountainside. The gomba door faces southeast, looking out over part of the village of Thami 500 feet below, and toward numerous gigantic waterfalls which cascade from the flank of 20,300-foot Mount Kwāngde. The ridge upon which the monastery abuts rises to 16,500 feet northwest of the enclave. To the west, the Thami River descends from 19,000-foot Tesi Lapcha Pass and discharges its water into the Bhote River one mile east of the monastery. Five miles east of Thami is the summit of Khumbila, and five days' journey north brings one to the Tibetan border via Nangpa La Pass.

The gomba is literally hewn out of the rock. The other monastic buildings cling precariously to the thirty-five-degree incline of the slope. The gomba itself is a two-story structure approximately forty feet square at its base. Immediately in front of the gomba lies the courtyard (*'cham-ra*) in which the dances are performed. It extends over the receding ground, and its outside edge is eight feet above the level of the terrain. The courtyard floor is braced up from the hillside with wooden shores every four feet along its thirty-foot length. Covered with hand-hewn rock slates, it is relatively flat; cracks between stones are packed with dried mud to give it a smooth surface. The courtyard extends twenty-five feet in front of the gomba and is flanked on the east by a small two-story building. This structure serves as a cookhouse in which the Abbot's food is prepared and from

[1] The main emphasis here is upon the Tengpoche Mani-rimdu performance, and consequently upon the Tengpoche courtyard in which the dances occur. Christoph von Fürer-Haimendorf has written a brief anthropological examination of the Thami Mani-rimdu in his book, *The Sherpas of Nepal* (London: John Murray, 1964), pp. 210-14. My study includes the Thami production, but emphasizes the Tengpoche performance. It was from the Abbot and lamas of the latter monastery that I obtained most of my information concerning the religious and aesthetic principles pertinent to Mani-rimdu. It was likewise from the Tengpoche Abbot that information concerning the historical background of the dance-drama was ascertained.

Five children from Khumjung who daily walk several miles, cut fire-wood, and carry it home in the baskets on their backs. Since wood is scarce in Khumbu, they must not cut live trees or shrubs. (Photo by Sabine Jerstad)

At right is the father of Nima Tenzing, the Sherpa climber in whose house I live in Thami. The sheepskin cloak is typical Tibetan costume for cold weather. At left is a Tibetan refugee, presently living in Thami.

The ten-year-old reincarnate Abbot of Thami monastery. His monastery is ruled by senior monks during the years of his minority.

Abbot of Tengpoche monastery. This monk supplied much of the information for this book.

which warm tea is served to dignitaries and lamas during the course of the performance of Mani-rimdu.[2]

West of the courtyard, forming its boundary, is a wooden structure about seven feet high, flat on top and open to the courtyard from below. Spectators sit on the stone floor in the edifice, and upon its flat roof, which is provided with benches and chairs. Other spectators crowd on the two-foot-wide raised stone walkway between the gomba and the courtyard floor. No special scaffolding or platforms are placed for spectators at Thami. Children line the outside edge of the courtyard and sit directly on the stone floor. Adjacent buildings provide other spots for viewing the dances, and some spectators even stand below the courtyard on the ground, although the view from there is poor. A maximum of five hundred spectators can witness the Thami festival.

One receives a fascinating view of the Khumbu world while witnessing the dances at Thami. Performers are etched against the glittering ice walls of Mount Kantega or the sheer rock precipices of Kwāngde. The colorful silk costumes of dancers are superimposed against the harsh and hostile immensities of the natural phenomena which surround the monastery. From the gomba wall, dancers appear to be promenading on the edge of space, with the village of Thami at their feet. If one were to believe in dancing gods, this spectacular setting could only enhance that belief.

Tengpoche monastery, though structurally more elaborate and ornate, does not afford a viewer the same awesome impression of the background which enhances the production at Thami. Located on the summit of an east-west ridge, the Tengpoche gomba faces east toward a 17,000-foot unnamed peak. To the southeast rise the precipitous walls of 22,340-foot Mount Kantega. Northeast of the monastery towers the wedge-shaped 22,500-foot Ama Dablam. Khumbila, to the northwest, appears

[2] Since no flat ground adjoins the monastery, the first day's ceremony of the Life-Consecration rite is held in the courtyard.

81

to guard the monastery, symbolic of the protective god it is supposed to house. To the northeast rises the highest land massif on
this planet, the triumvirate of Nuptse, almost 26,000 feet in
height, Lhotse, nearly 28,000 feet, and Everest—Chomo-lungma,
"The Goddess (chomo) Mother of the Wind (lungma)" to
Northern Buddhists—which soars more than 29,000 feet above
sea level.

The southern flank of the ridge on which Tengpoche is located falls away one thousand feet to a river gorge which drains
Mount Kantega. The northern side of the ridge drops another
thousand feet to the Imja River, which drains the Everest-
Lhotse massif. Behind (west) and below the monastery grounds
is the confluence of these two rivers with the Dudh River. In
front of the grounds, beyond the open field, is a seventeen-thou-
sand-foot peak. Tengpoche is located on the only raised level
piece of ground for seven miles in any direction. The name
Tengpoche means "sacred bowl," and the connotation is apro-
pos, for the surrounding mountains form the walls of the bowl,
with the monastery as the base.

The gomba is an important structure for worship as well as
for the dances. At Tengpoche it is a forty-foot square, three-
story, ochre-colored structure. The main floor, where almost all
worship transpires, is an open room provided with benches for
lamas and a throne for the Abbot. The walls and ceilings contain painted frescoes depicting gods, demons, and scenes from
the life of the Buddha. In this room, dimly lit by butter lamps,[3]
Sherpa lamas pass many hours in chants and services each day.
The second floor houses Buddhist scriptures, as does the first
floor, plus more paintings and gilded statues. The third floor, a
cupola-like structure, is set atop the pagoda-shaped roof, and it
also culminates in the same architectural form.

North and south, adjacent to the gomba and monastery courtyard, are the homes of the monks. These tiny one-story huts reflect their owners' lack of worldly materialistic concern. The

[3] A shallow bowl, two or three inches in diameter, filled with butter,
which has a wick floating in it.

homes are simple and bare of furnishings save for a bed, an open-hearth stove, and a few small statues and manuscripts. East of the gomba is a large open field about two hundred yards square. At its eastern end is a schoolhouse constructed by Sir Edmund Hillary in which lamas are taught, and where the children of nearby laymen may also receive an education. On the northern flank of the field, the lamas have constructed a guest house, using funds donated by mountaineering expeditions. Near the trail that connects Namche Bazar with Tengpoche, at the southeastern edge of the ridge, are located the only two private dwellings which are not associated with the monastery.

South and west behind the monastery is a field where the first day's ceremony is performed. A three-sided building fifteen feet long, eight feet deep, and seven feet high houses the altar, the ritual objects, and seats for the Abbot and the senior lama. The front of the building is open and faces east, the auspicious direction. The structure is probably a yak hut during the remainder of the year, but for this first day's ceremony it becomes an altar room. The frame of the structure is outlined by bright Chinese brocades. The Abbot's throne is placed behind the altar inside the edifice, at the southern end. To the left of the throne, also inside the structure, is a lower seat for the senior lama. The altar is a table covered by Chinese silk.

East of the building, in front of the open side, are two raised benches, fifteen feet long, arranged at right angles to either side of the opening of the structure. Covered with long, colorful, Tibetan wool carpets, these benches provide seating for the lesser lamas of Tengpoche. Behind the raised platforms novice monks and nuns from Devuche (a Buddhist nunnery north of Tengpoche) sit on Tibetan carpets placed directly on the ground.[4]

[4] Nuns are segregated because they are given a respected place in the theater, not because they are women. Sherpas do not distinguish seating arrangements by sex. Men and women mingle within the Mani-rimdu audience. In daily society, Sherpas do not relegate women to a subservient position. Men and women work side by side in fields, carry loads to markets together, and worship conjointly. Women are generally free and equal to men. They may marry whom they choose, and divorce their husbands for

Between the rows of lamas there is a kneeling carpet where devout laymen present donations to the monastery during the course of the ceremony to follow. Teapots and charcoal warmers are placed between the benches, and the lamas are served refreshments during the proceedings. Spectators sit south of the lamas' benches, in the open and partially hidden from the Abbot inside the building.

For the Mani-rimdu dances, however, the main element of the monastery is the courtyard, set amidst the splendid scenery. Immediately in front of the east door of the gomba lies the dancing area, the stone courtyard called the 'cham-ra. It can accommodate more than four hundred spectators. Like the Thami courtyard, the floor at Tengpoche is composed of gray rock slates. The over-all dimensions are approximately the same as their counterparts in Thami. It is not known whether the courtyard dancing area corresponds to any architectural format, but it resembles the Vikṛṣṭāvara design of ancient Indian theaters in slightly smaller dimensions.[5] The concept for the form of the area designed for theatrical presentations may have originated

---

any number of reasons, just as men are free to do likewise. They are not admitted to the village council, but this restriction is practically the only form of discrimination which exists between the sexes in Khumbu.

Devuche is a Buddhist nunnery approximately one hour's journey north of Tengpoche. The nuns in no way enter into the dances of Mani-rimdu, nor do they have any official function except as honored guests. They carry out their function in the nunnery, and a Sherpa may commission a nun to chant prayers for him, receiving the same benefit as he would from a lama. Sherpas distribute gifts of food and money among these female Buddhists during the course of Mani-rimdu. The nuns thoroughly enjoy the performance.

[5] One variation of the ancient Jyestha theater in India was the Vikṛṣṭāvara, which measured thirty-two by sixteen hastas, that is, forty-eight by twenty-four feet. It had greenrooms behind the acting area (the gomba in Khumbu), and seating in front of the stage. This stage form was used for dramas in which gods were the heroes of the performance. A curtain screened the acting area from the greenrooms. In Khumbu, a curtain separates the courtyard from the porch of the gomba, where costume changes are made. For further information concerning this and other ancient Indian theater architectural forms, see D. R. Mankad, *Ancient Indian Theatre* (Anand, India: R. C. Patel, 1960), pp. 2-32.

with Indian sages who fostered the Lha-mo in Tibet. It is distinctly possible that architectural forms accompanied the Buddhist tradition to Tibet and consequently to Khumbu, but this hypothesis is, of course, strictly suppositional.

The courtyard at Tengpoche is enclosed on the north, east, and south by a covered wooden structure to protect the audience from the elements. About fifteen feet high from the courtyard to the crest of the roof, the structure consists of a balcony and a main floor, open on the courtyard level. The lower portion is used for the storage of wood, but during Mani-rimdu it is a spectator area, seven feet deep and six feet high. Its back wall is constructed of dried mud bricks, which constitute the external structure of the entire courtyard area. No chairs or benches are placed in this area. The members of the audience sit directly upon the stone courtyard floor or on cushions.

The second story, or balcony, is approached by means of four stairways. It is six feet deep and eight feet high at the crest of the roof, and is guarded by a wooden railing on the courtyard side of the balcony. Three rows of benches or chairs can be placed in it for spectators. The south and east sections of the balcony are occupied by spectators. The north portion of the three-sided seating arrangement is reserved for the lamas and musicians. Seven lamas and the Abbot, who chant the scriptures, are seated on carpet-covered benches behind a red curtain in the balcony. As the performance is about to begin, the curtain is drawn aside, revealing the ecclesiastical authorities.

Musicians at Thami are seated on the courtyard floor. The Abbot and senior lamas occupy a spot on the raised stone walkway immediately in front of the gomba. At Tengpoche, however, they are all in the balcony, where they look down upon the performance. Musicians leave their posts, descend the stairs, accompany some of the dances from the courtyard floor, and return to their original places, where they either chant or accompany chants with their instruments.

The ten-foot-long brass horns, *dung-chen,* require special places because of their inordinate length. At Thami the *dung-*

Figure 1. *Dung-chen,* the ten-foot-long brass and copper trumpets. The trumpet end must be supported by a human or by means of a wooden stand, seen here.

Figure 2. *Rkang-gling,* the trumpet fashioned from a human thigh bone.

Figure 3. *Rgya-gling,* the three-foot-long trumpet.

86

Figure 4. *Sil-snyan* cymbals.   Figure 5. *Sbug-'cham* cymbals.

Figure 6. *Chos-rnga,* hand drum
mounted on a two-foot handle.

chen-pa (players of the *dung-chen*) are seated in the northwest corner of the courtyard on the floor itself. These two players never leave their posts. The horns are too cumbersome to be portable without the aid of two boys to support the flared end. The *dung-chen-pa* sit upon the stone floor with their instruments projecting into the courtyard, much like the famed alp horn players of Europe.

Other musicians at Thami are seated beside the Abbot, northeast of his throne, on the raised stone walkway. Their instruments include the smaller brass and wood trumpets, *rgya-gling;* the large brass cymbals with high dome handles, *sbug-'cham;* the smaller flat cymbals, *sil-snyan;* the trumpets made of a human thigh bone which has a snake's head on its trumpet end, *rkang-gling*; hand drums about four inches in diameter with double heads placed back to back, *damaru;* and a two-foot drum supported by a wooden handle, *chos-rnga* (see Figures 1-6 for diagrams of these instruments).

The same instruments are used at Tengpoche, but the musicians occupy different places. The *dung-chen-pa* sit in the northeast corner of the balcony. A wooden structure, which juts into the courtyard, supports the flared end of the trumpets. The other musicians are seated in the balcony, to the east of the Abbot. Two *rkang-gling* are kept in the gomba; prior to some dances they are sounded from inside the temple, and a refrain is echoed from the other two *rkang-gling* by musicians in the auditorium.

The lamas' grade, or status of learning in the monastery, determines which musical instruments they may play. A lama of high standing, but not an elder, controls the beat of time with the cymbals. The drums are played by the next lower grade of lamas, while the trumpets and conch shells are reserved for younger lamas who have resided in the monastery for fewer than five years. The *rgya-gling* is considered to be the most difficult of all instruments to master. Lamas with talent in music distinguish themselves by being accomplished on instruments, while lamas with no musical inclinations are exempted from such training in the practical form of music.

These instruments do not play tunes in Western modes, rhythmic patterns, or melodic lines. They do not strike a note which lamas emulate in their chanting. There is no pitch or key relationship between the notes of the chants and those of the instruments. Lamas growl their chants in deep-throated tones. Musicians accompany the dancers and chanters, adding the emotive power of sound to heighten the effect of the spectacle. They announce the beginning of the dances, provide a beat for dancers, and mark the conclusion of the act. Two drawn-out notes of the *dung-chen* signify the termination of the action. At climactic moments, such as the saving of a man from demons or the tossing of offerings to the gods, the horns blast notes to enforce the culmination of emotion.

Music is not written down in Khumbu. There are no scores on which notes are inscribed or from which lamas receive their information about timing and the type of instrument to be used. The player of the cymbals, for example, reads the liturgy and prayers from religious texts, which are written with seven, nine, or eleven beats to each verse, and arbitrarily marks the time with his cymbals. The drums carry this responsibility at times, but it falls primarily to the cymbals player. Dancers and chanters take their cues from the musicians. Each dance lasts approximately twenty minutes, an arbitrary time duration set by tradition. The cymbals player controls both the dancers' movements and the chanters in order to insure that the proper time is kept. He uses no stop watch or metronome. From long hours of practice and study, he mentally calculates the time.

Trumpets are sounded on certain key phrases, generally at the culmination of prayers. At the conclusion of the prayer, all instruments are played. The sound ceases, and the cymbals player again leads the chanters into the next prayer, and the dancers into the next series of steps. Dancers remain motionless after one series of movements and await the time cue from the cymbals. If no prayers are being chanted, the dancers move in symbolic action, such as the offering of gifts to a deity, to the accompaniment of the cymbals. Upon termination of the symbolic actions by the dancers, the other musical instruments join the cymbals in a loud crashing finale. The use of instruments is noted in greater detail in connection with the individual dances in Chapter VI.

In the exact center of the courtyard is a flagpole, which is supported by a socket recessed in the stone floor. Approximately thirty feet high, the pole is adorned with prayer flags, good luck symbols, and charms. The Khumbu and Tibetan versions of this flag insure wealth, happiness, and health. The central figure is usually a horse carrying the Buddhist book of law. It is probably a corruption of the Chinese horse-dragon, a symbol of grandeur in China.[6] This Pegasus-like creature is symbolic of the happiness one receives from being wealthy and secure. As this is definitely not a Buddhist concept, it undoubtedly derives from the materialistic Bon doctrines.

West of the flagpole and adjacent to it is a ritual altar which contains various religious objects used in the dances. Most of these articles appeared on the altar during the first day's *Tshe-dbang* rite (see pp. 103-5). These objects are vestiges of the ordinary altar adornments in the gomba that are used in the daily worship services. They represent the sacredotalism and idolatry of Northern Buddhism and its obsession with gods and tutelary deities. They are not unlike Roman Catholic ritualistic objects, such as rosaries, miters, copes, crosses, and images of Christ or Mary upon the altar. Each article on the Buddhist altar represents a certain aspect of the faith and depicts differing forms of worship.

Some of the articles are images made from butter and dough (*tor-ma*),[7] which represent certain deities. The deities may be

[6] L. Austine Waddell, *The Buddhism of Tibet or Lamaism* (Cambridge: W. Heffner and Sons, 1894), pp. 410-12.

[7] *Tor-ma* (Tib. *gtor-ma*) is an unbaked cake made from ordinary parched flour and butter, molded into a form. The form usually produced is that

peculiar to the Khumbu people, such as Khumbu yul-lha, the
protector of the region. A brass or *tor-ma mchod-rten*[8] reminds
Buddhists of the five elements of the universe and the Buddha's
Nirvana. In the center of the altar is placed a large dough cake
for Padmasambhava and for one of his fierce demoniacal forms,
Guru Tak-po. An image of the Buddha is also upon the altar, as
is a representation of Sanga Rdo-rje. It should be noted here
that these *tor-ma* representations of deities are in no way repli-
cas of a human form. They appear to have three body segments
—lower trunk, upper body, and head with a triangular-shaped
hat. Impressions of facial characteristics may be applied, but not
necessarily. The figure may be two- or three-dimensional,
painted upon a flat surface or molded from *tor-ma*. Only by in-
quiry is one able to identify them.

The altar itself resembles a Western cupboard, with two
doors which open out. Drinking vessels, beer, water, and *tor-ma*
balls, which are utilized in the course of some dances, are stored
on the shelves. When these objects are required, the *Ldab-ldob*[9]
enters the courtyard and serves as a stage assistant, filling vessels,
passing out cups or *tor-ma* to the dancers. His duties completed,

of a cone; however, in the case of images, *tor-ma* may take the shape of a
human likeness. Junior lamas create these prior to Mani-rimdu. *Tor-ma*
may also be in the form of a dough ball which is distributed during the
Life-Consecration rite. From Chapter III it will be remembered that effigies
of humans were substituted in sacrificial rites. It is probably from this same
concept that *tor-ma* originated, a vestige of ancient human sacrificial offerings and perhaps cannibalism. Padmasambhava is given credit for having
altered this form of worship.

[8] A *mchod-rten* is a religious reliquary of the Indian stupa, a mound of
earth which originally was a burial mound. Also known as "chaityas," these
mounds housed bones and relics of saints. In Northern Buddhist countries,
Tibet and Nepal, it became an architectural form made of masonry, stone,
or brick.

Its form is always the same: the bottom square portion symbolizes earth;
its upper rounded globular section represents water; the thirteen spiral
rings represent fire and the thirteen Bodhisattva heavens; air is represented
above this by a crescent; and ether by a circle tapering upward into space.
It serves to remind Buddhists of the elements which made up the universe.

[9] See p. 93.

the assistant reshelves the items, closes the doors of the altar, and returns to the gomba, leaving the dancers in the courtyard to complete their performance.

Nuns from Devuche are seated in the southwest corner of the courtyard on the floor itself. They are provided with thick woolen Tibetan carpets on which to sit. Other spectators who cannot find room in the covered auditorium sit partially in the east, north, or south portions of the dancing area, or upon the raised six-foot-wide walkway which extends the full length of the courtyard and is connected to the gomba.

The gomba door opens onto a porch about six feet deep. Three steps lead eastward from the porch and down to the stone walkway. Another flight of five steps intrudes and descends into the dancing area itself. A cream-colored canvas curtain about fifteen feet square masks the porch of the gomba from the spectators. This curtain is very plain. It displays no elaborate designs as do those of the Chinese opera or the Kabuki theater, nor does it draw apart or rise on mechanical devices as in the Western theater. It simply conceals dancers, who are about to enter the acting area. Its primary use is to protect the gomba porch from rain and snow during the remainder of the year. Dancers descend from the gomba through the curtain, between the audience on either side of the porch steps on the walkway, and into the courtyard. Their performance begins when they step through the curtain.

From the description above it is apparent that some spectators intrude into the dance arena while some view the proceedings from aloft in the balcony. Dancers come dangerously close to striking spectators during some acts, but no one seems to mind. The spectator will laugh, move away momentarily, and then return at the conclusion of the dance to his original seat on the courtyard floor. Children derive much merriment from the dancers who whirl near them.

If crowds are so large that they impede the progress of a dance because of their physical instrusion into the acting area, a monitor clears the way. Known as a *"Ldab-ldob,"*[10] this lama is chosen and noted for his physical prowess more than for his intellectual abilities. He carries a whip which symbolizes his power, but it is rarely used. The *Ldab-ldob* good-naturedly moves the audience back from the acting area, and Sherpas obey his orders with respect. In Tibet the *Ldab-ldobs* also acted as bodyguards for lamas on official journeys to afford protection from bandits and wild animals.

Audience members at Mani-rimdu do not shrink in fear from devil-dancers, nor do they show any sign of terror at their approach. They talk, smile, and enjoy the dances, frequently without recognition of the god who is being represented. They chuckle if an actor is so near as to endanger the spectator, even though the dancer is a god.

The Mani-rimdu dances present illusion. They allow a spectator to witness an action which does not involve him personally in the physical world. It does, however, involve him personally in the moral world, because the actions of the drama deal with human precepts. Sherpas witness life, themselves, and their religion from different points of view. The religious view is not afforded by their normal lives, for demons and saints do not walk the village pathways. Because the spectator does not participate in the action, he can view it clearly and with perspective. The only two dancers who are known by name to most Sherpa onlookers are the comic performers, Mi-tshe-ring and Rtogs-ldan. The remainder hold the audience's attention and provide colorful spectacles, but their doctrinal significance is lost on the populace. It is a performance to the laymen and to the actors. The over-all impression one receives is that the monastery is a theater in which monks perform for the benefit of the audience, using costumes, properties, and masks to enhance their performance.

[10] For further information concerning the *Ldab-ldob,* see Thubten Jigme Norbu, *Tibet Is My Country: As told to Heinrich Harrer* (London: Rupert Hart-Davis, 1960), pp. 94-95.

The dances of Mani-rimdu are not technically difficult by comparison with the training and skill required for classical ballet. Mani-rimdu dance steps do not demand as great physical strength or control as those of the ballet. There is one ingredient in the Khumbu dances, however, which renders them more difficult, even for Sherpas, than most other dances anywhere in the world. That is the factor of environment, for the altitude and air temperature are detrimental to physical activity.

Dances at Thami occur at elevations greater than anywhere in continental United States, excepting Alaska. At 14,500 feet, atmospheric pressure and oxygen content in the air is reduced almost 50 per cent from what it is at sea level. This shortage of oxygen causes rapid exhaustion and demands great stamina on the part of the dancers. The Sherpas, naturally, live at these elevations and are physiologically well acclimatized to them, but great exertion takes its toll, even among them. The panting of breathless dancers is audible thirty feet away. Their costumes are voluminous and heavy, and the masks weigh more than five pounds, the burden of which is borne by the dancer's head and neck. For this reason, rest periods are periodically required during the course of the performance.

Another environmental difficulty encountered during Mani-rimdu is the temperature. Tengpoche produces its festival in November or December, a time when Khumbu is extremely cold. Temperatures may dip to ten degrees below zero, and Mani-rimdu is produced in an outdoor theater with no facilities for external production of heat. The average daily temperature at Tengpoche is approximately twenty degrees. Many spectators sit upon the stone courtyard floor, which is extremely cold. If the wind blows, the chilling factor reduces the temperature even further. The dance area is enclosed, but freezing winds sweep through the theater nevertheless. The cold is more discomforting to the spectators than to the dancers, who stay warm by physical exertion. The audience huddles in heavy woolen garments and fur-lined parkas and caps. The sun, which is very warm in this southern latitude, shines on only half of the audience, for it is low on the horizon in late fall and early winter. The temperature was low enough to freeze the ink in my pen and render my hands too numb for legible writing. With the combination of cold and high altitude, Mani-rimdu becomes an endurance contest to spectators and dancers alike.

The Thami festival is produced in May when the sun is warm. Temperatures in the sun may soar to above ninety degrees. The altitude, then, severely hampers the dancers by sapping the strength which is not drained by the heat. The elements are far more favorable to the spectator, however, and this undoubtedly accounts for the fact that more people attend the Thami festival than the Tengpoche dances. Even though Thami monastery cannot accommodate spectators as readily as Tengpoche, the overflow crowd at Thami clambers upon roofs beyond the courtyard, or stands downhill of the dance area. As many as five hundred persons regularly attend the dances at Thami, while an average of three hundred attend the Tengpoche Mani-rimdu.

The color and texture of the rich brocaded costumes, the excitement of a regional gathering, and the opportunity to relax and celebrate combine to offer the Sherpas a spectacle unique in their daily lives. Given the beauty of the scenery which surrounds them and the occasion to accrue religious merit through an enjoyable endeavor, the Sherpas eagerly look forward to Mani-rimdu each year. The entire festival is a sensuous venture, for there is movement and dynamism, a novel interruption of their difficult existence. Mani-rimdu adds spice to the Sherpas' lives, providing them with a chance to thrill at a performance of their own cultural heritage.

V. The Opening of Mani-rimdu

THE TERM "Mani-rimdu" is derived from the name of a sacrificial prayer chanted by the lamas on various occasions. The Abbot of Tengpoche claims that the dances are performed after this prayer as a celebration of its completion. Known as *Mani Ril-sgrub,* it is believed to benefit the people of Khumbu by assuring them long life, bringing rain for crops, and propitiating the mountain gods who surround the Sherpa communities. *Mani Ril-sgrub* is also an appellation for the *tor-ma* offering which is distributed during the first day's Life-Consecration rite. The same *tor-ma* offering is presented during the dances to the various deities. The term "Mani-rimdu" is a corruption of *Mani Ril-sgrub.* Through oral transmission, the former has come to designate the dances which celebrate the prayer of *Mani Ril-sgrub.* Mani-rimdu has no denotative meaning in the Sherpa language other than this monastic festival; therefore, it is a term which refers only to these particular dances.

The dances are performed once each year, but the prayer itself may be chanted many times. According to the Abbot of Tengpoche, the prayer might be said whenever there is a long drought and rain is desired. The power to produce the desired precipitation resides in the efficacy of the prayer. The Abbot

96

also claims that the dances are a manifestation of joy, a celebration of the definite onset of good omens which directly result from the invocation. This, however, is not exactly valid. If the lama were correct, the dancers would technically have to delay their actions until the rains actually fell. The dances may have originated in such a concept, but they are not produced for that purpose in present-day Sherpa monasteries.

No other monastic authorities mentioned anything about rain, or dancing for the onset of rain, nor did any audience members. The dances are produced regardless of the results expected from the prayers. The prayer of *Mani Ril-sgrub* cursorily invokes the power of all the gods of Buddhism, not a specific rain god. Mani-rimdu may have been an innovation which was originally added to the prayer, but at the present time the dances overshadow the religious elements. The performance is designed to simplify concepts and deities, and to depict those elements in a visual and entertaining form. It explains the complex symbolism of Buddhist doctrines, especially that of the victory of virtue over vice. The spectators, however, comprehend little of the symbolism and sacred theories. They know only that the dances are somehow religious, and they witness them for sheer entertainment.

It is upon the Abbots of Tengpoche and Thami that the responsibility rests for the production of Mani-rimdu. Despite what an audience may surmise about the dances, the Abbot claims that it is only a festival of prayer. Sacred texts are chanted by lamas while the dancers perform. The Abbot may be the only one who truly understands the doctrinal basis of the festival, and it is his burden to insure the religious efficacy of the proceedings. Mani-rimdu is generally produced at the time of the full moon—in May at Thami and in November at Tengpoche. The Abbot, however, may cancel or change the date at will. It is usually arranged so that the dances do not interfere with large trading missions, or with the planting or harvesting of crops.

Mani-rimdu does not appear to celebrate any particular

97

saint's birthday or death. A large dance festival in Tibet cele-
brated the anniversary of the death of Tsong-kha-pa,[1] but that
could hardly be the case in Khumbu. Tengpoche and Thami
produce their festivals six months apart, and according to their
respective lamas they utilize identical dances, costumes, and
masks, and have the same religious purpose. That purpose, they
claim, is a prayer festival. The reason for producing festivals six
months apart is not clear, but since many people from the entire
area of Khumbu attend both performances, it was probably sur-
mised that one festival might compete with the other if they
were produced on the same day. This is another reason for assuming that the Khumbu festival pays more heed to the audience than is true in Tibet.

The Tengpoche Abbot claims authority not only over the
Mani-rimdu precepts at Rong-phu, but over the Abbot of
Thami as well. The current Thami Abbot is a boy whose monastery is governed by a senior monk during the Abbot's years of
minority. It is probably true that Thami lamas turn to the older
Abbot of Tengpoche for instruction. The lamas of Thami and
Tengpoche who actually perform the dances do not know the
ecclesiastical foundation of the festival. They rely, as do the laymen, upon the Abbot to direct them in the proper indoctrina-
tion. The implication here is not to disclaim the lamas' knowledge of Buddhist doctrines, but to indicate that, in the matter of
Mani-rimdu, only the Abbot and a few senior monks know the
full import of the festival. This implies, I think, that the Abbot
provides the religious basis in order to guard against heresy and
to protect the populace from evil, while the younger monks perform a dance strictly for the entertainment of the audience. In
the minds of the monks who actually dance, merit which accrues
from attendance at the festival carries little more emphasis than
the entertainment value afforded the spectators. Dancers suffer

---

[1] Tsong-kha-pa was born in 1357 and died in 1419. He was the founder
of a reformed sect of Tibetan Buddhism. Known as the Dge-lugs-pa, or
Yellow Hat, sect, it sought greater austerity and a return to strict monastic
discipline. Austerity did not denote Theravāda strictness, however,

from stage fright, and they gain prestige by performing superbly. The dancers are admonished to produce a good performance, and the Abbot and senior monks guarantee the religious efficacy.

Laymen display their finest wearing apparel at Mani-rimdu, and the entire festival takes on the air of a nineteenth-century county fair as it is known in America. While the women wear their most expensive jewels and Chinese brocades, the men are decked out in their Tibetan hats and their treasured woolen garments. Children, likewise exquisitely dressed, accompany their parents and gleefully enjoy the dances.

Laymen receive merit for attending Mani-rimdu. Their *bsod-nams* is automatically recorded, and no extra effort is required of them except to attend with a pure heart. There are no demerits distributed for enjoyment or for laughing at a dancer who portrays a god. No ecclesiastical authority oversees the crowd unless a fight should ensue, or unless spectators should impede the progress of a dance. Liquor flows freely among the spectators, and frequently among the dancers as well. At the conclusion of the dances, after the lamas have finished their religious service in the gomba, the monastery often provides beer for the laymen, who dance in the courtyard until the early hours of the next morning. Lamas join in the festivities freely, for sheer enjoyment.

Even though liquor may affect the outward performance of Mani-rimdu, it does not affect ecclesiastic control of its religious efficacy. Sherpa Buddhists believe that truth and correctness are located mysteriously on a spatial "wave-length." When one strikes the chord which corresponds with that "'frequency," truth in religious concepts is expressed, manifested, and recorded on the *bsod-nams* ledger. The Abbot, being a reincarnate Bodhisattva, is in touch with that frequency, and consequently when he controls the service and chants religious texts, he is automatically correct. He cannot fail, unless he should fall into apostasy. This renders the festival of Mani-rimdu undeniably correct, in religious terminology, no matter what the condi-

99

tion of the production. The actions of dancers and laymen cannot change what the Abbot utters in truth. Therefore, everyone can enjoy himself, realizing that the Abbot is insuring the religious verity.

The religious edification for laymen occurs on the opening day of the festival. First there is a procession and a few chants, then amulets, pills, *tor-ma* balls, and holy water are distributed to the faithful, who drink and eat, and rub the water into their heads as tokens of protection from disease for the coming months. When this is over, the people look forward eagerly to the next day's dancing. There is rejoicing because the Abbot, a living god, has laid his hand upon them, blessed them, and presented amulets to them. The dances are joyous diversion from the hard life of the Sherpas.

On the third day of Mani-rimdu the lamas conclude the religious chants and burn writings which represent evil. However, the monastery is conspicuously devoid of spectators on this day. The Sherpas need not remain, for the lamas are capable of handling the responsibilities which concern the religious welfare of the entire community. Laymen witness and delight in the dances, but they depart for home before the conclusion of the festival. To them, the entire atmosphere of Mani-rimdu is the thrill of a performance.

Costumes and masks utilized in Mani-rimdu are stored in the gomba or in buildings adjacent to it during the year. Three weeks prior to the production they are brought out of storage and repaired. The monastery hums with activity for a full week before Mani-rimdu is actually to be presented. Preparation of the gomba, courtyard, ritual objects, masks, and costumes, and rehearsals of the dances occupy the lamas' time. The day before the festival dances, there is a dress rehearsal. Known as a "dance of showing" (Tib. *tsam-ki-bulu*),[2] the rehearsal is complete with music, chants, and ritual articles, but minus the masks, costumes, and audience.

[2] Christoph von Fürer-Haimendorf, *The Sherpas of Nepal: Buddhist Highlanders* (London: John Murray, 1964), p. 213.

The main chapel in the gomba serves as a dressing room and a greenroom[3] during Mani-rimdu. Costumes are laid out, and junior lamas assist the dancers with their voluminous robes and large masks. Like all greenrooms, the gomba is a flurry of activity on the day of the performance. Last-minute alterations are made, and performers rehearse difficult steps before entering onto the stage. The confident actors laugh and joke, while others nervously pace the floor awaiting their entrance cues. Once the actor leaves the gomba and steps through the curtain, he begins portraying his role. No words are spoken once the actor enters the courtyard. It is not uncommon to hear the laughter of dancers subside three or four minutes before they enter, and to see them quietly assuming the role of a deity, feeling the part inwardly.[4] When the actor enters the arena, he becomes the god whose mask he wears. The time for joking is past, for the lama is a performer, and he accepts his role seriously and with dignity. Chapter VI explains more of the aesthetics of characterization and significances of the masks.

Festivities of the opening day of the festival at Tengpoche[5] begin about 1:00 P.M., after the daily rituals and morning services in the gomba are completed. *Rgya-gling* and *dung-chen* herald the beginning of Mani-rimdu three hours before the first ceremony actually starts. Monks play their instruments from the roof of the gomba as a call to worship. Inside the gomba, other monks busy themselves with arranging the standards they will carry in the procession to come. The standards convey good luck charms, the colors of the monastic order, and symbols from Tibetan Buddhism.

[3] The greenroom is the name applied to a room near the stage where actors await their entrance cues, relax, or greet friends. Actors are already made up and costumed when they occupy the greenroom during the performance. It was first called a greenroom in seventeenth-century theaters. The term came from the tradition that these rooms were usually hung or painted in green.

[4] Although this concept might sound sophisticated, and could be termed as identification or a form of empathy, it is primarily used to steady the nerves of the actor, who mentally rehearses his forthcoming action.

[5] These festivities are identical at Thami.

When all is ready, the parade forms inside the gomba and snakes its way down the steps leading into the courtyard, through the east door of the gomba. It circumambulates the courtyard several times, while the musicians perform and other lamas chant. *Sbug-'cham, sil-snyan, rkang-gling,* and *chos-rnga* complete the musical complement. The parade of lamas then exits through the east gate of the courtyard toward the Sherpa audience, which has been waiting for more than an hour. Musicians lead the column, and the Abbot is midway in it under a canopy held by two lamas. While the musicians play, the procession slowly winds its way south and west behind the monastery and into the field where the first day's ceremony is performed.[6]

The ceremony which occurs on the first day of Mani-rimdu is known as the "Life-Consecration" rite (*Tshe-wang*)[7] or *Tshe-dbang*[8]). It is a ritual performed in Tibet and in monasteries in Khumbu periodically. "The Life-Consecration rite," Fürer-Haimendorf writes, "is intended to bestow on the recipients the blessing of long life, and this is symbolized by the distribution of live-giving liquids and pills."[9] During this ritual at Mani-rimdu, however, the Sherpas have added another touch. A clown is included in the service, a lama who wears a yellow, grinning mask of a wrinkled old man. He is known to the Sherpas as Mi-tshe-ring, the "long-life man." He takes his place in front of the structure, sitting or standing just below the altar. He enacts a few antics, to the delight of the crown, but does not elicit the boisterous laughter which will meet his act during the next day's dances.

The entire ceremony is tinged with Bon concepts, for the idea of striving for long life is not Buddhist. "It seems to incorporate a good deal of pre-Lamaist [Buddhist] ritual," states Waddell,

[6] At Thami the setting is inside the courtyard of the monastery.

[7] Fürer-Haimendorf, *Sherpas of Nepal*, p. 214.

[8] David Snellgrove, *Himalayan Pilgrimage: A Study of Tibetan Religion by a Traveller Through Western Nepal* (Oxford: Bruno Cassirer, 1961), p. 141.

[9] Fürer-Haimendorf, *Sherpas of Nepal*, p. 215.

"and its benedictions and sprinkling of holy water are suggestive of Nestorian or still later Christian influences."[10] The ceremony deals with a detachable life and the nourishment of this supernatural life (*bla-tshe*), typically a Bon belief. The *bla*, as René de Nebesky-Wojkowitz points out, is a "soul" or "life power" which an individual or community possesses.[11] The *bla* is generally attached to a certain being or place, that is, an animal, tree, or mountain. In Khumbu, the *bla* is Khumbila, the nineteen-thousand-foot peak southwest of Tengpoche. In ancient Tibetan legends it was believed that if the *bla* were destroyed by evil, the individuals who were connected to it would also be destroyed. To counteract this, the ceremony of Life-Consecration was inaugurated. It prevents evil from destroying the *bla* and provides magic amulets to insure the longevity of the individual and the community. Sherpa laymen do not believe that if Khumbila were destroyed they would die, but they do respect the mountain as a sacred place.

The procedure of the ceremony depends upon several ritual objects upon the altar. These include water vases of different sorts which contain holy waters and the "life-spirit" (*tshe-chang*), which will be mentioned below. *Tor-ma* balls are used as ritual objects in this cermony. They are called *tshe-ril*, "pills of life." Special wafers, divining daggers, and *rdo-rjes* are also used here.[12]

The ritual begins with the invocation of Padmasambhava, the "Lotus-Born," who is now envisioned as being identical with the Buddha of Infinite Life, Amitāyus. Snellgrove provides a lengthy translation of the lamas' chants and invocations during the ceremony. The following excerpts are examples of Buddhist liturgy which illustrate this rite. The lamas chant:

[10] Waddell, *Buddhism of Tibet*, p. 444.
[11] René de Nebesky-Wojkowitz, *Oracles and Demons of Tibet: The Cult and Iconography of the Tibetan Protective Deities* (The Hague: Mouton, 1956) , p. 481.
[12] Waddell, *Buddhism of Tibet*, p. 445.

> O Lord Protector Boundless Life!
> Bestow thy consecration on these worthy sons,
> That life and knowledge may be widely manifest.

The fluid referred to next is from a skullcup filled with spirit, consecrated as the "Thought of Enlightenment" (*bodhicitta*), the regenerative fluid which is conceived of as pervading the whole of existence. The chant continues:

> Infusing as the Great Bliss, it mingles in the single flavor of the flow of the Thought of Enlightenment of the Father and Mother (Amitāyus and his partner Pānduravāsinī). It falls from the unseen heavens and whirls around in the skull-cup. You taste it in your throat and the whole body is pervaded with bliss. Let the threefold world vanish in clear light, and the arteries, breath and vital fluid be perfected as absolute knowledge.[13]

These chants are consecrations of the amulets to be distributed later, and the laymen understand little of what is spoken. They know only that they are being preserved from dangers which lie in their path.

The "life force" that is spoken of next has the ability to bring great happiness to the Sherpas, but it can be lost through evil. This does not mean, however, that a layman will perish physically if the force is destroyed by evil. He will lose spiritual merit and perhaps suffer in his religious life, either in this world or in the next incarnation. Nebesky-Wojkowitz' statement about the *bla* was in the context of Bon beliefs. The Sherpa Buddhists have altered that belief into a manifestation of the mind, that is, spiritual destruction, not physical. It is another example of Buddhism's ability to infuse its precepts into a popular rite from primitive folk beliefs. The chant continues, consecrating the sacrificial vase which contains "life force":

> From this life-abode (tshe-brang), this sacred place of the five lights of wisdom, where dwell the immortal Lotus-Born [Padmasambhava, that is, Guru Rinpoche] and all the masters of his

[13] Snellgrove, *Himalayan Pilgrimage*, pp. 141-42.

succession, from this sacrificial vase the flow of nectar streams and percolates the summit of your head. May your inner body be filled and may you receive the life-consecration of the unchanging adamantine body.[14]

The fluid is poured into the spectator's hand. He drinks part of the magic water and rubs the remainder on his head.

The ceremony continues with a chant to the "life spirit": "Having tasted in your throat this life-spirit (tshe-chang), which is the very essence of all things stationary and moving, compounded into a nectar possessing the Thought of Enlightenment, having tasted this, may you receive the life-consecration of the unobstructed adamantine word." The spectator drinks this fluid also. The last consecration is of the life pellet, a ball of dough which the spectator eats.

Eat this life-pellet (tshe-ril) consisting of the pure essence of the root of being manifested as a living seed. Eat it and may you receive the life-consecration of the unchanging adamantine mind. . . . May the pure life-essence sink into the center of your heart, the indestructible vital syllable HRĪH! May your whole body be clad with the adamantine armour of the seven doctrines, so that you may be sealed with the adamantine seal of permanence and stability which is ever free from the destitution and destruction of birth and death.[15]

Spectators have waited patiently for the signal to rush forward and receive their amulets and blessings from the Abbot. Only the village headmen and wealthy citizens who donate large quantities of goods, food, and money to the monastery are anointed by monks at their seats. A clamor of crushing bodies accompanies the signal to come forward, and it is obvious that Sherpas do believe in the power of lamas to grant them long life.

It is interesting to note that this ceremony is not accompanied by lama dances in Tibet. The Khumbu lamas have combined the popularity of both the Life-Consecration rite and 'Cham

[14] Ibid., p. 144.
[15] Ibid., pp. 144-45.

into one festival, in which the welfare of the community is secured and entertainment is offered.

After a final benediction, the lamas conclude their chants, take up their instruments, and queue up for the return parade to the gomba. The return is effected exactly in reverse of the arrival of the lamas. The procession marches northeast in front of the monastery courtyard, turns west and proceeds through the courtyard and into the gomba, well past sundown. The entire proceedings consumed five hours outdoors in below freezing temperatures at Tengpoche.

The laymen return to their places of residence near the monastery and await the next day's theatrical performance. *Tshe-dbang* is a religious ceremony which benefits the Sherpas. It is rather sobering to most, and hence a time for meditation. A night of meditation prepares the Sherpas for the morrow; the reason for attending Mani-rimdu is to enjoy the drama. It is with that thought in mind that Sherpas retire for the evening.

VI. The Performance of Mani-rimdu

THE SECOND day of Mani-rimdu is described by the Abbot of Tengpoche as a drama in thirteen acts. Each act is a dance performed as a unit independent of the others. There are no plots or scenarios utilized in the purely religious dances. Different characters or dancers appear in each act of Mani-rimdu (see Appendix II). Certain individual acts are sequels to the dance immediately preceding, for example, following the *Dur-bdag* dance in which skeleton dancers destroy an effigy of evil, there is a dance of pleasure, which serves as a celebration of the victory of good over evil. However, most of the presentations could be placed anywhere among the thirteen acts without disturbing the sense or purpose of the presentation. The only thread which connects the individual dances is a religious idea, a manifestation of good overcoming evil.

The acts of Mani-rimdu do not represent Buddhism as a whole. They are a form of Mahāyāna, and they present specific deities who are primarily concerned with magical powers, supernatural events, and the furtherance of Buddhism in Tibet and Khumbu. A Theravāda Buddhist monk would not comprehend the tantric import of the Tibetan deities. These are alien to the Hinayāna system of Buddhism. The dances, consequently, are specifically Tibetan and Sherpa in their peculiar implications.

107

The Abbot of Tengpoche added this notation concerning the dances of Mani-rimdu:

> The Gar-hchams [tantric dances] are accompanied by the blowing of trumpets, beating of drums and clashing of cymbals. The tantric deities are symbolized by many gestures expressing grace, valor and terror. The deities are clothed with elaborate dresses, ornaments and weapons. The dresses and ornaments represent a gift of devotion to the deity and the weapon is a symbol of protection against the enemies of the faith.[1]

Costumes and ornaments are specific in their meanings. The sleeve of a gown denotes an entire epoch of history. A sword specifically represents the awesome power of Padmasambhava. A certain color designates a particular deity. The language is highly symbolic, and without several years of study of the Buddhist pantheon it is obscure. To the initiated it is very plain language, and to a Buddhist lama it is so elementary that he is loath to explain it. (It must be mentioned that Buddhist tantric language is not secret. It is available to any who choose to study it.)

For the most part, the disposition of the dances has been established by tradition. Furthermore, the movements of each dancer are determined by custom. Ritual objects, magic swords, daggers, offerings of food for the gods, and other symbolic articles which appear in the performance are also firmly established by tradition. These customs, however, are practiced because of religious tradition, not because of theatrical convention. There is no place for an individual actor's experimentation with his role except in the two comic performances, which are performed from a crude scenario. One utilizes dialogue to convey the story lines, and it is the only act in Mani-rimdu which is transmitted by oral discourse. These humorous acts are homespun presentations of local humor, lampooning the entire idea of religious worship.

Prior to the opening of the ceremony of Mani-rimdu, a red silk curtain masks the Abbot, monastic chanters, and the musicians from public view. This curtain must not be confused with the

---

[1] Short essay written by Abbot of Tengpoche, December, 1965.

curtain mentioned in Chapter IV, which hangs on the gomba door and masks the dancers. The red curtain (yol-ba) indicates to the audience that the dances will soon commence. Affixed to the upper portion of the balcony on the north side of the auditorium, this curtain is used only for Mani-rimdu performances. The lamas file into the balcony and take their seats behind it. For ten minutes they chant prayers for the general well-being of the citizens and the monastery. When the chants are completed, the curtain is rolled up by hand and attached to the roof of the auditorium structure. Devout spectators bow three times to the Abbot as a sign of great respect to a living god. They present the Abbot, laymen, and lamas with offerings of tea, rice, rupees, or beer. Kitchen helpers constantly supply lamas with boiling tea, never allowing their cups to stand empty.

Immediately before the dances there is a three-part prayer. The first part is dedicated to Ri-rgyal Jo-mo glang-ma (Mount Everest). It commences with the mystic Sanskirt syllable, "Om-svasti," which invokes the world forces and the Buddha-mind (suchness). The prayer praises the mountain and says its majestic beauty is unsurpassed and its height is a banner on top of the world. The concluding expression is, "May the Queen of the mountains, Ri-rgyal Jo-mo glang-ma, be victorious forever." Everest and other peaks are believed to be the abode of a group of goddesses called the Five Sisters of Long Life (Tshe-ring mched-lnga). The goddesses are listed below, with the names of the corresponding mountain peaks in brackets:

1. Bkra-shis Tshe-ring-ma [Gaurisankar]
2. Mthing-gi zhal-bzang-ma [Menlungtse]
3. Blo-bzang-ma [Kangchenjunga]
4. Mgrin-bzang-ma [Kusam Kang]
5. 'Gro-bzang-ma [I was unable to identify this peak].[2]

The Five Sisters belong to a class of feminine deities known as

[2] Antoinette K. Gordon, The Iconography of Tibetan Lamaism (Rutland, Vt.: Charles E. Tuttle, 1959), p. 82.

109

Lha-mo, who inhabit a realm outside of the worldly sphere of mortals. The sisters' abode is on the high mountain peaks. Originally they were ancient Tibetan deities who were defeated by Padmasambhava. They took an oath of Buddhist fidelity and were subsequently incorporated into the Tibetan pantheon of Buddhist divinities. At the foot of each mountain abode are five glacial lakes with water of different colors which have been dedicated to the five sisters.[3]

According to the Tibetan text, *Mi-yo Lang-zang-mei-chotrin-zhook-so (Mi-gyo gLang-bzang-ma'i mchod-sprin-bzhugs-zo),*[4] the goddess who resides on Jo-mo glang-ma is Mi-g.yo glang-bzang. This appears to be a corruption of the third sister listed above. She was one of the goddesses who worshiped the great magical wizard of Buddhism in Tibet, the poet Milarepa.[5] Each of the Five Sisters of Long Life gave Milarepa special offerings. Mi-g.yo glang-bzang presented him with cattle. During the chanting of the prayer to Everest, a yak, tied in the courtyard, is anointed with butter and milk, and draped in silk banners by a lama and a layman. The animal's head, ears, shoulders, and tail are consecrated in symbolic offering to Mi-g.yo glang-bzang. The dedication of the yak is the end of the prayer of Everest.[6] This animal will do no more work after its consecration. It is theoretically turned loose to roam the Khumbu mountainsides as a living offering to the goddess who resides on Mount Everest.

[3] René de Nebesky-Wojkowitz, *Oracles and Demons of Tibet: The Cult and Iconography of the Tibetan Protective Deities* (The Hague: Mouton, 1956), p. 177.

[4] This text was partially translated by Rimshi L. Surkhang, a Tibetan refugee now living in Seattle, Washington.

[5] See W. Y. Evans-Wentz (ed.), *Tibet's Great Yogi Milarepa: A Biography from the Tibetan Being the Jetsun-Kahbum or Biographical History of Jetsun-Milarepa, According to the Late Lama Kazi Dawa-Samdup's English Rendering* (2nd ed.; London: Oxford University Press, 1951).

[6] This could be another substitution for an animal sacrifice. The yak is cut loose from his tethers and sent out of the courtyard. The animal is either donated to the monastery by a wealthy merchant or is owned by the monastery. It is sometimes sold to a Sherpa, thereby exonerating the monastery from blame if the Sherpa chooses to utilize the animal as a beast of burden.

The second part of the prayer is dedicated to the praise of Tengpoche (Tib. Steng-chen-dgon), the monastery itself. In addition to religious references, the prayer indicates that this monastery is located near the base of the great Ri-rgyal Jo-mo glang-ma. The concluding phrases proclaim that Tengpoche's fame is known throughout the world, and that it will be victorious forever.

The third and last portion of the prayer praises the Khumbu Valley in which Tengpoche is located. "Here," the text claims, "the steady drum of Mahāyāna beats forever. Surrounded by crystal white snow mountains, the light of the sun and moon shines above."[7] The chanting concludes with the statement that Khumbu, surrounded by these mountains, is always favored with good luck.

Upon the completion of the prayer, the musicians leave their posts in the balcony and enter the gomba. Ten minutes later they begin playing their instruments from within the temple. Almost immediately they file into the courtyard in the following manner. Two *rgya-gling-pa* (players of the small brass trumpets) emerge first, followed by two *rkang-gling-pa* (players of the thigh-bone trumpets) and two *chos-rnga-pa* (one who sounds the religious [*chos*] drum [*rnga*]). Next in the procession are two lamas who carry incense burners which hang suspended from two-foot poles carried horizontally. The pungent fragrance of this incense burner (known as *bsangs-phor*) is supposed to purify the atmosphere of the courtyard. Six cymbals players complete the procession. When the entire parade is in the courtyard, the cymbals players begin the "dance of the heralds," or *Rol-'cham*. They whirl clockwise around the altar in slow rotating steps, marking time with their cymbals. The *Rol-'cham* signals the beginning of the festival dances. During it, the Abbot and other lamas chant a Tibetan prayer of blessing. The cymbals clash on each ninth beat of the chant, symbolic of good

[7] This and other information quoted or attributed to the Abbot was obtained by the author in personal interviews, or from notes accumulated between 1963 and 1966.

111

luck. This type of rhythm also signifies that the prayers will reverberate on the wave length of the universal Buddha-mind and be recorded as merit for the lamas and the spectators in attendance. The entire name of the dance of the heralds is *Rol-'cham bkra-shis dgu-brdung,* which means the good-luck *(bkra-shis)* dance *('cham)* of nine *(dgu)* beats *(brdung).*

The *Rol-'cham* lasts approximately five minutes, and the only dancers are the cymbals players. The musicians remain behind the altar facing the gomba door. As the dance ends, the *dung-chen-pa* blast two loud wailing notes to signify the termination of the act. The musicians file back to the gomba as the long trumpet players complete their notes. Tea is served to lamas and special guests while the next dance is being prepared.

As noted above, the musical instruments are an integral part of the performance. In daily ritual the *sil-snyan* are used in worship of the higher deities, that is, the true Bodhisattvas and Buddhas of Mahāyāna origin. Another instrument used mainly for worship of the Buddha is the *chos-rnga.* The *sbug-'cham, rkang-gling,* and *rgya-gling* are utilized to summon demons and deities from Bon pantheons. These traditional and regular uses of instruments for daily ritual are not particularly adhered to in Mani-rimdu. All were used simultaneously either from the balcony or the courtyard during the *Rol-'cham.* For the purposes of Mani-rimdu they provide background accompaniment to the dances. The only exception to this is when an instrument is handled by a specific dancer who represents a particular deity. By noting which instrument or ritual object an actor carries, it is possible to establish the sacred identity of the dancer.

GSER-SKYEMS

The first actual dance act of Mani-rimdu is the *Gser-skyems,* the "golden-drink dancers." Two *rkang-gling* are sounded from within the gomba. They are answered by the *dung-chen* in the balcony, and then the four instruments play simultaneously.

The first day's processional awaiting the arrival of the Abbot and monks from the gomba. Standards, drums, musicians, and audience join in the parade. The *dung-chen,* brass and copper horns ten feet long, are visible in the foreground.

Outdoor setting for *Tshe-bdang,* the Life-Consecration rite on the first day of Mani-rimdu. The three-sided building faces east and contains ritual objects used in the ceremony.

The same field during the rite. The populace is seated to the right of the building, the Abbot and two senior monks inside, senior monks left and right in front of the building, and the nuns from Devuche on the ground facing the building.

Monk bestowing *tor-ma* balls to spectators during the *Tshe-bdang* rite. He also pours sacred water into the spectators' hands.

An ancient wooden mask found at a gomba in Topke Gola in northeastern Nepal. It probably represents a local protective deity. (Photo by Terry Beck)

Part of the audience witnessing Mani-rimdu at Tengpoche, Nepal. They are seated near the gomba on the stone courtyard floor.

The first set of performers in Mani-rimdu, the *Gser-skyems* dancers. Note the long-sleeved gowns (*phod-kha*) and a poncho-like garment (*rdor-gong*) worn by the actors. Each also wears a ceremonial apron, black hat, and wig.

Ging-pa, the second act of Mani-rimdu. This masked actor is guardian king of the west and is also a king of the Nagas.

The *rkang-gling* cease and cymbals join the long trumpets. All music stops, and when it commences again the cymbals accompany the entrance of the dancers.

All eight *Gser-skyems* dancers are supposed to be dressed identically.[8] However, probably owing to the lack of money to purchase eight silk costumes of the same color, there were three different hues in the long gowns or robes (*phod-kha*). Covering the actor from the shoulders to the ankles, they are slipped on over the head and worn over the monks' regular woolen monastic garb. The sleeves are long and flowing, about thirty inches wide at the wrist. Three royal blue, three chrome yellow, and two magenta silk brocaded robes are utilized at Tengpoche. The Thami *gser-skyems* all wear royal blue gowns. Three-inch silk bands of vermillion, grass green, and chrome yellow encompass the ends of the sleeves.

Over the *phod-kha* the actor wears a thirty-inch-square silk poncho-type garment (*rdor-gong*). Its four corners point down the arms, front, and back of the actor. Each dancer also wears a bright colored silk apron or *spang-gdan,* which extends from the waist to the knee. It, like the sleeves of the gown, is bordered by vermillion, grass green, and chrome yellow silk stripes about three inches wide. The color of the *spang-gdan* varies from dancer to dancer, even though they should be identical. Each dancer wears white woolen Tibetan boots (*ras-zom*) used only for ceremonial occasions. The *ras-zom* are individually owned by the lama dancers, but the remainder of the costume belongs to the monastery. Costumes are either purchased ready-made from gombas in Tibet or manufactured by the lamas themselves.

Each performer carries in his right hand a silver-shafted cup

---

[8] The descriptions of costumes and ritual objects in these dances are the ones which I witnessed. In some cases the Abbot ascribed certain colors to garments which in reality did not correspond to those which the dancers wore. In such instances, the ideal color is mentioned, as well as the actual one which was displayed either at Tengpoche or Thami.

containing a *tor-ma* ball, which the actor throws to one of the five directions. It is a form of offering to the particular deities which this act worships and to which it pays homage.

The dancers wear black papier-mâché hats which resemble pith helmets. The brim is wide and circular and is surrounded by a conical form which culminates in a design. Painted and molded on four of the hats is a mask of Mgon-po, who is a protective deity of tantric Buddhism in Tibet.[9] A wide lemon-yellow sash of silk attached to the hat extends down the dancer's back and is tucked under the apron string at the small of the back. The actor also wears a wig (*skra-tshab*) of long black stringy hair, which hangs down his neck and over his face, giving him a grotesque appearance. A piece of black silk (*skra-len*) worn under the wig and over the shoulders of the costume keeps the gown and the actor's head clean, for the dye used in the wigs is not fast.

Moving singly, the dancers descend the stone steps from the gomba and into the courtyard at ten-foot intervals. Once in the *'cham-ra,* they move about as a group, keeping their original spatial isolation. From the steps they whirl to their left clockwise (the auspicious direction for passing mani walls), pay homage to the Abbot, and continue to their left until all eight dancers occupy the arena. The dance steps are slow and reserved; the dancer hops first on one foot and then on the other, always circling the arena clockwise.[10] After they have circumambulated the flagpole and altar several times, the cymbals bring the action to a crashing halt. The *Ldab-ldob* enters the courtyard and dis-

[9] Mgon-po belongs to a class of tutelary, or protective, deities called *yidam*. He serves as the "fiend-general" of the Rnying-ma-pa sect of Buddhism. Each sect in Tibet chooses a chief defender of all its doctrines. They are pictured as fierce in appearance and number some seventy-five in all. L. Austine Waddell, *The Buddhism of Tibet or Lamaism* (Cambridge: W. Heffner and Sons, 1894), p. 365.

[10] I was unable to discover any symbolic significance for the hopping or whirling motions of the dancers. These steps resemble the folk dances of the Sherpas. It is probable that their origin lies in the remote past of folk dancing, and was inherited by the 'Cham.

tributes drinking vessels to each dancer. He places a *tor-ma* ball in each silver cup and pours *chang* in each drinking vessel.

The cymbals take up the beat once again, and the dancers, carrying their cups, slowly whirl and hop, circling the courtyard one more time. As lamas chant and musicians play, the dancers halt to a loud crash of the cymbals. On the next loud clash the dancers toss the *chang* and *tor-ma* into the air to the five directions. This action of receiving the offering, circling the courtyard, and tossing the contents of the cups is done twice. After the second time the *Ldab-ldob* replaces the drinking vessel beneath the altar and returns to the gomba. The dancers whirl in more rapid motion, circling the *'cham-ra* three times, and then exit into the gomba. Two long, wailing, deep-throated blasts on the *dung-chen* signify the end of the act.

Several elements of symbolic, tantric language appear in this dance. To understand the nature of the "hidden" discourse, this symbolic phenomenon should be examined in some detail. No words are spoken to the audience, nor do the spectators understand the words which the lamas chant. No signboards or other descriptive insignia indicate who the dancers are or what the dance reveals. The entire ceremony is couched in language understandable only through symbols.

As was mentioned, the term *"gser-skyems"* means "golden drink." The dance portrays the offering of the "golden" drink to a local deity, Zur-ra Ra-rgyan. This deity is not generally known in Tibet, but has come to represent a manifestation of Kun-tu bzang-po in Khumbu contexts. This latter deity is considered to be the Ādi-buddha, or primordial Buddha, to the Rnying-ma-pa sect. The Ādi-buddha is self-creative and self-existent, of the highest intelligence.[11] The Rnying-ma-pa sect claims Kun-tu bzang-po as the founder of tantric Buddhism. The five

---

[11] The concept of creative powers, here, must not be taken literally. The Ādi-buddha is the first Buddha, not an anthropomorphic or anthropopsychic god who physically created the world from a void. Kun-tu bzang-po is blue in color, and in Tibetan *thang-kas* appears near the top of the painting. See Gordon, *Iconography of Tibetan Lamaism*, p. 32

manifestations of this primordial Buddha are called the Buddhas of Meditation, and their reflex forms are known as Bodhisattvas.

One form of Kun-tu bzang-po is Rdo-rje thig-le, a contemplative figure exclusively, who possesses no physical manifestation. His active form is Zur-ra Ra-rgyan, a demon who was defeated by Padmasambhava and who now serves as a protective deity, even though he is, by association, a form of the Ādi-buddha, Kun-tu bzang-po. "Ra-rgyan" (Tib. Ru-skyes) means "born of a horn," and he is frequently known as Nag-po krag-med to the Buddhists of Khumbu. That he was "born of a horn" probably links him to Mi-g.yo glang-bzang, whose form of offering is a yak. This latter aspect ties the primordial Buddha's celestial power to the protective strength afforded by the goddess of Mount Everest. The duty of Zur-ra Ra-rgyan is to protect tantric Buddhism. His realm is primarily in the Himalayas of Nepal and on the Indo-Tibetan border where there are high snow mountains and great rock peaks. The fact that he roams the mountains also serves to link him to Mi-g.yo glang-bzang.

The dance not only presents an offering to the local deity, but also to Kun-tu bzang-po. It is from the latter deity that the concept of "golden" derives. It symbolizes an offering to a celestial deity, not merely a local protector. Religiously speaking, the dance implies that Khumbu religion is derived directly from the hand of the Ādi-buddha and that one of his manifestations personally protects it.

This dance is not unknown in Tibet, although it is not as popular there as in Khumbu. Masks with horns protruding from the top represent yaks and cattle in Tibet. These animal impersonators dance for the god Zur-ra Ra-rgyan, symbolically offering themselves to the god.

The black hats of the *Gser-skyems* indicate that the actors are tantric. The black wigs are symbolic of the Indian tantric yoga, or practitioner of tantric theory. The sadhu, as the Indian ascetic is called, allowed his hair to grow long and refrained from shaving his beard as a sign of worldly disinterest. Although the wig alludes to an Indian, and therefore a different form of tantrism, to the audience it symbolizes the general notion of this practice. Tantrism developed in India, and, because of the intercourse between Indian and Tibetan forms of mystic worship, common principles underlie Hindu and Buddhist practices, which date from the second century. The wig exemplifies tantrism in general, making no distinction between Tibetan and Indian forms.

Another element of the "hidden" language found in the costume of the "golden-drink" dancers is the wide sleeve of the *phod-kha*. In conjunction with and affording the same meaning as the sleeve is the *skra-len*. These two elements find their significance in Tibetan history. Chapter III mentioned the enemy of Buddhism, Glang-dar-ma. To recapitulate the story briefly, Buddhism was in its infant stages in ninth-century Tibet. Glang-dar-ma had his brother, the pro-Buddhist king, assassinated and assumed the throne himself. He sought to uproot Buddhism and return the country to Bon rule of the Tibetan aristocracy. Many Buddhists were persecuted and exiled from the country, but many toiled and planned to restore Buddhism.

While the Tibetan king, Glang-dar-ma, was reading the inscription on a pillar in Lhasa, Lha-lung Dpal-gyi rdo-rje prepared to kill the Bon ruler. He approached the King in a disguise and bowed three times before him. The suspicious King was disarmed by this move and thought the lama to be another apostate. However, the Buddhist had hidden a bow and arrow in his long flowing sleeves, and he wore a sash similar to that worn in Mani-rimdu dances. At an opportune moment, the lama drew his weapons and slew the king. The slayer then rode away to freedom, and eventually Buddhism was restored in Tibet.

The sleeves of the *phod-kha* and the *skra-len* have since then symbolized this act by Lha-lung Dpal-gyi rdo-rje. The very costume signifies the bravery of the Buddhist protector of religion.

117

Each gown and sash of this nature evince his action. An entire legacy of history is signified by the appearance of the costume. The hat, wig, sash, and gown all transmit symbolic importance.

The over-all purpose of the dance is to praise the Buddhist deities who coerce and defeat the enemies of the faith. The dancers themselves represent priests of tantrism, *Zhwa-nag* ("Black Hat"), who are capable of performing magical deeds. Their necromancy is too powerful for evil ones to oppose, and they are forced into submission. Bound by an oath, the defeated demons vow to protect Buddhism.

During the course of the dance the *Zhwa-nag* perform a different action after each five steps to their left. As they circle the courtyard they move only five steps at a time, then step backward, whirl, and hop before moving forward again. Then the actors progress five more steps, repeating the same forward and backward moves. Following the lateral measures they place their hands on their hips, whirl, and take three steps backward. This action is symbolic of worship to the following deities: (1) Guru Rinpoche; (2) the Khumbu tutelary deity; (3) the *Ḍākinī* or demi-goddesses of Buddhism; (4) the Dikrāja, protector of the faith; and (5) the local deity. Each act of worship to these five figures is represented by the five lateral steps. Following the three backward moves, the dancers retrace their movement forward. This return symbolizes the self-protection one receives from worship of the former deities.

Another tantric element appears in conjunction with the tossing of the *tor-ma*. The *chang* and *tor-ma* offering is proffered to the five directions. These directions correspond to the Five Celestial Jinas, as the Buddhas of Meditation are sometimes called. The Buddhas of Meditation have the "body of Dharma" (Dharmakaya), the form of the absolute Buddhahood.[12] They owe their origin to their spiritual father, the Ādi-buddha, from

---

[12] Alice Getty, *The Gods of Northern Buddhism: Their History, Iconography, and Progressive Evolution Through the Northern Buddhist Countries,* trans. J. Deniker (Rutland, Vt.: Charles E. Tuttle, 1962), p. 28.

whom they received their wisdom and capacity for meditation. The Bodhisattvas are the result of the exercising of the Celestial Buddha's power. The following table lists their functions, the color that symbolizes each, and their corresponding Bodhisattvas:

Buddha	Location	Element	Mantra*	Color	Corresponding Bodhisattva
Vairocana	center	sight	*om*	white	Samantabhadra
Akshobhya	east	sound	*hūm*	blue	Vajrapāni
Ratnasambhava	south	smell	*trah*	yellow	Ratnapāni
Amitābha	west	taste	*hrih*	red	Avalokiteśvara
Amoghasiddhi	north	touch	*ah*	green	Viśvapani†

* A mantra is a special magical spell which is vocally pronounced. Here "mantra" refers only to the first syllable of that formula or spell which is chanted to the particular deity in question. An entire formula, such as *"Om mani padme hum,"* is called a mantra.
† Getty, *Gods of Northern Buddhism,* p. 28.

As dancers offer gifts to the five directions—east, west, north, south, and zenith—they pay homage to the Buddhas of Meditation. The offering is a tantric union of sight, sound, smell, touch, and taste. It represents the amalgamation of the audible and touchable with mind, speech, and body in the final state of completeness and enlightenment. It combines the world of matter with the world of the spirit, the microcosm with the macrocosm. It establishes the "inner relationship" of things both phenomenal and noumenal. The physical offering in the dance signifies the tantric union of all doctrine, wisdom, and action into a single element which overpowers all evil.

It cannot be said that this dance contains a plot. This term indicates that a story is revealed through characters and actions which have a beginning and generally come to a conclusion. A plot involves conflict between characters, or between a person and outside events. It generally denotes tension and action. Mani-rimdu dances do not tell a story except in the comic acts. The spectators feel no affinity for the religious characters. They are symbolic deities who do not interact with each other. The *Gser-skyems* does move forward in time, but it is "other world" time which contains no months or years. Evil once ruled, but virtue and compassion overcame it. Homage is paid to the protectors and defenders of religion as well as to the spiritual father of Buddhism. The entire concept is unfolded through highly symbolic language, comprehensible only to the initiated or learned.

GING-PA

Ging-pa, the second dance at Mani-rimdu, is performed by four dancers. The costumes differ quite radically from those of the previous dance. The basic color of the entire costume is royal blue and its material is cotton. Each dancer wears a pair of ornamented trousers known as *spud-shub*. Yellow, vermillion, and Nile green stripes about three inches wide spiral from the crotch downward and outward to the cuff of the trousers. Over this the dancer wears a short, skirt-like piece of cloth with vermillion trim around the edges, which extends from the waist to mid-thigh. The dancers also wear short jackets. The body of each jacket is blue, but the long silk sleeves of two are dark pink, while the other two are chrome yellow. All four wear poncho-like brocaded silk *rdor-gong*, identical to those of the *Gser-skyems.*

Unlike the *Zhwa-nag* of the previous act, all the *Ging-pa* wear different colored masks, *zhal-'bag*. They are white, green, red, and yellow, and on the crest of each is a small white skull. These, and all masks of Mani-rimdu, have a highly polished, glazed finish. The *zhal-'bag* is not fierce or demoniacal in appearance. The mouth is smiling and the teeth are human, unlike the fangs and terrifying features of masks in later acts. The

eyes are painted a pale lemon color, and the eyebrows extend
upward, slanting well above the ear line. The mask is about sixteen inches high and twelve inches wide. It is positioned so that
the actor can see through the nostrils of the mask. It is held in
place by a headpiece inside the vizard which fits the actor like a
cap. Since Mani-rimdu dancers make no violent or quick moves,
there is little chance that the mask will be disengaged. Masks are
made of papier-mâché almost exclusively, but a few are molded
from a type of mortar which resembles plaster of Paris. Older
masks were carved from a solid block of wood, but such large
chunks of wood are scarce in Khumbu and Tibet. Since 1961 all
masks at Tengpoche have been of the papier-mâché type.

The white- and green-masked dancers carry the *chos-rnga,*
while the other two carry *sbug-'cham* cymbals. The dancers
whirl around the altar much more rapidly than the *Gser-skyems*
dancers. After several turns around the courtyard, the red- and
white-masked dancers pair up and move in unison while the
green- and yellow-masked performers do likewise. They maneu-
ver through two complete circlings of the *'cham-ra* in pairs. The
pairs then unite and form one dance in unison. This action is
symbolic of another tantric "union."

The red-masked dancer is considered to be male, the white female. Their synchronous movements indicate an alliance between male and female. Green symbolizes the male and yellow
the female in the other pair. The four become a coalition representing two, and the fusion of the two represents the existence
of a mystical union which culminates in enlightenment. The
red and green dancers represent *thabs,* the active principle
which signifies the "pursuit of enlightenment." It embodies all
aspects of study, meditation, and religious acts, for these are the
means by which one approaches enlightenment. The female
symbol is *shes,* which means ""knowledge." In the mystical tantric union *shes* represents transcendental wisdom or enlightenment, and it is passive. According to Mādhyamika doctrine, one
gains enlightenment only by constantly pursuing it. One ap-

proaches noumenal transcendent wisdom (*shes*) only through phenomenal means (*thabs*). Only by the union of *thabs* and *shes* can enlightenment be obtained.[13]

At the beginning of the dance there appeared to be four separate elements, but by the end of the act these elements are shown to be inseparable. What appear to be disparate entities are in reality equal and indivisible, for in tantric Buddhism all phenomena coalesce to produce *prajñāpāramitā*. The principles of tantric Buddhism were mentioned in Chapter I. The difference should be noted again between the Hindu and Buddhist forms, however. Hinduism employs the female as the active principle. She is generally shown in a physical embrace with her male counterpart. Buddhism, however, makes the male the active, driving force. Buddhism also chooses to use this sexual union as a father-mother (*yab-yum*) union, which produces the desired product, enlightenment.

There is also another union in this dance. The *Ging-pa* represent the guardian kings of the four quarters. These kings must not be confused with the Buddhas of Meditation, however, for the latter are contemplative and passive, while the guardian kings are active. The guardian kings are minor protective deities. They are frequently referred to as the four *Lokapāla*, known in Tibetan as *Rgyal-chen bzhi,* the four kings. Getty says of them:

> The four Guardian Kings are mentioned in the earliest Buddhist writings as visiting Gautama while he was in the Tushita heaven waiting for the time to come for him to manifest himself on earth as Mānushi-Buddha. They are alluded to in the "Nidāna-Katha" as having been present when Māyā's couch

[13] By contrast to this pursuit of enlightment, Zen doctrine maintains that one cannot actively pursue enlightenment by phenomenal means (*thabs*) because such an act is selfish, and therefore "wisdom" (*shes*) will not be achieved.

For a discussion of the various aspects of this mystical union, see David Snellgrove, *Buddhist Himalaya: Travels and Studies in Quest of the Origins and Nature of Tibetan Religion* (Oxford: Bruno Cassirer, 1957), chap. ii, "Tantric Buddhism," pp. 51-90.

was carried to the place of incarnation of the Buddha. [Māyā is Buddha's mother.] They assisted at his birth, and received the Buddha "on the skin of a spotted tiger." They held up the hoofs of the horse Kanthaka when Gautama secretly left his palace to go into the wilderness. After his fasting and meditation under the Bodhi-tree they offered the Buddha four bowls of food, which he miraculously merged into one. In fact, they assisted at every important event in the life of the Buddha, and were present at his parinirvāna [death of Buddha].[14]

In paintings and sculpture the four guardian kings are pictured in this manner:

North: Rnam-thos-sras (Skt. Kuvera). King of the Yakshas (supernatural beings who bring disease). Symbols: *dhvaja* (banner) in right hand and mongoose in left. Color: yellow.

South: 'Phags-skyes-po (Skt. Virūḍhaka). King of the Khumbhanda (giant demons). Symbol: sword. Color: blue or green. Instead of the usual helmet, he wears the skin of an elephant's head.

East: Yul-'khor-bsrung (Skt. Dhritarāshtra). King of the Gandharvas (demons feeding on incense). Symbol: stringed instrument. Color: white. He wears a high helmet on top of which is a plume and from which hang ribbons and bows.

West: Spyan-mig-bzang (Skt. Virūpāksha). King of the Nāgas (serpent gods). Symbol: *mchod-rten,* a jewel, or a serpent. Color: red.[15]

These deities guard Buddhism against attack from demons. Together they act as one defender through the mystical union of tantrism. By offering prayers to them one receives protection from disease and demons which constantly plague the populace. The King of the North, Rnam-thos-sras, is also considered to be the God of Wealth, and he is prayed to for that end.

[14] Getty, *Gods of Northern Buddhism,* p. 166.
[15] *Ibid.,* p. 84.

RDO-RJE GRO-LOD

Dance number three presents one actor called Guru Rdo-rje gro-lod. His maroon *phod-kha* has long sleeves with several bright stripes. A green band circling the forearm contains dark pink rose brocade on a green background. On either side of this band are two vermillion and two lemon yellow silk stripes receding from the middle in both directions. The dancer's apron is a rich cream brocade with pastel designs. It is bordered with pink brocaded silk, and the hem is fringed with colors which run the spectrum. The gown itself is bordered on the bottom by an eight-inch magenta and silver design. This silk costume is probably the most colorful of all those in Mani-rimdu.

Rdo-rje gro-lod wears a terrifying brown mask, emblematic of a protective deity. It is fiendish in appearance and has orange and black eyes surrounded by white eyeballs. Gold paint represents his beard, mustache, and eyebrows. The mask measures eighteen inches from chin to crest, and is twelve inches wide. It is topped by a black wig which is tied up in a knot on top of the dancer's head. The nose is flattened and turned upward like a snout. Two fangs protrude from the sides of the frowning mouth. Elongated earlobes and five skulls attached to the forehead of the mask further distinguish it. The earlobes indicate a Bodhisattva, and the skulls signify a deity of tantric origin. The shock of black hair is symbolic of the Indian sadhu, and signifies that the actor impersonates a deity of Indian origin who is tantric in religious precepts.

In his left hand Rdo-rje gro-lod carries an elongated arrow-shaped magic dagger with an elaborately designed handle. This dagger conveys special significance for tantric Buddhists, as does the *rdo-rje* that he holds in his right hand. To understand the significance of these items it is necessary to know Rdo-rje gro-lod's place in the Tibetan pantheon.

Practically every deity in the Mahāyāna sphere portrays both a peaceful and a wrathful mood. The pacific aspect represents the mercy and compassion which results in good bestowed upon his followers. The wrathful mood warns enemies that the deity can also destroy those who oppose Buddhism. Rdo-rje gro-lod is one of the eight fierce manifestations of Padmasambhava (see pages 16, 33), a tantric wizard who, legend relates, traveled widely through Tibet, Sikkim, and Nepal, coercing and converting demons or destroying them. It was in a manifestation of his fierce form, Rdo-rje gro-lod, that he defeated the demons of Khumbu and forced them to swear an oath of fidelity to Buddhism. For this chore, he used several magic tools. Among them was the *rdo-rje*, the thunderbolt of the gods. It literally means "diamond," or "that which destroys but is itself indestructible." "It is likened to the Mystic Truth which cannot be destroyed," writes Getty, "'and also to wisdom that destroys all passion.'"[16] It was introduced to Tibet by Padmasambhava and is used presently in all Sherpa rituals to exorcise demons and to praise certain Buddhas. In the dance it symbolizes Rdo-rje gro-lod's tantric (mystic) powers.

The dagger (*phur-bu*) in his left hand represents more magical power. Its handle contains a carving of the fierce defender of Buddhism, Rta-mgrin, the protector of horses (which could loosely mean cattle [yak] in Khumbu). Rta-mgrin used the *phur-bu* to stab demons and destroy the enemies of Buddhism. In many paintings and sculptures, he is shown with disheveled hair, symbolic of a horse's mane. Consequently, Rdo-rje gro-lod's hair may signify the power of Rta-mgrin as well as the locks of an Indian sadhu, one of whom was Padmasambhava.

In the Thami performance of this dance, Rdo-rje gro-lod carries green and yellow silk streamers in his right hand instead of the *rdo-rje*. (From the *Ging-pa* dance it will be remembered that masks of green and yellow symbolized a tantric union.)

Padmasambhava is not only a saint in the Rnying-ma-pa sect, but he is honored by the reformed Dge-lugs-pa order also. To display his universal recognition in Tibet and Khumbu, Rdo-rje

---

[16] *Ibid.,* p. 200.

gro-lod wears a bright yellow silk sash tied across his chest. The yellow evidences his acceptance by the Yellow Hat Dge-lugs-pa sect.

Rdo-rje gro-lod is ushered into the courtyard by lama musicians, who exit after the dancer's appearance. He backs out of the gomba and upon reaching the top step of the courtyard turns to reveal his fiendish appearance. Slowly whirling and gesticulating with his two magic weapons, he descends into the arena. He moves to his left, circling the altar in stately, majestic movements.

Although such a hypothesis is tenuous at best, one could interpret this act as possessing a crude plan of action, a primitive plot. It appears that the dancer's actions have three segments. His first two turns around the altar are extremely decelerated and grand. They perhaps symbolize his arrival in Tibet as a highly revered saint and worker of magic. Following this, the beat of the cymbals accelerates the tempo slightly. Rdo-rje gro-lod's actions become almost imperceptibly more pronounced and violent. He remains imposing, but stabs at the air, apparently encountering demons and defeating them. Lamas chant praises to the deity and list the demons whom he is destroying or converting to Buddhism. The basic actions of his steps never change throughout the entire performance. Like all other dancers he whirls and hops on one foot and then on the other. His actions are slower than in most other dances, however, for it requires a full three to four minutes for him to circle the courtyard.

The *Ldab-ldob* enters the acting area and places a chair in the southeast corner of the courtyard. Rdo-rje gro-lod advances to the chair and sits in it, all in slow motion. The stage assistant then serves him a *chang* and *tor-ma* offering while the lamas chant. He tosses the offering into the air, as homage to the Buddhas, and continues to dance. The offering probably represents Buddhists paying honor to Padmasambhava, and to this manifestation in particular, for ridding the countryside of demons and rendering it safe for the peaceful practice of religion. This

third segment of his actions represents the realization of his trip
to Tibet, his coercion of demons, and his acceptance of the role
of protector of religion.

After Rdo-rje gro-lod has finished his dance and entered the
gomba, there is the usual fifteen-minute delay before the next
dance. Lamas are served tea, and pious citizens present offerings
to ecclesiastic authorities or to the poor. The audience members
are free to stretch, move about, partake of more food and drink,
or simply converse with their neighbors. Upon the first note
played by the *rgya-gling,* people return to their seats and await
the next act. Cymbals and drums from the gomba herald the
entrance of the fourth set of dancers.

RNGA-'CHAM

Four *Rnga-'cham,* or "drum dancers," appear through the
curtain. They move in pairs as they descend into the *'cham-ra.*
One set plays the mounted drums, *chos-rnga,* and the other pair
wields the *sbug-'cham* cymbals. Their costumes are almost identical to those of the *Gser-skyems,* except that all four *phod-kha*
are chrome yellow in this act, and there are no masks of Mgon-
po, the protective deity, on their hats. Replacing the mask is an
abstract triangular form, encompassed by flames, which is affixed
to the upper portion of the black hat. The triangle is about
twelve inches high and eight inches wide at its base, with a jewel
superimposed in the middle. This two-dimensional gold-painted
structure is called a *tri-ratna,* the "three jewels."

The entrance of the *Rnga-'cham* dancers is accompanied by
thigh-bone trumpets from the gomba and the balcony. The
dancers also add to the sound by playing their drums or cymbals.
In general, the act symbolizes what the Abbot of Tengpoche
termed "the eternal beat of the heavenly drum which vibrates in
the world as life and death [vibrates]." It signifies the Buddha's
message of truth to the world, and it is a dance of joy. Perhaps
metaphoric terminology would more nearly describe the significance of the "heavenly drum." Life and death, in Buddhist

127

terms, exist eternally as phenomenal effects of ignorance. They
are operated by the forces of the universe which exist of and for
themselves, dependent upon natural law. As was mentioned earlier, Tibetan Buddhists believe that truth resides mysteriously
on a "wave-length or frequency," which, if it can be monitored,
becomes comprehensible and attainable. Gautama discovered
enlightenment through his own efforts and put himself and others on that pattern. The drums, here, symbolize the expounding
and transmitting of truth on the wave-length of the universe.
Truth exists as life and death exist. Truth also vibrates (is a
universal force) as life and death vibrate, or occur by process of
natural law in the phenomenal world. The truth of the Buddha's enlightenment and teachings, of course, reverberates so
forcefully that life and death are overcome.

The *tri-ratna* further enforces the religious understanding of
the beating of the "heavenly drums." The triangle represents
the three jewels: the Buddha, Dharma (the law), and Sangha
(the community or order of monks). By adhering to the precepts of these three "jewels," one can attain truth, that is, hear
and respond to the heavenly drum. Getty provides further iconographic information concerning the *tri-ratna:*

> In the Buddhist scriptures it is written that Ādi-Dharma [con-
> sort of the Ādi-buddha] revealed herself from a point in the
> center of the triangle. From one side of the triangle she pro-
> duced Buddha; from another side Dharma; and from the third
> side, Sangha. Ādi-Dharma is therefore the mother of the Buddha
> that issued from the first side (right side of the triangle—all
> Buddhas are born from the right side of their mothers). The
> Dharma that issued from the second side is the wife of the
> Buddha of the first side and the mother of the other Buddhas.
> . . .
> According to the esoteric [tantric] doctrine, Buddha repre-
> sents the spiritual essence, the "efficient cause of all." Dharma
> is the material essence, the "plastic cause." . . . "a co-equal by-
> unity with Buddha." Sangha is the compound of Buddha and
> Dharma, "the immediate operative cause of creation."[17]

[17] *Ibid.,* p. 197.

128

Rdo-rje gro-lod. This is the third act of Mani-rimdu, and the lone actor represents one of the eight fierce manifestations of Padmasambhava. He wears a yellow sash across his chest, indicating that he is venerated by the Yellow Hat Dge-lugs-pa sect, as well as the Red Hat Rnying-ma-pa sect.

The four *Rnga-'cham* (drum dancers) as performed at Thami. This is the fourth dance at Mani-rimdu. Note that Thami monastery has no balconies for seating, and the Abbot, monks, and musicians are seated on the courtyard floor.

The first of the comic acts, *Mi-tshe-ring,* is the fifth act on the program. He is the "long-life" man. The mask represents Hwa-shang Mahāyāna, an eighth-century Ch'an monk from China.

Mi-tshe-ring and his assistant prepare a *tor-ma* offering.

The seventh act of Mani-rimdu, the *Chos-skyongs*. The actor shown here is Lha-mo, the protectress of the Dalai Lama.

Rtogs-ldan is the eighth act of Mani-rimdu and the second comic act. It is the only act that uses dialogue. Rtogs-ldan is seated on his cushion, Bkra-shis don-grub to the left.

The ninth act of Mani-rimdu is *Gnas-srung,* and the character pictured here is Zur-ra, one of the class of deities whose duty it is to guard the holy places of pilgrimage.

One of the two *Mi-nag* in the *Gnas-srung* act. The *Mi-nag* protect the life, property, and health of the people of Khumbu.

The dance signifies that all these powers exist, as represented in the *tri-ratna*. The teachings of the Buddha are mystically fused with the universal powers, and this unified tantric coalition reverberates eternally via the transmitting force of the "heavenly drum."

In a sense this dance could be considered as a sequel to the Rdo-rje gro-lod dance. The fierce manifestation of Padmasambhava magically converted or defeated all demons who opposed the doctrines of Buddhism. The "drum dance" celebrates the victory over evil and broadcasts the true teachings of the Buddha via a drum. The *chos-rnga* is used only in worship of the Buddha, and it represents a phenomenal manifestation of the mystical heavenly drum.

MI-TSHE-RING

The fifth performance at Mani-rimdu is a comic act by Mi-tshe-ring, the "long-life man" who appeared in the previous day's Life-Consecration rite. No music or chanting brings him into the courtyard. He suddenly appears peering through the curtain. There are giggles and snickers as he stares at the audience, as though he were afraid to step out into the crowd. He provides the audience with ample time to make a mental adjustment from serious dancing to this humorous act. As he begins to emerge from behind the curtain he is greeted by peals of laughter and shouts from the onlookers. (Sherpas do not show approval by hand clapping as is customary in the West. Upon completion of an act, the performers leave the stage, and the audience indicates neither approval nor disapproval.)

This enactment, like all the dances of Mani-rimdu, is performed by a monk. He performs in this role exclusively and works diligently on his pratfalls and comic antics. Monks generally state that a novice must spend three years of study prior to his first appearance in Mani-rimdu. Those with rhythmic movements and a desire to perform specialize in particular roles until

129

they become senior members of the monastery. When he is approximately forty-five years old, a monk's dancing days are terminated. The Mi-tshe-ring actor has been in the Tengpoche monastery for more than ten years and has performed his role since 1957. The movements of the role are communicated orally to the dancer, who adds innovations from his own imagination. Unlike other dancers in Mani-rimdu, the comic actors are relatively free to do whatever they wish. Monks enjoy these roles, for they elicit audience response, and they can perform for the audience, not for deities or worship alone. The comic actor also acquires prestige by his portrayal and is respected for it.

The subject foundation of Mi-tshe-ring is based upon Buddhist theory, but laymen are not aware of it. They see it as a comic act which pleases them immensely. They join in the performance as active participants, not mere viewers of a highly symbolic language of dance and costume which, for the most part, is not understood. The comic actors interact with the spectators, bringing them into the show as well.

The costume of Mi-tshe-ring is akin to the other flowing gowns, but it is much simpler. Over his magenta monk's gown the actor wears a lemon yellow brocaded *phod-kha* of Chinese silk. The sleeves on this costume are tight, not voluminous and wide as in some previous dances. The Chinese pattern on the silk depicts dragons and flowers. Over the *phod-kha* he wears an old cream-colored cotton gown, open in the front and sleeveless. His shoes are old boots, supposedly Chinese. Around his neck hangs a rosary made of seeds, wood, bones, and rock,[18] which he uses in mock worship.

Mi-tshe-ring's face is covered by a flesh-colored mask of an aged man, bald and benign. Scores of age wrinkles line the mask and are accentuated by its smiling appearance. It has bushy gray

[18] Rosaries symbolize the necklace of pearls referred to in the "Lotus of the Good Law" sutra, which was offered to the Chinese manifestation of Avalokiteśvara, Kuan-shih-yin, as an offering. The necklace, then, is a symbol of the above God of Mercy in his Chinese manifestation. See Getty, *Gods of Northern Buddhism*, pp. 190-91.

eyebrows and a gray beard, which resembles the "Man jan" beard of the Chinese opera.[19] The lips of the mask are red and the teeth human. Attached to the back of the mask is a stringy gray wig. The actor's entire appearance is emblematic of extreme old age.

Before explaining his actions on stage, we should delineate briefly Mi-tshe-ring's historical background. He is not wholly a figment of the Khumbu lamas' imagination, but an impersonation of an ancient Chinese scholar. During the eighth century many religious disputations were in vogue in Tibet. King Khri-srong Lde-btsan had ended the reign of Bon as the state religion in Tibet,[20] and three main movements of Buddhism were all trying to gain an exclusive upper hand in religious affairs. The tantric followers of Padmasambhava were opposed by disciples of the more scholarly and sedate teachings of Indian ascetics. A third school, however, also competed for influence in Tibetan religion. This form of Buddhism, known as Ch'an (Japanese Zen), had been introduced to Tibet through China. Its leader was a Chinese monk named Hwa-shang Mahāyāna, and the school was known in Tibetan as Ston-mun-pa.[21] There was great confusion and intimidation from all sides of the argument. Finally the King called the Chinese and Indian leaders together for a debate. Hwa-shang represented the Chinese, and Kamalaśīla spoke for the Indian-based philosophy.

Hwa-shang and his followers were defeated in the debate. The King ordered their teachings banned, and he placed their manuscripts under lock and key. Henceforth, only the "Middle Path" (Mādhyamika doctrine) with infusions of tantrism was allowed.

[19] The Man jan completely obscures the mouth. The beard of Mi-tshe-ring begins below the mouth but extends in a broad swath over the chest. See A. C. Scott, *The Classical Theatre of China* (London: George Allen and Unwin, 1957), p. 170; and Sis-Vanis Kalvadova, *The Chinese Theatre*, trans. Iris Urwin (London: Spring Books, 1957), p. 27.

[20] Helmut Hoffmann, *The Religions of Tibet*, trans. Edward Fitzgerald (New York: Macmillan, 1961), p. 74.

[21] *Ibid.*, p. 75.

Mi-tshe-ring in Mani-rimdu represents Hwa-shang, the erroneous teacher of Buddhism. He is pictured as a decrepit old man who cannot even control his own actions, much less lead others in religious philosophy. The comic dance of the schoolmaster in Chapter III was the Tibetan version of Mi-tshe-ring. He was a bumbling schoolteacher, and his students represented his disciples, who poked fun at him and made him the butt of their pranks. He exercised no control over them, symbolic of Hwa-shang's disregard for Buddhist order. To the Buddhist monks of Tibet, his teachings opened the portals to nondisciplined Buddhism, a world without order.

In Khumbu, Mi-tshe-ring has no children or pupils, nor does he represent a teacher. Rather, he emulates a devout man who is unable to pay respectful homage to the deities. Every act of religious devotion which he attempts backfires, for he utilizes the wrong methodology. According to one Buddhist informant, the enactment of this dance was possibly begun around the turn of the twentieth century during the reign of the thirteenth Dalai Lama. He resided for several years in Peking and apparently saw a dance of Hwa-shang at a Buddhist monastery outside the Chinese capital. Upon his return to Tibet the Dalai Lama instituted the dance for his people. In China, Tibet, and Khumbu it evinces the supremacy of Tibetan Buddhism over other forms of the same religion.

Mi-tshe-ring walks with a senile hobble, using a bamboo stick for support. His aged back is bent forward, and his shoulders are hunched in weakness. As he moves down the stone steps into the courtyard, he slips and falls, clutching at the raised walkway. Gaining his feet once more, he tries to back down the first step, but sprawls on the walkway again. He then attacks the steps straight away and tumbles down two of them, lying on his back rubbing his bruised parts. He angrily shakes his fist and stick at those spectators near him who laugh at his awkwardness. Gaining his balance again he feebly makes a successful attempt to descend one step without falling. In his glee at his agility he promptly tumbles the remaining two steps, ending spread-eagled on the stone floor of the courtyard. At this the audience roars with laughter.

For some minutes Mi-tshe-ring writhes in agony on the 'cham-ra, gingerly rubbing his wounded limbs and backside. He attempts to rise without the aid of his walking stick, and again finds himself in a crumpled heap on the floor. Upright at last, he slowly advances on the audience, stretching his arms wide, imploring them, as if to say, "Why do you laugh at a poor old man?" He hobbles toward the Abbot and monks in the balcony, but cannot reach them to offer a gift. Eventually he drags an unwilling "audience member" into the courtyard to help him.

This assistant, of course, is part of the act and is himself a monk. He is a purely local innovation in Khumbu, and serves to involve the entire audience, since he is chosen as one of its members. The actor plays his part well, pantomiming an argument with Mi-tshe-ring, refusing to step out of his secure seat and portraying embarrassment at being asked to do so. No words are spoken during the entire performance.

Ultimately the man gives in, and Mi-tshe-ring sends him away to locate an object upon which he can stand in order to reach the Abbot in the balcony. Finally the monk returns with a ladder, which he leans against the balcony railing. Mi-tshe-ring takes up a ceremonial scarf (kada) and prepares to climb the ladder, intending to place the scarf around the Abbot's neck. Before embarking on his ascent, he kneels and bows to the High Lama, banging his head against the stone floor. After rubbing his head, he tries it once more, with the same result, much to the delight of the audience. Failing at this, he takes two steps up the ladder and slides all the way to the floor. The second attempt terminates with Mi-tshe-ring hanging under the ladder, a leg caught between the rungs. The assistant extricates the old man, and they decide to give up this form of homage.

The "long-life man" is discouraged at his failure, but he promptly orders his assistant to prepare another type of offering. Seated before the altar he begins to mold tor-ma from barley flour and water. The result of this work is a pasty mess which is spilled on the floor, the assistant, and Mi-tshe-ring himself. The old man tries to toss the *tor-ma* to the gods, but it sticks to his hands. As he scrapes it off one hand he discovers that it is stuck to both. After much consternation and scolding he orders his assistant to kneel in front of him, and he proceeds to wipe his hands on the monk's robes. Exasperated with his futile efforts, he dances once around the courtyard, stumbling and falling, and slowly creeps up the steps and into the gomba.

Mi-tshe-ring is a caricature of a human being, symbolizing man's rigidity, both physical and mental. His act plumbs no profound emotional depths; rather the audience sees Mi-tshe-ring on the surface, catching the outward form of life with the innocence of a child. Obviously the act is not taken seriously or an audience member would surely help the poor fumbling gentleman down the stairs before he could harm himself.

Although this dance could be rationalized as having religious merit, no one thinks of it in those terms. It is a comedy to the audience and the monks alike. A mockery has been made of religious offerings, and sacred *tor-ma* has been used as material for this buffoonery. Religion, which is embraced seriously and practiced diligently, is used as subject matter for the pranks of Mi-tshe-ring. Yet the Abbot, senior monks, dancers, and laymen wipe tears of laughter from their eyes. How can mockery be tolerated in a supposedly serious festival of worship?

In the first place the festival carries no overtones of a serious act of worship. It is a portrayal of religious personages symbolically overcoming evil. It is a demonstration of the deities' power, a visual enactment of the spirit of the deity, not a presentation of the deity in person. The festival is aesthetically removed from physical encounters with actual gods and demons.

Second, the dancers add color, form, rhythm, order, space, and time to the performance. That is, they create something before an audience at a specific time in a specific place. The created object exists only for the elapsed time of the duration of the act. Afterward only the memory remains, the object is gone.

This places the actual act (worship?) of performing on a plane removed from the mundane world of phenomenal encounters. The act is illusory, a created manifestation of a deity.

Third, another element has been imposed upon the drama. This factor is the human element, for comedy is in the realm of the reasoning power of man. The ability to poke fun at one's institutions is a mark of maturity. It is an admission of being human, together with all its frailties and inconsistencies. Laughter keeps men young and flexible. When it dies, a people die. If a society lacks the ability to laugh, a rigor-mortis-like attitude descends which will never permit corrective measures, for no admission of purgative requirements would be conceded. George Santayana writes: "Where the comic spirit has departed, the company becomes constraint, reserve eats up the spirit, and people fall into a penurious melancholy in their scruple to be always exact, sane and reasonable, never to mourn, never to glow, never to betray a passion or a weakness, venture to utter a thought they might not wish to harbour for ever."[22]

The Sherpas have an ability to view themselves humorously, to see their own lives through a jaundiced eye, and it is their faculty for laughter, their admission of being human, that permits a Mi-tshe-ring to mock everything which they hold sacred. This comic figure affords the people of Khumbu a view of themselves as others might see them. He exaggerates their eccentricities and misguided devotion. He exposes their frailties and ostentations. He lifts them out of their mundane work-a-day world and allows them to view man through a roving omniscient eye which superficially witnesses their actions.

DUR-BDAG

The sixth dance presents one of the subhuman elements of the Buddhist pantheon in Khumbu. The *Dur-bdag* are ghoulish

[22] George Santayana, "The Comic Mask," *Theories of Comedy,* ed. Peter Lauter (Garden City, N.Y.: Doubleday, 1964), pp. 416-17.

characters whose costumes are designed to represent a human skeleton. These two dancers wear cream-colored, close-fitting garments that resemble Western long-sleeved pullovers, and trousers that resemble tights. Superimposed on this costume are red lines which outline the bones of a skeleton. The bones of the rib cage, arms, and legs are drawn in this fashion on the shirt and trousers. The tights extend over the feet, which are also painted to mark the foot bones and toes. The dancers wear royal blue skirts eighteen inches long, which reach to mid-thigh. Their hands are bare.

Their masks are painted and shaped to represent human skulls. They have sunken eye sockets, massive grinning mouths, and enormous sets of teeth. The masks are cream colored, and are outlined in red and yellow to accentuate the shape of the skull. Five small skulls are affixed to the crown of each mask, extending from one ear over the top of the head and down to the other ear.

This dance is a visual explanation of some of the functions of the Lord of the Dead, Gshin-rje Chos-rgyal, or, as he is known in Sanskrit, Yama. Getty relates the legend of Yama:

> There was once a holy man who lived in a cave in deep meditation for fifty years, after which he was to enter Nirvāna. On the night of the forty-ninth year, eleventh month, and twenty-ninth day, two robbers entered the cave with a stolen bull, which they proceeded to kill by cutting off its head. When they discovered the presence of the ascetic, they decided to do away with him as a witness of their theft. He begged them to spare his life, explaining that in a few moments he would be entering into Nirvāna, and that if they killed him before the time he would lose all benefit of his fifty years' penance. But they refused to believe him, and cut off his head, whereupon his body assumed the ferocious form of Yāma, King of Hell, and taking up the bull's head, he set it on his own headless shoulders. He then killed the two robbers and drank their blood from cups made of their skulls. In his fury and insatiable thirst for victims he threatened to depopulate the whole of Tibet. The Tibetans appealed to their tutelary deity, Mañjuśrī, to protect them from this formidable enemy, whereupon he assumed the ferocious form of Yamāntaka and waged war against Yāma. A fearful

struggle ensued, in which Yamāntaka (lit. "he who conquers death") was victorious.[23]

Yama judges those who venture into hell after their earthly demise. He conducts them to the appointed spheres of the underworld. Yama has many helpers who assist him in his duties. Two of them are known as the *Citipati* (Tib. *Dur-khrod bdag-po*), and they are usually depicted in paintings and sculptures with Yama.[24] They, too, were beheaded and now are fierce enemies of the thieves of life, such as demons, murderers, bandits, and the like. They have vowed eternal vengeance upon the evil spirits. In Khumbu these *Citipati* are called the "Masters of the Cemetery" (*Dur-bdag*), and they are subordinate to the protective deities (*Sa-bdag*), the country gods. Even though they are associated with the Lord of the Dead, the *Dur-bdag* are protective beings.

Cymbals and thigh-bone trumpets announce the beginning of the dance. The two *Dur-bdag* enter the arena together, to the accompaniment of the drums, trumpets, and cymbals. The music ceases as the dancers whirl beneath the Abbot. Moving clockwise around the *'cham-ra*, the two actors rotate on one foot, stamping the pavement with the other. Their actions resemble those of an American Indian war dance. The stamping probably symbolizes their duty as depicted in Tibetan iconographical works. In these paintings and sculptures the *Citipati* (*Dur-bdag*) are represented as dancing on corpses of humans to signify their revenge, which is wreaked upon demons, especially those evil ones who deprive men of their phenomenal life.

After they have completed one turn around the courtyard, the *Ldab-ldob* brings out an eighteen-inch effigy of a human corpse. The effigy is called a *bskang-ba*,[25] an offering to the Lord of the Dead. This corpse is either a substitute for a human or a representative evil, a demon. The latter is probably nearer the truth,

[23] Getty, *Gods of Northern Buddhism*, p. 512. Also see Chapter II.
[24] Gordon, *Iconography of Tibetan Lamaism*, p. 95.
[25] In Tibet this effigy of the corpse is called a *"ling-ga."* In Mani-rimdu, however, the object is not only a corpse, but an offering to the Lord of the Dead.

137

for although it is offered to Yama, it is presented by the *Dur-bdag,* who have vowed to protect life and destroy evil. Tied into the middle of a ten-foot string, the effigy is dragged about the courtyard two times. Each dancer holds one end of the string, and the effigy is pulled, whirled in the air, and banged against the stone floor.

Halting before the Abbot's seat, the two dancers release the figure and let it lie on the pavement. They then circle the courtyard again, but this time with increasingly rapid and violent moves. At the culmination of their dance the *Dur-bdag* circle the effigy, with the cymbals accompanying. With menacing stamps and hand gestures they symbolically destroy the enemy (effigy). They toss the corpse to the gods and pace themselves around the altar once more, then the music brings the dancers to a complete halt.

From behind the curtain of the gomba, two other actors appear. They halt on the top step, look at the *Dur-bdag,* and slowly descend into the courtyard. They walk directly toward the altar, turn left, and take up positions between the altar and the Abbot.

When the music commences again, they join the pair of skeleton dancers. The four dance in the courtyard, and the two acts become one performance. The newcomers are *Zhwa-nag* ("Black Hat"), tantric priests, who are noted for their magical ability to coerce demons. They are dressed as they were during the *Gser-skyems.* Each priest carries a *phur-bu,* the magic dagger of Padmasambhava, which was noted in Rdo-rje gro-lod's dance.

The four dancers circle the altar five times, but their actions are different. The *Dur-bdag* pound their feet against the courtyard floor, and the *Zhwa-nag* slash at the air with their daggers. According to the Abbot the *Zhwa-nag* "kill the enemies of Buddhism in such a manner that their souls are led to higher spheres." This refers to the spirit of the departed demon or enemy. Since the *Zhwa-nag* are such powerful wielders of magic, only demons of some importance are worthy of their attention. When these demons are overcome by the wizards, their bad karma is purged, and they consent to being converted and to using their strength to protect Buddhism. They are, therefore, reborn in a higher realm.

"The *Zhwa-nag* obtain their reward," the Abbot commented, "by eating the flesh and drinking the blood of the deposed enemy." This action, however, was not performed. After several turns of the courtyard, the four dancers—two skeletons and two priests—gather around the corpse. While they remain motionless, the monks chant an invocation to the Lord of the Dead. When they have completed the scripture, the cymbals take up the beat, and the dancers whirl around the effigy, symbolically striking at it. The two *Dur-bdag* throw the corpse in the air as the final act of the offering. (At one Tengpoche performance the effigy landed in the crowd, and children eagerly clutched at it as a souvenir of the festival.)

The drums, cymbals, and *rgya-gling* trumpets accompany the four dancers as they circle the *'cham-ra* in more rapid steps for the last time. The skeleton dancers move up the steps into the gomba; as the *Zhwa-nag* complete their circle, they also depart from the courtyard. The music halts as the dancers reach the stone walkway. Two *dung-chen* sound a pair of long low notes to signify the completion of this dance. The act is a combination of two dances, but it is referred to here, and at Mani-rimdu, as a single act.

The *Dur-bdag* are subordinate to the *Zhwa-nag* in spiritual spheres, and it is not certain why the two pairs united in this act. My hypothesis is that the *Zhwa-nag* were required to consummate the final destruction of evil. Since the *Dur-bdag* are a subhuman form of protector—active, vengeful, and violent by nature—the serenity of Buddhism's power is displayed by the *Zhwa-nag*. The skeletons' costumes and masks are fierce and gruesome; they are on the lowest echelon of the Buddhist pantheon. The *Zhwa-nag*, on the other hand, wear gorgeously colored and designed costumes; they are revered tantric priests. Their part in this act signifies their overwhelming might and genius, indicating that they are even more powerful than the physical protectors of Buddhism. The *Zhwa-nag*'s knowledge of spells and magic is potent enough to defeat any demon. If the *Zhwa-nag* could not cope with a demon, it would be necessary to summon for assistance an emanation of Padmasambhava, the chief of all wizards, perhaps in the form of Rdo-rje gro-lod. There is a deity, or a manifestation of a deity, whose superior omnipotence can always be elicited to combat demons. It is a matter of having the proper tool for the specific job at hand.

CHOS-SKYONGS

The seventh act is the dance of the eight *Chos-skyongs*. The skeleton dancers and priests of the previous dance are junior and minor to these figures. They are known as *Dharmapāla* in Sanskrit, and are frequently referred to as the "Eight Terrible Ones." Their duty is to defend the law or doctrine of Buddhism, and they are considered to have the rank of Bodhisattva. Nebesky-Wojkowitz characterizes these eight figures:

> To protect the Buddhist religion and its institutions against adversaries, as well as to preserve the integrity of its teachings, is a task assigned, in accordance with precepts common to the various sects of Tibetan Buddhism, to an important group of deities, best known under the name *Chos-skyong* (Skt. *Dharmapāla, dvārapāla*), "Protectors of the religious law." Another appellation frequently given to the gods and goddesses of this particular group is *btsan-srung-ma*, "guardians of the Buddhist doctrine...." In accordance with the deities they have to fulfill, the *Dharmapāla* are usually depicted in fierce aspect, brandishing weapons and crushing the human or supernatural enemies of Buddhism under their feet.[26]

The eight *Chos-skyongs* are: Lha-mo, the glorious goddess (Skt. Śrīdevī); Tshangs-pa dkar-po, the White Brahma; Beg-tse, God of War; Gshin-rje chos-rgyal, the Lord of the Dead (Skt. Yama); Rnam-thos-sras, God of Wealth (Skt. Kuvera); Mgon-po, the Great Black One, a protector of Buddhism (Skt. Mahākāla);

[26] Nebesky-Wojkowitz, *Oracles and Demons of Tibet*, p. 3.

140

Rta-mgrin, Protector of Horses (Skt. Hayagrīva); and Gshin-rje-gshed, conqueror of the Lord of the Dead (Skt. Yamāntaka).[27]

These divinities are all tantric, and they wage war without mercy against all demons and enemies of Buddhism. They are not malignant, but are represented in ferocious form to inspire malignant spirits with fear.[28] They are "demon-generals or com-manders-in-chief who execute the will of the tutelaries—the demon-kings."[29] The *Chos-skyongs* also symbolize the four tran-quil or peaceful methods employed by divine beings (Bodhisatt-vas) for the salvation of sentient creatures—compassion, fondness, love, and stern justice.[30]

The first two figures to enter the arena are dressed in royal blue brocaded silk gowns with mustard yellow capes. Each dancer wears a necklace made of bones. Their royal blue masks are adorned by five skulls and contain a third eye in the fore-head, the symbol of a Bodhisattva's omniscience. Hanging down from the back of the mask is a sash. A shock of unkempt black hair, tied up on a conical form on the head, straggles down the actor's back and over his eyes. The over-all appearance of the costumes is identical to those of the *Csor skyems* dancers.

One of these royal-blue-masked dancers is Lha-mo, the only goddess among the group. Her features are designed to display ugliness and ferociousness. The mask is frowning and fiendish, the eyes staring wildly. Her mop of hair emphasizes the gro-tesque fangs that are visible in her mouth. This goddess is re-garded as the protectress of the Dalai Lama.[31] As a female de-fender of the Mahāyāna doctrine, she is armed with weapons. In her right hand she carries a sword and in her left hand a mace, a

---

[27] Gordon, *Iconography of Tibetan Lamaism*, p. 36.
[28] Getty, *Gods of Northern Buddhism*, p. 148.
[29] Waddell, *Buddhism of Tibet*, p. 363.
[30] W. Y. Evans-Wentz (ed.), *The Tibetan Book of the Dead: Or the After-Death Experiences on the Bardo Plane, According to Lama Kazi Dawa-Samdup's English Rendering* (New York: Oxford University Press, 1960), p. 121.
[31] Jacques Marchais, *Objects from the Tibetan Lamaist Collection of Jacques Marchais* (New York: Comet Press, 1941), p. 23.

club used for breaking the armor of demons. A legend about Lha-mo further delineates her ferocious character. She vowed to convert her husband and her relatives to Buddhism. If she failed in her appointed task, she would kill her own son as a demonstration of her animosity toward the enemies of Buddhism. Finding it not in her power to influence her husband, she "flayed her son alive, drank his blood, and ate his flesh."[32]

The other blue-masked figure with Lha-mo is Mgon-po, "the Great Black One."[33] His costume is identical to that of Lha-mo, but he carries different objects in his hands. In his left is a trident, a three-pronged spear which resembles Poseidon's spear. It is called a *triśūla* in Sanskrit, which means "three points." The exact meaning of the trident is obscure, and Buddhist theories of it vary. They range in meaning from the doctrine of the Buddha to a representation of the *tri-ratna,* to the tree of life and lightning, to the Buddha's first sermon at Benares. The trident is a symbol which has become associated with Mgon-po.[34] In his right hand he carries a *phur-bu.*

Nebesky-Wojkowitz describes the way that Mgon-po is usually represented in paintings:

> According to the rules of Tibetan iconography, he is depicted in the following way: The color of his body is blue or black, he has one face, is three-eyed and six-handed. In his first right hand he holds a chopper with a thunderbolt-shaped hilt, in the middle one a rosary of human skulls—with this hand he lifts simultaneously the elephant hide which covers his back—and with his lowest right hand he whirls a *damaru* [small hand drum]. The main left hand holds a blood-filled kapāla [skull bowl] in front of his breast, his middle left hand, which holds another corner of the elephant hide, wields a *trident,* and the lowest one clutches a snare with two thunderbolts attached to its ends. The face of the deity is set in a most fierce manner with gaping mouth, the fangs bared and the tongue rolled backward; a blue snake winds itself around his hair. . . . He treads on a white "ganesa" or on a defeated obstacle-creating

[32] Getty, *Gods of Northern Buddhism,* p. 150.
[33] For further information see the glossary of terms in *ibid.*
[34] Gordon, *Iconography of Tibetan Lamaism,* p. 18.

demon.... [His body] ... is covered with numerous ornaments:
bangles of bells are on his hands and feet, he wears a green
necklace, red earrings, ornaments of human bone, a crown of
five skulls, and a garland of fifty freshly severed human heads;
the whole figure is surrounded by fiercely blazing flames.[35]

Mahākāla was a Hindu divinity of the highest order. He was
permitted entry into the Buddhist pantheon as Mgon-po, a protector and defender of the doctrine. He is usually painted on the
main east wall of a gomba near the door, and is a favorite Tibetan defender. One of his manifestations is the God of Wealth
and the special protector of the Mongolian Buddhists. Other
forms of this god serve as the protector of science and the protector of tents.

The next pair of dancers to enter the courtyard in the *Chos-
skyongs* dance are costumed in vermillion masks and gowns with
chrome yellow capes. They also wear necklaces, but instead of
skulls over their masks they display five jewels. These represent
the five Buddhas of Meditation. A third eye adorns the forehead
of each mask.

The first figure is Beg-tse (literally, "hidden shirt of mail").
He is represented in paintings as the God of War and the Protector of Horses. Since he is a warrior, he wears a breastplate in
paintings, but this is not utilized in Mani-rimdu costumes. The
face of the mask displays a closed mouth and large bulging eyes.
Red hair hangs from the conical form on top of the head in a
straight fall. It does not lie about the ears or face. This deity was
converted to Buddhism in Mongolia, where he witnessed the superior power of Avalokiteśvara.

In his right hand Beg-tse carries a sword (*khadga*), which symbolizes the enlightenment of the world, for "as the sword cuts
knots, so does the intellect pierce the deepest recesses of Buddhist
thought."[36] The *khadga* is a special symbol of Mañjuśrī and is
used both to defeat demons and to direct them to the proper
path, Buddhism. In iconographical representations this deity

[35] Nebesky-Wojkowitz, *Oracles and Demons of Tibet.* p. 39.
[36] Getty, *Gods of Northern Buddhism*, p. 189.

143

should be ferocious, wearing a crown of skulls and carrying a bow and arrow. In his Mani-rimdu form, however, the latter elements are missing, and his appearance is much more benign than that of the two previous blue-masked dancers.

The other vermillion-masked actor is Gshin-rje-gshed, the conqueror of the Lord of the Dead. He is sometimes referred to as "the exterminator of the Lord of the Dead." This deity is the fierce manifestation of Mañjuśrī, the Bodhisattva of Transcendental Wisdom. Technically he should be depicted with a bull's head, but in Mani-rimdu his mask is identical to that of Beg-tse. Both of these very ferocious gods appear rather subdued in Mani-rimdu.

In his right hand Gshin-rje-gshed wields a *gri-gug*, or tantric knife, shaped like a small hatchet. It is used to overpower demons. His left hand holds a *kapāla*, the skull bowl. This bowl originated in the legend of Gshin-rje-gshed. Before waging war on the Lord of the Dead, he killed three robbers; making cups of their skulls, he drank their blood.[37] This legend is closely associated with that of Gshin-rje Chos-rgyal, who likewise killed enemies and drank their blood from cups fashioned out of their skulls.

The next figure who descends from the gomba is Rnam-thos-sras, God of Wealth to Northern Buddhists. This actor wears a white brocaded gown of silk. Red, blue, yellow, and green designs adorn the *phod-kha.* He wears a yellow cape, and a sash attached to his mask extends down his back to the waist. The mask is white, although ideally it should be yellow, and it is pleasing in appearance. The third eye of foreknowledge is implanted in the forehead. The features of the face are smiling and more feminine than masculine. No beard, bushy eyebrows, or large bulging eyes appear in this characterization. Getty further explains this god, who is derived from Hinduism:

Kuvera [Rnam-thos-sras] was the son of a sage called "Visravas."

[37] In present-day tantric ceremonies, lamas fill such cups with water to represent blood, and offer it to the god who conquered death, Gshin-rje-gshed. Also see *ibid.,* p. 188.

144

He is said to have performed austerities for a thousand years, in reward for which Brahma gave him immortality and made him god of Wealth, guardian of all the treasures of the earth, which he was to give out to whom they were destined. *Kuvera's* abode was said to be on Mount Kailās. . . . *Kuvera* was also worshipped by the Buddhists, and was looked upon as one of the *Lokapāla,* regents of the Four Cardinal Points. As Regent of the North he was called "Vaisravana," and his abode Alaka in the Himā-layas, abounding in wealth and magnificence.[38]

In one hand the representation of Rnam-thos-sras carries a *dhvaja,* a banner of victory, the symbol of this god. In the other hand he should hold a *nakula,* but instead he carries a water vase on which is inscribed a picture of the *nakula.* This symbol is a bag made of the skin of a mongoose, which signifies Rnam-thos-sras' victory over the Nāgas, the traditional Indian guard-ians of treasure.

The last three dancers to enter the courtyard wear fiendish masks of chocolate brown, outlined in gold paint to emphasize their angry mood. They all wear white brocaded gowns of Chinese silk and mustard yellow capes. Each mask contains the third eye and is topped by a crown of five skulls. Straggly brown hair is tied up in a knot and hangs down the back and sides of the head.

The first actor represents Tshangs-pa dkar-po. He is one of the "Eight Terrible Ones," but little is known of him. Gordon calls him the "White Brahma," and he is a warrior god like Beg-tse, but beyond this his identity and duties are a mystery.

The second chocolate-brown-masked actor is Rta-mgrin, "with the neck of a horse." He is worshiped by horse dealers in Tibet because he frightens away demons by neighing like a horse. The horse is one of the "seven precious things" in Tibet.[39] (See page 125 for further description of Rta-mgrin.)

---

[38] *Ibid.,* p. 156.

[39] The "seven previous things" are known as the "Seven Gems." They are: (1) the wheel with a thousand spokes (represents the symmetry and completeness of the law) ; (2) the jewel (a wish-procuring gem) ; (3) the jewel of a wife; (4) the gem of a minister (business regulator); (5) the

The third figure with a brown mask in the *Chos-skyongs* dance is Gshin-rje Chos-rgyal, the Lord of the Dead. In most iconography he is represented as dark blue, red, white, or yellow in color, but he is depicted as brown in Mani-rimdu. This probably owes to the lack of properties, and not to deficiency of knowledge of his proper form. The legend of Gshin-rje Chos-rgyal is related briefly on pages 136-37.

Deceased Buddhists are brought before this god in the underworld. They must answer his questions and submit to his final judgment. It is Gshin-rje Chos-rgyal and his helper who total up the karmic record of Sherpas after death. They place black pebbles for evil deeds and white pebbles for virtuous acts on the universal scales. There is a symbolic physical weighing of black and white. If the evil side of the scale descends below the horizontal, the man's next incarnation will be on the same level as the present, or in a lower realm, perhaps not even in the sphere of mortals.[40]

All eight figures make up the dance of the *Chos-skyongs,* and it appears to be a celebration of the victory of good over evil. It may chronologically follow the previous dance in which subordinate deities physically coerced demons, for the former gods were assistants to these eight. However, if this dance logically follows, I was unable to ascertain why. It may be an act of celebration, for it is also called *dga'-ba,* which means pleasure. If it truly represents pleasure at the victory of the deities in the previous dance, however, it would be more logical if a Buddha performed the dance, for these eight are converted demons, or Hindu gods, who rely upon the Buddhas for direction. The dance could be only a display of pleasure for the monks who witness this powerful group of protectors. The lamas were un-

---

white elephant (symbol of universal sovereignty); (6) the horse (the horse from the good-luck prayer flags mentioned in Chapter IV); and (7) the gem of a general (who conquers all enemies). See Waddell, *Buddhism of Tibet,* pp. 389-90

[40] Evans-Wentz, *Tibetan Book of the Dead,* pp. 35-37.

willing or unable to state whether it logically followed the previous dance or not.

During the entire ceremony the eight dancers circle the courtyard. At times they move in circular fashion, and at other moments they group in fours facing each other across the *'cham-ra.*
They whirl in their positions and rest, then exchange places on
opposite sides of the arena, shortly to return to their original
places. As they circle the courtyard, whirling and hopping, they
stop eight times. At each halt a different figure is directly below
the Abbot. A chant is intoned, invoking the protection of the
particular deity who faces the Abbot at that time. Cymbals pick
up the beat, and dancers circumambulate the altar once more,
this time stopping with the next deity in line with the Abbot.
Again the chant, music, and movement, until the third deity
comes to rest before the High Lama. This action continues until
all eight gods have been praised. The dancers circle the courtyard three times to the accompaniment of all instruments in a
loud energetic beat, and finally they proceed up the courtyard
steps and into the gomba. Two droning notes from the *dung-
chen* mark the conclusion of the act. The monks have completed
their tribute to all the *Chos-skyongs,* the defenders of their faith.

Once again the monks' and musicians' teacups are replen-
ished. Spectators move about freely, conversing, eating and
drinking, or distributing more offerings. A short musical piece
announces the beginning of the next act.

RTOGS-LDAN

The eighth act is another comic dance, and it is the only performance which utilizes dialogue. The name of the dance derives from the main character, Rtogs-ldan. This act is a caricature of an Indian sadhu, a holy man or ascetic. Probably it
mocks the present-day sadhu rather than the ancient holyman,
for it was from eighth-century Indian ascetics that the Buddhist
impluse reached Tibet. It will be recalled that Buddhism practi-

147

cally succumbed during the twelfth century in India, and it was
never revived to its original position of grandeur. The present-
day Indian beggar, sadhu, or holyman is looked upon by Buddhists as being somewhat odd and eccentric. The monks of
Khumbu never go into the streets to beg, nor do they seek audiences to witness feats of yoga mysticism. The Hindu Indian ascetics, however, are prone to such vainglorious "religious" practices. The fakirs and snake charmers are an outgrowth of this
type of action. On almost any street in Indian cities one can witness their actions, generally performed for money. Their appearance is shabby, and their manner is crude. The Buddhist monks,
on the other hand, are generally clean. Their heads are shaved,
and their robes are in order. When a Buddhist in Tibet or
Nepal becomes an ascetic or meditates for long periods, he does
so in solitude, not on a city street. It is this Buddhist dislike for
ostentation and eccentricity which forms the subject matter of
Rtogs-ldan's act.

Rtogs-ldan means "one having true perception," but in
Mani-rimdu the term is used sarcastically, for the actor is a
comic buffoon. He wears a distinctly human mask, painted light
brown like an Indian's skin color. His eyebrows, teeth, jaw, and
eyes are characteristic of the Indian. The mask has a black
moustache, small beard, and smiling features. It is neither de-
moniac nor exaggerated, nor does it particularly evince folly.
His wig is black and tied up in a knot on top—again symbolic of
a sadhu's hair. In his earlobes are two long silver rings.

The costume of Rtogs-ldan is that of an Indian beggar and is
generally a representative dress of northern India. He wears a
faded red *arti*, a toga-like garment, beneath which is an old
white cotton lower garment or gown. The toga is sleeveless,
showing a long-sleeved shirt of red silk print beneath it. A white
sash is tied around his waist. The actor's only non-Indian garment is his Sherpa footwear. The sadhu generally travels bare-
footed, but in winter in Khumbu a shoeless dancer would become very chilly walking on the stone courtyard.

Rtogs-ldan is not heralded by any music, except that which

148

calls the spectators back to their seats. He appears at the gomba doorway arguing with spectators. Unlike Mi-tshe-ring, Rtogs-ldan speaks through his mask. In fact, he chatters rapidly during his entire performance. He carries a five-foot walking stick, also symbolic of a sadhu. Over his shoulder he bears a burlap sack which contains all his earthly possessions. This actor specializes in this one role, as did the Mi-tshe-ring impersonator. Rtogs-ldan is not old like his comic counterpart, but middle-aged, approximately thirty in Khumbu.

Once in the courtyard, the actor announces that he has come to pay homage to the respected Abbot of the monastery—but he cannot remember the name of the place. Perplexed over his lack of memory, he calls for his companion, who is lost. He searches for him throughout the audience, and peers into the corners of the courtyard, but is unsuccessful in his quest. Finally he returns to the steps leading to the gomba and shouts for him. A very tattered man enters the arena to the accompaniment of abuses from Rtogs-ldan.

This companion is called Bkra-shis don-grub; he is a Sherpa who accompanies the holy man, apparently aspiring to become a sadhu like his master. Bkra-shis don-grub wears a tattered Sherpa toga made of homespun wool and worn out Sherpa boots. His mask is slightly grotesque, although it is humorous and human. Its color is ashen gray, and it is wrinkled with toil, not old age. It is expressionless save for an appearance of dull-wittedness. He has no wig, his head being covered by a grimy cotton cloth.

This act, I think, is purely a local innovation, although one lama claimed some sort of derivation from Tibet. He did not know from what it had originated, for his knowledge was from hearsay. If there is a prototype in Tibet, it is probably from the comic interludes of the Lha-mo dramas, rather than anything from 'Cham. Between the acts of Lha-mo, purely comic plays of local humor are presented. These have no relation to the drama, however, and they are in no way religious. The actors in the interludes sometimes wear masks, but not always. Duncan mentions one of these interludes in Batang that was "Replete with vulgar jokes, tinctured with obscenity," which were "ludicrous pantomimes" [words are used, however].[41] This is not the traditional theatrical fare presented in 'Cham dances. It is a local innovation, an addition to the 'Cham or Mani-rimdu, even though it may have originated in the interludes of Lha-mo. As far as I could determine, Rtogs-ldan is not a caricature of any specific Indian ascetic. The act caustically ridicules the whole concept of the begging hermit. It is an expression of creative instinct, utilizing local imagination and ideas instead of altering an already established genre of drama. Few, if any, of the Khumbu monks have ever witnessed a performance of Lha-mo, or the comic interludes of that genre in Tibet. Since it was not transported to Khumbu with religious dances or intent, and since it may not have been imported at all, it should be considered as a Sherpa creation.

The act is not recorded in texts, nor are the words written down for the actor. From a concordant and practiced scenario, the two actors perform their actions, improvising dialogue spontaneously. If guests are in the audience, the actors freely refer to them or crack jokes about them, totally localizing this act. The performance is not in the past, but here and now. It does not occur in heavenly realms, nor in the imagination, but on the Khumbu stage.

During the entire act, Bkra-shis don-grub plays straight man to Rtogs-ldan. Bkra-shis is embarrassed by some of his master's actions. Bkra-shis is a Sherpa, and he knows the Sherpa people and their deeds. No Sherpa would beg, or be ignorant of the correct method of paying homage to an Abbot, or forget the name of the monastery. After Bkra-shis refreshes the sadhu's memory, the act gets under way.

The two men empty the knapsack. They pull out a drum mounted on a wooden handle, and a water pitcher. These items

[41] Marion H. Duncan, "The Tibetan Drama," *China Journal*, XVII, No. 3 (September, 1932), 107

150

are carefully placed on the courtyard floor. Next Bkra-shis hands his master a teapot, which is also delicately handled, for these articles are ritual objects that are used in their worship. The next item Bkra-shis passes is an old boot which Rtogs-ldan assiduously sets down before realizing what it is. In anger he swings the boot at Bkra-shis, for his servant has lost the other one, and one boot is useless. The next object produced from the sack is a wooden *rtsam-pa* (parched flour) bowl. The last article is a carpet which Bkra-shis carefully spreads, measuring it this way and that, making sure it is directly behind the ritual objects, and facing the Abbot, but he places it in the wrong direction. When the carpet is properly centered, Bkra-shis sits down upon it, only to be instantly removed by Rtogs-ldan. He reminds Bkra-shis that he is only a pupil, and that he must put himself through hardship before he attains the status of his master. Bkra-shis is ordered to sit on the cold floor, but he dislikes this. He attempts to place the extra boot beneath him, but the sadhu snatches away all his goods and stores them behind himself. Finally, with much grumbling, Bkra-shis takes his place on the floor, reminded frequently by Rtogs-ldan that suffering is the way to enlightenment.

Settled at last, the master announces that he will teach his pupil the proper method of preparing offerings of food. They remove the lid from the flour bowl and set the water pitcher beside it. Rtogs-ldan admits that he is ignorant of this kind of offering, for his system of religion does not engage in such foolishness. Bkra-shis also claims that, as far as he can see, such offerings are only a waste of food; and since he has not eaten for some time, he tosses a handful of flour into his mouth. Rtogs-ldan strikes him and tells him that he is no better than a dog, for he thinks only of his stomach and is very selfish. When Bkra-shis explains that he has eaten nothing for three days because Sherpas are not charitable to beggars. Rtogs-ldan again reminds him that he must suffer in order to attain perfection. The pupil retorts that the only good starvation will do is to produce a perfect corpse. They then proceed to mold a food offering (*tor-ma*), but it becomes a sticky mess, which they spill on themselves and the courtyard.

Bkra-shis grows impatient and takes up a *kada* to present to the Abbot. He remembers that this is one form of homage which all Sherpas pay. However, his hands are sticky with the flour paste, and the scarf becomes soiled. An argument ensues concerning whose fault it is, and they decide they should forget it. They attempt another form of worship. For this they will utilize an idea from one of the Mani-rimdu dances that they have witnessed.

Rtogs-ldan produces a doll from his knapsack and hands it to Bkra-shis to lay on the courtyard floor. With a knife in his hand the sadhu dances about the doll, emulating the skeleton dancers and their actions of stabbing and stamping on the effigy of a corpse. Rtogs-ldan stamps the pavement and waves his arms wildly as he closes in on the corpse. Noticing that Bkra-shis stands aloof from all this, the holy man hands him a knife and entreats his pupil to join in the dance. The two cease their dancing and prepare to sacrifice the doll. Bkra-shis is to hold it while Rtogs-ldan stabs it.

The Sherpa assistant, however, begins to stroke the image and caress it. Rebuked by the master, Bkra-shis says that he has grown fond of the doll and does not wish to see it harmed. He claims that he would suffer first, for he never had such a fine toy in his poor childhood. He cradles the doll in his arms and walks away from the Indian. Asking himself what people will think of him when he fails to offer sacrifice because his dim-witted assistant fell in love with a doll, Rtogs-ldan heaps abuses upon Bkra-shis. The latter retorts that he has no concern for others' opinions. When the master attempts to retrieve the doll forcibly, Bkra-shis begins to cry. Disgusted with his helper Rtogs-ldan returns to his cushion, proclaiming that he will redeem himself in the monks' eyes by performing a yoga trick.

Producing a two-foot knife, Rtogs-ldan mutters prayers and incantations over his sharp instrument. He announces that he will prove to Bkra-shis that the master's superior discipline and study have transformed him into an indestructible man. He will puncture his skin with the knife and never feel pain. Bkra-shis warns him that men bleed when their bodies are pierced by such instruments. Rtogs-ldan replies that such a concept is held only by those who believe in the body, and by those who love and become hungry. Kneeling before his cushion, the sadhu places the knife in front of him. Slowly he leans into the blade, which appears to pierce his body, but in reality partially retracts into the handle.

Rtogs-ldan's concentration upon his act is intense. He looks to neither side and makes no comments. The suspense tears at Bkra-shis, who believes his master's predicament is his fault for being dull and not disciplining himself to follow the sadhu's teachings. Bkra-shis covers his eyes, moves forward to stop him, but then backs away in fear. The audience, too, is hushed, for the knife is real, and they all know it. At last Bkra-shis can stand it no longer, and he screams at his teacher to stop. Alarmed by the loud shout, the sadhu slips and falls onto the knife, which penetrates his body and kills him. The poor assistant stares down at his master, mumbles something about pseudo-religious quacks, picks up the doll with a shrug of his shoulders, and sits down to finish eating the flour. With a roar of approving laughter from the audience, the act is finished.

The monk who enacts the part of Rtogs-ldan fasts and prays for seven days prior to the performance, because his part is considered dangerous, and indeed it is. The knife only partially retracts into the handle, the remainder must penetrate the actor's clothing, narrowly missing his body. As he falls, the actor turns slightly to his side in order to avoid the blade. His timing must be perfect, or the knife, which is quite sharp, would surely enter his chest. As his act moves toward its climax, an uneasy silence falls over the audience, for they realize the serious consequences which could result from misjudgment. Only when Bkra-shis picks up the doll does the audience relax and begin to laugh again.

The knife act is a form of realism which could be deadly. The pratfalls and slapstick antics are humorous to the audience. The Sherpas understand that it is pretense and that no actual physical harm results, because the two men are portraying a role. They are pretending. The spectators also know, however, that the knife is real. For the few seconds, at the end of Rtogs-ldan's act there is no psychical distance between audience and actor. The spectators fear for the actor's life, and they are drawn emotionally and physically into the actual world of the monk impersonator—not the world of Rtogs-ldan. Once the act of falling on the knife is safely completed, the audience is aesthetically removed again almost instantaneously, once they realize that he is not harmed. The act is an admixture of the sardonic caricature of sadhus, slapstick comedy, and frightening reality. It is not, however, the illusion of reality, that is, the arrangement of symbols to appear familiar and recognizable. It is a potential disaster, for a man's life is actually at stake.

Lamas, laymen, and musicians laugh at Rtogs-ldan's inane antics. No one is spared from his biting satire. He ridicules worship and parodies the use of offerings. Bkra-shis indicts Sherpas for being stingy and acting like country bumpkins. The two deride Buddhism and Hinduism, ascetics and priests, citizens and visitors. The object of their barbs is primarily religion—its manifold theories and practices. Bkra-shis is an iconoclast who fails to understand how anyone could believe that he does not exist, for his stomach tells him that he does. To him the body is obviously real, for Rtogs-ldan stabs his "illusory" frame with an "illusory" piece of steel and dies. He declares that philosophies only serve to confuse him.

When the courtyard has been cleared of the debris from the comic dance, the *rkang-gling* sound from the gomba and are answered by the *rgya-gling* in the balcony. Drums and cymbals join the musical introduction while monks chant. When the chanting is finished, the music ends, and a brief lull in the activity ensues. When all is ready, the cymbals mark the beat for the next set of dancers.

GNAS-SRUNG

The *Gnas-srung* are a class of deities whose duty it is to guard the holy places of pilgrimage.[42] Their dance involves three actors. According to one lama, the three comprise a single act, called the dance of the *Gnas-srung* (deities), but the Abbot claimed that there are two separate dances. One set of actors is called the *Mi-nag* (black men), and the lone third performer is known as Zur-ra.[43] The latter means literally "the side one," perhaps the "extra one" or the "added one" with regard to this dance. These two sets of dancers are considered here as one act, the ninth.

The two *Mi-nag* are local deities, subordinate to Zur-ra. Their duties are to protect and supervise the defense of local villages and gombas. They are truculent and violent, wielding long swords. Their master Zur-ra outlines their duties, and they carry out his wishes, wreaking punishment and destruction upon local demons. Their job is to protect life, property, and health.

Each *Mi-nag* wears black trousers, a long-sleeved black jacket, and everyday black woolen Sherpa boots. Their tattered white aprons painted with mustard yellow signify tiger skin, and they also wear a yellow silk sash around the waist. The actors' faces are hidden by fierce black masks, with gold paint outlining the busy eyebrows, the goatee, and the corners of the mouth. The nose is turned up as a pig's snout, and the enormous eyes—which have orange irises, black pupils, and white eyeballs—enhance the ferocious appearance. A pink and blue silk scarf hangs from the back of the mask.

The actions of these dancers are violent and forceful. To the accompaniment of the *rkang-gling* and *sbug-'cham,* they circle the courtyard, slashing at the air with their weapons. The

[42] Nebesky-Wojkowitz, *Oracles and Demons of Tibet*, p. 5.

[43] Zur-ra was mentioned in connection with the *Gser-skyems* dancers, who offered a "golden drink" to him. Here, Zur-ra actually appears as a deity and dancer.

monks chant verses to summon the evil spirits and natural phenomena which plague Sherpas. As each demon is invoked, the
Mi-nag whirl rapidly, striking at the supposed image, bringing
it to the ground, and then stabbing it.

After each act of destruction the musicians halt, the dancers
cease their activity, and a lull ensues. The monks locate the next
text and begin chanting; the music joins them, indicating to the
dancers that the next portion of the act is to begin. Ten minutes
of such activity transpires before the *Mi-nag* go back into the
gomba. Four musicians leave their posts and also enter the temple. After a ten-minute time lapse, the musicians reappear from
the gomba and return to the courtyard.

Two *rgya-gling-pa* enter first, followed by two *rkang-gling-pa*.
All wear their magenta ceremonial monastic dress and their
high, crested hats. Behind them is a hatless monk who carries a
khatvāṅga, the magic ritual wand of Padmasambhava. Its handle
is surmounted by a *rdo-rje* and three skulls, and it is a model of
the stock which the saint used to defeat the local demon, Zur-ra.
The musicians play as they march, stopping behind the altar in
a row facing the gomba. After several minutes of music a figure
emerges from the gomba.

The new dancer is Zur-ra, one of the major local deities in
Khumbu. He wears a white sleeved gown of silk, brocaded with
gold, red, and royal blue designs. Like many other dancers, he
wears a mustard yellow cape and apron. The apron is designed
with the fierce face of Dgra-lha, the "Enemy-God" (sometimes
the symbol of greed). He is a form of the Indian god, Mārā, the
God of Desire. His purpose is to symbolize the three major
causes, or evils, which lead to rebirth: lust, ill-will, and
ignorance.[44] Padmasambhava and other Buddhist wizards waged
war against Dgra-lha and other beings who led Buddhists down
these baneful paths of desire. Zur-ra specifically protects the
Khumbu region from the reinfiltration of these once-destroyed
forces.

[44] Waddell, *Buddhists of Tibet,* pp. 88-109.

It is not exactly clear who Zur-ra is, but most lamas agree that he is their chief country god, Khumbu yul-lha, who resides on Mount Khumbila, a few miles from the monastery. He is a symbol of towering strength, the epitome of the protection afforded Sherpas by their gods, especially those of tantric, magical origin. Zur-ra wears a bone necklace, which symbolizes his tantric powers. The two *Mi-nag* are his servants, or helpers, who carry out the country god's wishes, and who are unceasingly at war with evil.

Zur-ra's mask is chocolate brown and menacing. Gold paint outlines his bushy eyebrows and beard. His eyes are huge and piercing. The third eye of foreknowledge is embedded in his forehead, and his teeth resemble fangs. Atop the mask is a single skull and an eight-inch conical form painted orange. Five two-foot flags mounted on sticks rise from the top of the mask. They represent the power of the five Buddhas of Meditation, the manifestations of the Ādi-buddha. His ornaments distinguish Zur-ra as a defender of the faith and as a fierce protector of the Khumbu region. The mask also displays earrings and a friendship scarf.

Before descending into the courtyard, Zur-ra slowly and nobly steps and whirls on the raised walkway for three minutes. The musicians play from the *'cham-ra* and the balcony with all their instruments while the monks chant prayers to this defender. Once he is in the courtyard, the actor takes almost five minutes to circle the altar because his movements are so deliberate and measured. Upon his second turn of the *'cham-ra* a chair is brought into the arena and the actor takes his seat. The *Ldab-ldob* presents him with a *tor-ma* offering.

The musicians herald the Sherpas' offering to Zur-ra with music. The two *Mi-nag* return to the courtyard and aid in the celebration of the offering to their spiritual master. They dance in front of the seated deity, whirling and moving toward him and away from him, symbolizing the protection he assures the people of Khumbu. The Zur-ra tosses his offering in the air and joins the dance. After the *Ldab-ldob* removes the chair, the mu-

sicians file out of the courtyard and return to their original posts
in the balcony or the gomba. The dancers whirl about the courtyard very slowly. The *Mi-nag* adjust their tempo to that of their
master. The two "black men" move up the courtyard steps and
into the gomba, and the Zur-ra actor follows. Two wailing notes
from the *dung-chen* terminate the dance.

MKHA'-'GRO

Perhaps the least impressive and colorful dance in Mani-
rimdu appears next. This tenth act presents the *Mkha'-'gro-ma,*
the five *Ḍākinī* The word *Mkha'-'gro* means "sky-goers," and it
designates those feminine deities who generally appear, icono-
graphically, in dancing attitudes. They are more universally
known by their Sanskrit name, *Ḍākinī,* even to the Sherpas.

There are three forms of feminine divinities: goddesses with
the rank of Bodhisattva; *Prajñā* (the females shown in an embrace with a deity); and *Ḍākinī.* Like most other deities in Buddhism, they have either a pacific or an angry form.[45] One of the
fierce Bodhisattva goddesses was mentioned in the *Chos-skyongs*
dance previously. The *Ḍākinī,* however, are of much lower rank
than the Bodhisattvas or the *Prajñā.*

The *Ḍākinī* dancers each carry a *khaṭvāṅga,* the magic divining stick invented by Padmasambhava. They are tantric deities
who gave Padma the books upon which he founded the doctrines
he preached in Tibet.[46] These books were supposedly in an
unknown language, further adding to the magical milieu in
which Padmasambhava operated. The five *Ḍākinī* of Tibetan
iconography are generally considered to be these:

1. Sangs-rgyas mkha'-'gro-ma (Skt. Buddha Ḍākinī).
2. Rin-chen mkha'-'gro-ma (Skt. Ratna Ḍākinī).
3. Pad-ma mkha'-'gro-ma (Skt. Padma Ḍākinī).

[45] Getty, *Gods of Northern Buddhism,* p. 119.
[46] *Ibid.*

4. Sna-tshogs Rdo-rje mkha'-'gro-ma (Skt. Viśva Vajra Ḍākinī).
5. Rdo-rje mkha'-'gro-ma (Skt. Vajra Ḍākinī).[47]

The dancers wear no masks or elaborate costumes, and their actions portray no real dramatic action. This dance serves as a recognition of these five deities. Their movements are rhythmic and ordered, like the other dances, and are intended to display the singing abilities of these heavenly creatures. However, they do not sing or utter any sound whatsoever. They are the pacific forms of the Ḍākinī, and their presence symbolizes the mercy and peacefulness of their duty. Their duty, like their pacific form, is to broadcast mercy.

LHAG-MA GNYIS

The eleventh act at Mani-rimdu is another whirling dance, the actions of which are identical to the others. It is called the Lhag-ma Gnyis, literally "the two remnants." The meaning of this act is unclear, and lamas were very vague about it. The Abbot claimed that these two dancers are "servants who are not supposed to feast with other deities, and so they enjoy the remnants of the meal by themselves." This must mean tor-ma offerings from previous dances.

Their costumes are identical to those of the Zhwa-nag priests except that they wear chocolate brown demon masks. The masks are the same ones worn by the Chos-skyongs dancers in Act 7. The process of "eating the meal" is never enacted. The dancers are not presented with an offering; they do not stop their actions, or in any way symbolize the partaking of food. The Abbot referred to the remnants of any of the offerings of tor-ma and chang, but neither the Ḍākinī nor the Chos-skyongs received such offerings.

The two Lhag-ma Gnyis actors are probably lesser Ḍākinī.

[47] Sometimes a sixth Ḍākinī is added, the Karma Ḍākinī. See Gordon, Iconography of Tibetan Lamaism, p. 34.

159

Besides the five mentioned earlier, there are a number of inferior goddesses of the same genre. Two of them, Makaravaktrā and Simhavaktrā, accompany the goddess, Lha-mo (who appeared in the dance of the *Chos-skyongs*), and carry out her orders. These ferocious acolytes follow Lha-mo, walking on a "lake of blood, in which float skulls and human bones."[48] Their duty is to protect Buddhism, and they are capable of attack and destruction. It is probable that the *Lhag-ma Gnyis* dance presents these two lesser divinities.

GRI-'CHAM

The next to the last act is a dance performed by four masked monks. It is called the *Gri-'cham*, or "sword-dance." These actors wear the same costumes as the *Mi-nag*, plus two chocolate brown masks of the *Chos-skyongs*. Each dancer carries a curved two-foot sword, *gri* (Skt. *churī*), which is used to destroy demons. It is sometimes thought to be a poisoned sword.

This dance is also obscure in its meaning, but one lama claimed that it represents the *btsan* class of demons, who were defeated by Buddhist wizards and who became protectors of the faith. These evil ones originated in Bon, and their domain was in the air. They are supposed to be savage huntsmen, wearing helmets and armor, who ride horses over the mountains. "Whoever is unfortunate enough to fall in with them in the loneliness of the mountains is pierced by their arrows and falls victim to a deadly sickness."[49] Their color is supposed to be red, but in Mani-rimdu they are black.[50]

These *Gri-'cham* dancers represent lesser divinities who now protect the people of Khumbu from diseases, plagues, and accidents. Their primary duty is to protect traders and herders in

[48] Getty, *Gods of Northern Buddhism*, p. 150.
[49] Hoffmann, *Religions of Tibet*, p. 19.
[50] Nebesky-Wojkowitz, *Oracles and Demons of Tibet*, p. 299. This difference in color owes to the lack of costumes, not to improper knowledge of demonological iconography.

Costume of a *Zhwa-nag* actor found at the ancient Kerok gomba near
Thami. (Photo by Terry Beck)

Gri-'cham, the "sword dance," twelfth act of Mani-rimdu. Four masked actors represent lesser deities, converted demons from Bon.

the mountains. As far as I could determine, they are not known by any particular name. Their actions are similar to all other dancers in this festival. They circle the altar, whirling and striking at the air, sometimes coming dangerously near the spectators. The monks chant only a short invocation. The musical accompaniment is primarily performed by the cymbals. No offerings are presented to these actors.

By this late hour in the dance festival, the audience is restless. They have been sitting for more than seven hours in the outdoor theater, and they pay little attention to the performers. The temperature dips to well below freezing by late afternoon at Tengpoche. They have consumed a great amount of *chang*, and some spectators care only for their conversations with nearby audience members. Several of the dancers also find it difficult to concentrate on their actions, for they too have drunk quantities of liquor.

ZOR-'CHAM

The last act, the thirteenth, is known as the *Zor-'cham*. It is performed by two *Zhwa-nag*,[51] and it marks the last offering of the day. It is the all-encompassing presentation of *tor-ma*. It signifies the supreme weapon employed in combating evil, for it symbolically denotes Buddhist doctrine, deities, defenders, and philosophy. It symbolizes an amalgamation of these elements offered as a whole by the Sherpas of Khumbu to all the gods of Buddhism in general. It sums up and characterizes their devotion to Buddhism and their opposition to the forces of evil.

The *tor-ma* balls are tossed to the five directions, and finally through the door of the courtyard by both priests. This signifies the banishing of all evil forces and the onset of good omens for the coming months. It is the termination of the prayer of *Mani Ril-sgrub*. The *tor-ma* is taken from the altar in the center of the arena. These actions and actors represent all the cumulative

---

[51] Costumes are identical to those of the *Zhwa-nag* in Act 6, pages 138-40.

forces of the doctrines of Buddhism. The dancers circle the altar several times holding the *tor-ma* in their hands while monks chant an invocation to all the gods of Buddhism, imploring their protection and mercy.

When the dance has ended, a final benediction is offered in the form of encore by most of the dancers who appeared during the day's activities. It is called the *Log-'cham,* or the "go back dance." Since a number of roles were doubled and many masks were utilized in two or three dances, the number of actors is limited to sixteen, the number of monks who actually performed. Rdo-rje gro-lod and Rtogs-ldan are missing from the group. The dancers are not supposed to represent any particular form of power in this last scene. It serves as a final glance at most of the deities who protect the Khumbu region, and it also furthers the progress of Buddhism.

The monks retire to the gomba for their evening prayer, and the spectators rush to warm themselves around fires. After the evening meal, most of the laymen will gather in the courtyard for a long night of folk dancing and singing. Not until around 3:00 A.M. do the Sherpas begin to retire for the remainder of the night. From 10:00 A.M. until early the next morning these hard-working people have enjoyed themselves, witnessing monastic dramas and dancing their own folk steps.

The final, third day, of Mani-rimdu heralds another ritual. Known as Zhi-ba'i sbyin-sreg, this rite culminates in the destruction of evil forces in Khumbu. Probably a form of the rite from Tibet which definitely destroyed all demons who may have been missed by the New Year's dances, Zhi-ba'i sbyin-sreg is performed by lamas in the monastery courtyard. It consists entirely of lamas' chants, which do not involve spectators, and the monastery is conspicuously empty, save for the lamas themselves.

A throne for the Abbot is placed in the courtyard, and lamas are seated in front of him at right angles on carpets, much like the first day's ceremony. A bonfire is lighted in front of the Abbot, who chants and burns rice offerings, *tor-ma,* and pieces of parchment on which are inscribed magic and evil symbols.

An over-all view of the Mani-rimdu festival, then, is as follows: On the first day laymen are assured of longevity and are presented with amulets to protect them from evil and disease. It is a joyous occasion that calls for entertainment, which is provided for them on the second day. They gain merit for attendance at Mani-rimdu, and are enlightened and pleased by the dances. They witness an art form, performed by skillful dancers, which imparts knowledge about the life they lead. They leave the monastery after a night of folk dancing. The lamas protect them further on the third day by destroying any demons which might return to plague them through the coming months. Mani-rimdu is entertainment, protection, security; a time of relaxation, and the chance to thrill at a spectacular performance.

Sherpas return to their work-a-day world where there are no dances, costumes, or masks and where they will not find the thrill of the crowd until the next Mani-rimdu performance six months hence. The festival provides the only organized dramatic shows in Khumbu. Literally hundreds of worship services transpire in the monastery before the onset of the next performance. If Sherpas sought only religious edification, they could acquire merit by attending these services, but they do not.

Mani-rimdu is not only worship. It is a dramatic production, and it is attended primarily because it is a performance: a chance to witness exciting dances. It is an art form. It communicates something to the audience. It depicts concepts and actions which surpass mundane existence. Its residue of ideas remains with the Sherpas throughout the year. Young people re-enact the comic roles of Rtogs-ldan and Mi-tshe-ring, and one can hear Bkra-shis don-grub's and Rtogs-ldan's quips repeated in family conversations. The Sherpas retain the ideas presented by Mani-rimdu, and their lives are thereby enriched. What they remember is the idea which was communicated by the art form. No one remembers what was chanted by the lamas from scripture, but each Sherpa can recall how Mi-tshe-ring tumbled down the stairs, or how he struck his head painfully against the stone courtyard during his mock prayer scene.

163

In short, the act is remembered. Mi-tshe-ring was an actor, not a real person. He only pretended to harm himself, and his actions caused no uneasiness in the audience concerning his physical well-being as a real person. He was above humanity. He was invested with the attributes of a new being which was previously nonexistent. He acted his part in a dramatic production. It is that which the Sherpas recall. Their lives have been enriched, their horizons expanded, their scope broadened. They witnessed an art, in the form of drama, and they will never forget it, for it has become a part of their very existence.

Mani-rimdu is of tremendous importance to the Sherpas, for it is the only type of organized and produced theatrical fare within that society. Besides its religious implications, Mani-rimdu exemplifies man's voluntary determination to enrich his existence. The result of this endeavor is an unconscious art form which lifts the Sherpas out of mundane existence and affords them a view of life which is not the normal one. They can put aside, temporarily, thoughts of physical survival, while they witness beauty and order, color and form, laughter and excitement.

This drama is a unique form of theater, evolved from the ancient 'Cham in Tibet and further developed by the Sherpas in Khumbu. It is not the only entertainment or diversion in Khumbu, but it is the most important one. It reflects the Sherpas' creativity and aesthetic sense, plus their ability to combine all aspects of life—pleasure, religion, fellowship, compassion, and intelligence—into one form of entertainment.

Appendix I: Glossary

THE BASIC language in this glossary is Tibetan; Sanskrit terms are designated by the abbreviation "Skt."; pronunciation forms of Tibetan words are designated by the abbreviation "pron." Words found in a standard English dictionary do not have the Sanskrit or Nepali diacritical marks. A few terms from Buddhist scriptures have been accepted into general English usage, and they are listed in the glossary under their English spellings.

Tibetan entries are listed in English alphabetical order according to the first letter of the word, regardless of Tibetan alphabetical order.

Abhidharma (Skt.): Collection of Buddhist canonical works consisting of commentaries on philosophy and metaphysics.

Amitāyus (Skt.): Name of the Buddha of Infinite Life.

Anātman (Skt.): Meaning "non-self" or "non-soul," this Buddhist concept denies the existence of a corporeal or spiritual soul.

Arti: A toga-like garment worn by Indians; used in Mani-rimdu by Rtogs-ldan in his comic act.

Aśvaghosha: First-century poet and writer of Buddhist works. Author of *Cāriputra,* an extant "prakaraṇa" play in Sanskrit.

Beg-tse: God of War and protector of horses for Sherpas and Tibetans.

Bimbisāra: According to tradition, a contemporary and patron of the Gautama Buddha, who had a play performed in honor of the Nāga kings.

Bkra-shis don-grub (pron. Tashi-tundup): Actor who impersonates a poor Sherpa in the *Rtogs-ldan* act.

Bkra-shis Tshe-ring-ma: One of the Five Sisters of Long Life, identified with Mount Gaurisankar. *See also Tshe-ring mched-lnga.*

165

--⟨ Appendix I: Glossary ⟩⋅--

Bla: Term for the prebuddhist Bon concept of a "soul" or "life force" often connected with an inanimate object, such as a tree or lake. The welfare of the individual depends upon the vitality of the inanimate object

Bla-tshe: Complete term for the Bon concept of a separate "life force" or "soul" that resides in all men and in numerous natural phenomena.

Blo-bzang-ma: One of the Five Sisters of Long Life, identified with Mount Kangchenjunga in Sikkim.

Bodhicitta (Skt.): "Thought of Enlightenment" or "awakened mind." In some contexts, means "supreme knowledge."

Bodhisattva (Skt.): An enlightened individual who delays entry into Nirvana in order to lead all sentient creatures to that goal. A more active aspect of salvation than the Buddha.

Bon (pron. Pön): The prebuddhist shamanism of Tibet.

Bsangs-phor (pron. sang-por): Incense burner used to grace religious celebrations of the Sherpas.

Bskang-ba: An effigy of a corpse, also called a *"ling-ga."* An expiatory offering to the Lord of the Dead (*see* Gshin-rje Chos-rgyal).

Bsod-nams (pron. sö-nam): Virtuous deeds which, if accumulated in sufficient quantity, lead to a higher rebirth and eventually to Nirvana.

Bsod-nams rgya-mtsho (1543-88): Third in a series of Dge-lugs-pa incarnations, and the first to receive the title "Dalai Lama" in 1578 from Altan Khan.

Btsan: Most powerful of the Bon class of spirits that dwell in the air. Subdued by Buddhist masters, they now serve as defenders of Buddhism.

Buddhas of Meditation: Also called the Celestial Buddhas or Celestial Jinas, these are the five manifestations of Ādi-buddha, the primordial Buddha.

Bundachendzen: Father of Lama Sanga Rdo-rje who selected sites for monasteries in Khumbu.

'Cham: Original name of religious drama from Tibet, out of which Mani-rimdu eventually evolved.

'Cham-ra: Name for the stone monastic courtyard in which Mani-rimdu is performed.

Chang: Fermented rice beer used by Sherpas for refreshment and as a ritual offering. Made from barley in Tibet.

Chomo-lungma: *See* Jo-mo glang-ma.

Chos: Tibetan equivalent for Sanskrit *Dharma.* Generally means "Buddhist doctrine."

166

—◦◦{ Appendix I: Glossary }◦◦—

Chos-rnga: Drum mounted on a two-foot handle, carried by Sherpa monks and used in worship of the Buddha. See Figure 6.

Chos-rnga-pa: Player of the *chos-rnga.*

Chos-skyongs (Skt. *Dharmapāla*): "Protectors of Buddhist Law." This important group of deities, usually depicted in a fierce aspect, is also called "Guardians" (Tib. *Srung-ma*) or "Oath-bound-ones" (Tib. *Dam-can*).

Citipati (Skt.): *See Dur-khrod bdag-po.*

Dākinī (Skt): *See Mkha'-'gro-ma.*

Damaru: Small, three-inch, double-headed hand drum used in various rituals.

Dbang-bum: "Empowering vase," a ritual vase used in Khumbu tantric worship.

De-nyid (Skt. *tatva*): "Suchness"; an ascription of the absolute reality, the "universal Buddha-mind."

Dga'-ba (pron. gawa): Pleasure.

Dge-ba (pron. ge-wa): Act of virtue which is recorded on the "universal ledger." Each act of *dge-ba* adds to the accumulation of *bsod-nams.* *See also Sdig-pa.*

Dge-lugs-pa (pron. Ge-lug-pa): The reformed Yellow Hat sect of Tibetan Buddhism founded by Tsong-kha-pa (1357-1419).

Dgra-lha (pron. ḍa-hla): "Enemy God" protects an individual from his enemies. Bon maintains each person has a Dgra-lha and a Pho-lha ("Male God") who protects against sickness.

Dgu-gtor 'cham (pron. gu-do cham): One of the names applied to various dances performed during the Khumbu New Year celebrations.

Dharmakāya (Skt.): "Dharma body," the absolute form of Buddhahood, which is essentially unmanifest.

Dharmapāla (Skt.): *See Chos-skyongs.*

Dhvaja (Tib. *Rgyal-mtshan*): "Banner of Victory," consisting of cloth cylinders draped on a flagstaff. Always displayed in a monastery (Tib. *dgon-pa*), it is carried about on ceremonial occasions.

Dikrāja (Skt.): Deity who defends the Buddhist doctrine.

Dung-chen: Ten-foot brass and copper horns used in worship and for religious festivals. See Figure 1.

Dung-chen-pa: Player of the *dung-chen.*

Dur-bdag. See Dur-khrod bdag-po.

Dur-khrod bdag-po (abbr. *Dur-bdag*) (Skt. Citipati): "Masters of the Cemetery," assistants to Gshin-rje Chos-rgyal, Lord of the Dead. They appear in the sixth act of Mani-rimdu.

Dza-rong-phu (pron. Rong-phu): The monastery north of Mount Everest in Tibet. Also known to Western mountaineering expeditions as Rong-buk.

Eight-fold Path: Last of the four Noble Truths, this code of ethics and morality was delivered by the Buddha in his first sermon at Benares following his enlightenment. It sets forth the antidotes to suffering and pain.

Four Noble Truths: Expounded by the Buddha at Benares, they are: (1) existence is suffering, (2) the cause of suffering is desire, (3) the end of suffering is the ending of desire, and (4) the eight-fold path which ends suffering.

Gdung-rje (pron. Dumje): Sherpa festival to celebrate the anniversary of the birth of Guru Rinpoche (Padmasambhava), traditional founder of Tibetan Buddhism.

Ging-pa: Second act of Mani-rimdu; four performers who represent the guardian kings of the four directions.

Glang-dar-ma: Ninth-century pro-Bon king of Tibet who followed his assassinated brother to the throne and began persecuting Buddhists. He was in turn assassinated by a Buddist monk, and Buddhism was eventually restored.

Gnas-srung: "Guardian of the Locale," the ninth act of Mani-rimdu. The main character is the chief country god of Khumbu.

Gri (Skt. *churī*): Magical curved sword used to destroy the demonic enemies of Tibetan Buddhism.

Gri-'cham: The "sword dance," the twelfth act of Mani-rimdu. Actors carry a *gri* to symbolize their relentless battle against enemies of the faith.

Gri-gug: Tantric knife, shaped like a small hatchet, wielded by Yamāntaka.

'Gro-bzang-ma: One of the Five Sisters of Long Life. (I was unable to discover what mountain peak is identified with this goddess.)

Grub-thob Thang-thong: Legendary founder of dance, theater, and entertainment in Tibet.

Gsang-ba rdo-rje: Legendary founder of monasteries in Khumbu.

Gser-skyems (pron. ser-kyem): "Golden-drink" dance, the first act of Mani-rimdu.

Gshin-rje Chos-rgyal (Skt. Yama): Lord of the Dead.

Gshin-rje-gshed (Skt. Yamāntaka): Conqueror of Gshin-rje Chos-rgyal, Lord of the Dead. Serves as a protector of life.

Gtor-ma (pron. tor-ma): Unbaked dough made from ordinary parched flour and butter, usually molded in conical shapes. Used as a disposable offering and icon in worship.

Guru Rinpoche: Epithet of Padmasambhava, traditional founder of

Appendix I: Glossary

Tibetan Buddhism. Guru is Sanskrit for "Teacher," and Rin-po-che is Tibetan for "Great Precious One."

Hayagrīva: *See* Rta-mgrin.

Hwa-shang Mahāyāna: Eighth-century teacher of the Chinese Ston-mun-pa school of Buddhism, who was defeated in the A.D. 792-94 debate with the Indian teacher Kamalaśīla. The "erroneous" teachings of the Chinese teacher are parodied by the comic act, *Mi-tshe-ring*, in Mani-rimdu.

Jo-mo glang-ma: The Sherpa name for Mount Everest. Frequently known in Western rendering as Chomo-lungma, it is called Sāgarmātā (Mother of the Skies) by Nepalis. "Ri-rgyal Jo-mo glang-ma" (Queen of Mountains, Willow Goddess) is the honorific name used in scriptures associated with Mani-rimdu. (NOTE: the Sherpa name *Glang-ma*, "Willow," must be a local variation. The more common name seems to be *Jo-mo rlung-ma*, "Goddess of the Wind." Mount Everest is also known in Tibetan as *Jo-mo gangs-dkar*, "Goddess of White Snows.")

Kada: Ceremonial scarf used by Mi-tshe-ring.

Kapāla: Bowl made from a human skull and used in Sherpa rituals.

Karma-pa: Semi-reformed sect of Tibetan Buddhism founded by the Bka'-brgyud-pa lama, Karma-pa (1110-93). This sect was divided into two orders, the Black Hat and the Red Hat.

Khaḍga (Skt.): A magical sword, symbolizing the power of Buddhism, used by tantric lamas to coerce demons.

Khaṭvāṅga (Skt.): Ritual wand capped with a *triśūla* carried by Guru Rinpoche.

Khumbu yul-lha: "Khumbu country god," the protector of the Khumbu region.

Kun-tu bzang-po: "All Good," Tibetan name of the Ādi-buddha for the unreformed Rnying-ma-pa.

Kuvera (also Kubera): *See* Rnam-thos-sras.

Las-bum: Ritual water vase.

Ldab-ldob (pron. dob-dob): Monastic assistant, marshall, monitor, and stage assistant for Mani-rimdu.

Lhag-ma Gnyis (pron. Hlang-ma nyi): "Two Extras," the eleventh act of Mani-rimdu. The two actors involved represent lesser *Mkha'-'gro-ma*.

Lha-lung Dpal-gyi rdo-rje (pron. Hla-lung pal-gi dorje): Buddhist monk who assassinated Glang-dar-ma for persecuting Buddhism.

Lha-mo (Skt. Śrīdevī): Buddhist goddess. "Lha-mo" also refers to a genre of Tibetan theater that utilizes dialogue and written dramas with laymen and women as performers.

169

--◆{ Appendix I: Glossary }◆--

Ling-ga: See Bskang-ba.

Log-'cham: The "encore" or "curtain call" dance which marks the conclusion of Mani-rimdu. This "go back" dance represents all the deities who protect Buddhism in Khumbu.

Lo-gsar: "New Year," the New Year festival in Khumbu.

Mādhyamika (Skt.): The "Middle Path" school of Buddhism founded by the second-century A.D. teacher Nāgārjuna. This school teaches that *samsāra* and Nirvana are relative aspects of the absolute reality, known as *śūnyatā,* or "voidness." This school of Buddhism is one accepted by all sects of Tibetan Buddhism.

Mahākāla: *See* Mgon-po.

Mani Ril-sgrub (pron. ri-drup): Name of the *gtor-ma* offering used in the Life-Consecration rite, as well as the name of the prayer that consecrates the rite. The term "Mani-rimdu" derives from the name of this offering and prayer.

Mañjuśrī (Skt.): Bodhisattva of Transcendental Wisdom.

Mārā: The Indian God of Desire. *See also* Dgra-lha.

Mchod-rten (pron. chörten): Tibetan name for the stūpa of Indian Buddhism. Originally a receptacle for sacred relics, it later served as a cenotaph and as a symbol of the mind of the Buddha.

Mda'-dar: "Arrow-silks," a divining arrow tied with silk of five colors.

Mgon-po (Skt. Mahākāla): Also called Nag-po chen-po (Great Black One), chief tantric defender of Buddhism for the Rnying-ma-pa sect.

Mgrin-bzang-ma: One of the Five Sisters of Long Life, identified with Mount Kusam Kang.

Mi-g.yo glang-bzang (pron. Mi-yo lang-sang): Goddess who resides on Mount Everest.

Mi-nag: "Black Men," local subordinate deities who appear in the ninth act of Mani-rimdu, *Gnas-srung.* Their duty is to destroy demons who threaten the local populace.

Mi-tshe-ring: "Long-life man," appears in the sixth act of Mani-rimdu and gives a performance parodying Hwa-shang Mahāyāna.

Mkha'-'gro-ma (Skt. *Ḍākinī*): A class of female deities that go about in the sky. *Mkha'-'gro,* the tenth act of Mani-rimdu, portrays five lesser goddesses who symbolize mercy and serenity.

Mong-doh (sp.?): A Khumbu festival which marks the termination of the old year and usually occurs in January.

Mthing-gi zhal-bzang-ma: One of the Five Sisters of Long Life, identified with Mount Menlungtse.

Nag-po chen-po: *See* Mgon-po.

Nag-po khrag-med: "Bloodless Black One," a local name for Kun-tu bzang-po.

Appendix I: Glossary

Nakula (Skt.): "Mongoose," a bag made from the skin of a mongoose filled with jewels to signify Rnam-thos-sras' victory over the Nāgas, guardians of treasures.

Pad-ma mkha'-'gro-ma (Skt. Padma Ḍākinī): One of the five *Mkha'-'gro-ma* who appear in the tenth act of Mani-rimdu.

Padmasambhava: *See* Guru Rinpoche.

'Phags-skyes-po. (Skt. Virūḍhaka): One of the four guardian kings (Rgyal-chen bzhi). Assigned to the south, he is also king of giant demons.

Phod-kha: Long-sleeved gown worn by Mani-rimdu actors.

Phur-bu: A magical dagger with a three-edged blade used to thwart evil spirits. Its *rdo-rje* handle is topped with a horse's head, signifying Rta-mgrin

Phye-mar (pron. chi-mar): Wafers made from rice flour and butter for use in tantric rituals, especially the Life-Consecration rite.

Prajñāpāramitā (Skt.): "Perfection of Wisdom," the ultimate goal of gnosis and enlightenment in the Mādhyamika school of Buddhism. Study and practice of *Prajñāpāramitā* literature can lead to transcendental wisdom.

Rakshi: Liquor made from rice, barley, potatoes, or corn.

Ras-zom: Tibetan or Sherpa boots with wool or leather soles and woolen uppers that extend to mid-calf.

Rdor-gong: A poncho or cape-like garment worn over the *phod-kha.*

Rdo-rje (pron. dorje; Skt. *vajra*): A ritual object representing the thunderbolt of the god Indra. Held in the right hand, it is used for various mundane and supramundane rituals and symbolisms.

Rdo-rje gro-lod (pron. Dorje Trolö): One of the eight wrathful manifestations of Padmasambhava.

Rdo-rje'i gtun-theg: Thunderbolt scepter with eight ridges, used in the "Life-Consecration" rite on the first day of the Mani-rimdu festival.

Rdo-rje mkha'-'gro-ma (Skt. Vajra Ḍākinī): One of the five *Mkha'-'gro-ma* who appear in the tenth act of Mani-rimdu.

Rdo-rje thig-le: A contemplative form of the Ādi-buddha, Kun-tu bzang-po.

Rgya-gling (pron. gya-ling): Small trumpet of wood and brass, blown as a trumpet but fingered as a flute, and used in Sherpa worship. See Figure 3.

Rgya-gling-pa (pron. gya-ling-pa): Player of a *rgya-gling.*

Rgyal-chen bzhi: "Four Great Kings," these four guardians of the cardinal points are also called *Jig-rten skyong* (Skt. *Lokapāla*).

Rin-chen mkha'-'gro-ma (Skt. Ratna Ḍākinī): One of the five *Mkha'-'gro-ma* who appear in the tenth act of Mani-rimdu.

Rkang-gling (pron. kang-ling): Trumpet fashioned from a human thigh bone. There is no fingering of notes as with the *rgya-gling,* and its

171

tone is uncontrolled. See Figure 2.

Rkang-gling-pa (pron. kang-ling-pa): Player of a *rkang-gling*.

Rnam-thos-sras (Skt. Kuvera): God of Wealth and, as guardian of the north, one of the *Rgyal-chen bzhi*.

Rnga-'cham: "Drum-dance," the fourth act of Mani-rimdu.

Rnying-ma-pa (pron. Nying-ma-pa): Unreformed and oldest sect of Tibetan Buddhism, traditionally founded in the eighth century by Guru Rinpoche.

Rol-'cham bkra-shis dgu-brdung: Generally known by the abbreviated title *Rol-'cham,* this dance of the heralds serves to introduce the main acts of Mani-rimdu.

Rta-mgrin (Skt. Hayagrīva): "Horse necked," protector of horses and one of the eight *Chos-skyongs.*

Rtogs-ldan (pron. Tong-den): The eighth act of Mani-rimdu, a comic performance parodying Indian ascetics.

Rtsam-pa: Ground barley which is a staple food to Sherpas.

Rus-krang (pron. Ru-rang): Skeleton dancers in Tibetan 'Cham.

Sa-bdag: "Soil-masters," protective local deities in the Khumbu region.

Śākti (Skt.): Active female principle, especially identified with Durgā, the consort of Śiva.

Samsāra (Skt.): Phenomenal existence, the orb of transmigration.

Sanga Rdo-rje: Lama from Rong-phu who selected sites for the monasteries of Khumbu, and an incarnation of Padmasambhava.

Sangs-rgyas mkha'-'gro-ma (Skt. Buddha Ḍākinī): One of the five *Mkha'-'gro-ma* who appear in the tenth act of Mani-rimdu.

Sa-skya-pa: Semi-reformed sect of Tibetan Buddhism founded by Sa-chen Kun-dga' snying-po (1092-1158). It has many followers in Khumbu.

Sbug-'cham (pron. bu-cham): Cymbals used in Sherpa Buddhist worship. See Figure 5.

Sdig-pa (pron. dig-ba): Evil deeds which detract from the store of *bsod-nams* and must be counteracted by good deeds, *dge-ba.*

Shes: "Wisdom," represents the passive female principle (as opposed to *śākti*) in Buddhist tantric ritual. When it is perfectly coupled with "means" or "compassion" (*thabs*), transcendental wisdom can be achieved.

Sil-snyan: Small shallow cymbals. See Figure 4.

Skra-len: A piece of black silk worn under an actor's wig to keep costumes clean.

Skra-tshab: "Hair substitute," a wig worn beneath helmets or over masks by actors in Mani-rimdu.

Smon-lam 'cham: "Prayer-dance," one of the names applied to the various dances performed in Khumbu during the New Year celebrations.

Sna-tshogs Rdo-rje mkha'-'gro-ma (Skt. Viśva Vajra Ḍākinī): One of the five *Mkha'-'gro-ma* who appear in the tenth act of Mani-rimdu.

Spang-gdan: An apron worn over the actor's gown.

Spud-shub: "Ornamented trousers" worn by actors in the *Ging-pa* act.

Spyan-mig-bzang (Skt. Virūpāksha): King of the Nāgas (serpent deities) and the guardian king in the west.

Spyan-ras-gzigs (pron. Chenrezi): Tibetan name of Avalokiteśvara, Bodhisattva of mercy. The Dalai Lama is regarded as the earthly manifestation of this Bodhisattva.

Śrīdevī: *See* Lha-mo.

Ston-mun-pa: Tibetan corruption of Chinese Tun-men-pa'i, meaning "Instantaneous System." This refers to Ch'an Buddhism, a Chinese derivation of the Yogācāra system, which maintained that enlightenment is achieved suddenly and thereby negated the necessity for virtuous deeds and religious merit. Defeated in the eighth century debate in Tibet, this system later developed in Japan into Zen Buddhism.

Thabs: "Means," or also compassion, represents the active male principle in Buddhist ritual. *See also Shes.*

Thanka (Tib. *thang-ka*): Religious wall scrolls depicting deities, demons, buildings, ritual circles (*maṇḍala*), or scenes from the Buddha's life.

Theravāda: Name for the southern school of Buddhism, also called Hinayāna (lesser vehicle).

Ti-bum: Ceremonial water vase with a pendant mirror affixed to it, used in the Life-Consecration rite.

Tor-ma: See Gtor-ma.

Trident: *See Triśūla.*

Tri-ratna: "Three Jewels," symbolic elements encased by a flame-shaped triangle representing the (1) Buddha, (2) Dharma, and (3) Sangha.

Triśūla (Skt.): A special three-pronged shaft carried by Mgon-po.

Tsam-ki-bulu (sp.?): Term applied to the rehearsal of Mani-rimdu performed the day prior to the festival.

Tshangs-pa dkar-po: "White Brahma," one of the eight *Chos-skyongs.*

Tshe-brang: "Life abode," sacred place where the wisdom of Padmasambhava abides.

Tshe-bum: "Life vase," with sacred water for ritual use.

Tshe-chang: "Life fluid," rice-beer for ritual use.

Tshe-dbang: "Life-Consecration" rite which occurs the first day of the three-day Mani-rimdu festival.

Tshe-ril: "Life pellets" (*gtor-ma* balls) used in ritual.

Tshe-ring mched-lnga: "Five Sisters of Long Life," protecting country deities. Mount Everest is identified with one of them.

Tshe-wang: See Tshe-dbang.

Tsong-kha-pa: Founder of the Dge-lugs-pa sect of Tibetan Buddhism.

Vinaya (Skt.): Section of canonical works dealing with the rules of monastic discipline.

Yab-yum: "Father-mother," term applied to the mystical psychosexual union and its symbols in tantric Buddhism.

Yama: *See* Gshin-rje Chos-rgyal.

Yamāntaka: *See* Gshin-rje gshed.

Yeti: Commonly known in the West as the "Abominable Snowman."

Yi-dam: Class of tutelary deities to which Mgon-po belongs.

Yogācāra (Skt.): Frequently referred to as the "Mind-only" school of Buddhism, it developed in the fourth century A.D. Proscribed in Tibet after the debate of 792-94. Also known as Ston-mun-pa.

Yol-ba: "Curtain," red in color, used to conceal the Abbot and monks before the beginning of the dances at Tengpoche monastery. Lowering of the *yol-ba* signifies that all is ready.

Yul-'khor-bsrung (Skt. Dhritarāshṭra): Guardian king in the east, he is also King of the Gandharvas, spirits that feed on fragrances.

Zhal-'bag: Generic term for masks, inclusive of all those used in Mani-rimdu.

Zhi-ba'i sbyin-sreg: Final day's ritual of Mani-rimdu, culminating in the destruction of all evil forces in Khumbu.

Zhwa-nag: "Black Hat," tantric masters possessed with magical powers who wear broad-brimmed black hats.

Zor-'cham: The last act of Mani-rimdu, a dance performed by two actors wearing "Black-Hats," or *Zhwa-nag.*

Zur-ra: *See* Zur-ra Ra-rgyan.

Zur-ra Ra-rgyan: A manifestation of Kun-tu bzang-po, Ādi-buddha of the Rnying-ma-pa sect.

Appendix II: Sequence of the Dances

THE DANCES of Mani-rimdu in order of their appearance at Tengpoche, Nepal, December 9, 1965:

1. *Gser-skyems.* Eight dancers who represent *Zhwa-nag,* tantric priests.
2. *Ging-pa.* Four dancers who represent the guardian kings of the four directions.
     North: Rnam-thos-sras (Skt. Kuvera)
     South: 'Phags-skyes-po (Skt. Virūḍhaka)
     East: Yul-'khor-bsrung (Skt. Dhritarāshṭra)
     West: Spyan-mig-bzang (Skt. Virūpāksha)
3. *Rdo-rje gro-lod.* One dancer who represents a fierce manifestation of Padmasambhava.
4. *Rnga-'cham.* Four drum-dancers who signify the Buddha's message of truth to the world.
5. *Mi-tshe-ring.* Two comic dancers who satirize Hwa-shang, the eighth-century Buddhist scholar from China.
6. *Dur-bdag.* Two *Dur-bdag,* also known as *Citipati,* who are assistants to the Lord of the Dead, and one *Zhwa-nag,* tantric priest.
7. *Chos-skyongs.* The "Eight Terrible Ones," known in Sanskrit as the *Dharmapāla,* who serve as protectors of the Buddhist religion:
     1. Lha-mo (Skt. Śrīdevī)
     2. Tshangs-pa dkar-po
     3. Beg-tse
     4. Gshin-rje chos-rgyal (Skt. Yama)
     5. Rnam-thos-sras (Skt. Kuvera)
     6. Mgon-po (Skt. Mahākāla)

175

7. Rta-mgrin (Skt. Hayagrīva)
8. Gshin-rje-gshed (Skt. Yamāntaka)

8. *Rtogs-ldan.* Two comic actors who satirize the actions of an Indian sadhu:
   1. Rtogs-ldan
   2. Bkra-shis don-grub

9. *Gnas-srung.* Two *Mi-nag,* local subordinate deities, and one *Zur-ra,* the master of the *Mi-nag.* Zur-ra is a local deity in Khumbu, probably the country god, Khumbu yul-lha.

10. *Mkha'-'gro-ma.* The five *Ḍākinī:*
    1. Sangs-rgyas mkha'-'gro-ma (Skt. Buddha Ḍākinī)
    2. Rin-chen mkha'-'gro-ma (Skt. Ratna Ḍākinī)
    3. Pad-ma mkha'-'gro-ma (Skt. Padma Ḍākinī)
    4. Sna-tshogs Rdo-rje mkha'-'gro-ma (Skt. Viśva Vajra Ḍākinī)
    5. Rdo-rje mkha'-'gro-ma (Skt. Vajra Ḍākinī)

11. *Lhag-ma Gnyis.* Two lesser *Ḍākinī* who are dressed as *Zhwa-nag* priests:
    1. Makaravaktrā
    2. Simhavaktrā

12. *Gri-'cham.* Four masked dancers who are lesser deities, converted *btsan* demons from Bon. They protect the people of Khumbu from disease, plagues, and accidents.

13. *Zor-'cham.* Two *Zhwa-nag* priests.

176

Bibliography

ARNOLD, EDWIN. *The Light of Asia; or, The Great Renunciation: Being the Life and Teaching of Gautama, Prince of India and Founder of Buddhism.* London: W. Heffner and Sons, 1883.

BEAL, SAMUEL (trans). *The Fo-Sho-Hing-Tsen-King: A Life of Buddha.* Vol. XIV of *The Sacred Books of the East,* ed. F. Max Müller. Oxford: Clarendon Press, 1886.

BELL, CHARLES. *The People of Tibet.* Oxford: Clarendon Press, 1928.

———. *The Religion of Tibet.* Oxford: Clarendon Press, 1931.

BISHOP, R. N. W. *Unknown Nepal.* London: Luzac, 1952.

BOWERS, FAUBION. *Japanese Theatre.* New York: Hill and Wang, 1952.

———. *Theatre in the East: A Survey of Asian Dance and Drama.* New York: Grove Press, 1956.

BROWNE, LEWIS (ed.). *The World's Great Scriptures: An Anthology of the Sacred Books of the Ten Principal Religions.* New York: Macmillan, 1961.

BUCHANAN, FRANCIS HAMILTON. *An Account of the Kingdom of Nepal, and of the Territories Annexed to This Dominion by the House of Gurkha.* Edinburgh: Archibald Constable, 1819.

BÜHLER, G. *The Laws of Manu.* Vol. XXV of *The Sacred Books of the East,* ed. F. Max Müller. Oxford: Clarendon Press, 1883.

BURTT, E. A. (ed.). *Teachings of the Compassionate Buddha.* New York: Mentor Books, 1955.

COOMARASWAMY, ANANDA K. *Buddha and the Gospel of Buddhism.* London: George C. Harrap, 1916.

———, and D. Gopala Krishnayya (trans.). *The Mirror of Gesture; Being the Abhina ya Darpana of Nandike-svara.* New York: Weyhe, 1936.

177

CORNFORD, FRANCIS MacDONALD, *The Origin of Attic Comedy*. Garden City, N.Y.: Doubleday, 1961.

CORRIGAN, ROBERT W., AND JAMES L. ROSENBERG (ed.). *The Art of the Theatre: A Critical Anthology of Drama*. San Francisco: Chandler, 1964.

DAVID-NEEL, ALEXANDRA. *Initiations and Initiates in Tibet*. London: Rider, 1958.

————. *Magic and Mystery in Tibet*. New York: University Books, 1958.

————. *My Journey to Lhasa*. New York: Harper and Brothers, 1927.

DAVIDS, THOMAS W. RHYS. *Buddhism: Its History and Literature*. 2nd ed.; New York: G. P. Putnam's Sons, 1907.

———— (trans.). *Buddhist Suttras*. Vol. XI of *The Sacred Books of The East*, ed. F. Max Müller. Oxford: Clarendon Press, 1881.

Dictionary of Philosophy, ed. DAGOBERT D. RUNES. 15th ed. rev.; Paterson, N.J.: Littlefield, Adams, 1963.

DOUGLAS, WILLIAM O. *Beyond the High Himalayas*. Garden City, N.Y.: Doubleday, 1952.

————. *Exploring the Himalaya*. New York: Random House, 1958.

DUNCAN, MARION H. *Customs and Superstitions of Tibetans*. London: The Mitre Press, 1964.

————. *Harvest Festival Dramas of Tibet*. Hong Kong: Orient Publishing Company, 1955.

————. *Yangtze and the Yak: Adventurous Trails In and Out of Tibet*. Ann Arbor, Mich.: Edwards Brothers, 1952.

ERNST, EARL. *Kabuki Theatre*. New York: Grove Press, 1956.

EVANS-WENTZ, W. Y. (ed.). *The Tibetan Book of the Dead: Or the After-Death Experiences on the Bardo Plane, According to Lama Kazi Dawa-Samdup's English Rendering*. New York: Oxford University Press, 1960.

————. *Tibet's Great Yogi Milarepa: A Biography from the Tibetan Being the Jetsun-Kahbum or Biographical History of Jetsun-Milarepa, According to the Late Lama Kazi Dawa-Samdup's English Rendering*. 2nd ed.; London: Oxford University Press, 1951.

FAUSBÖLL, V. (ed.). *Buddhist Birth Stories of Jātaka Tales: The Oldest Collection of Folk-lore Extant, Being the Jātakatthavannāna*, trans. Thomas W. Rhys Davis. London: Trübner, 1880.

FRAZER, JAMES GEORGE. *The Golden Bough: A Study in Magic and Religion*. Abridged ed.; New York: Macmillan, 1922.

FÜRER-HAIMENDORF, CHRISTOPH VON. *The Sherpas of Nepal: Buddhist Highlanders*. London: John Murray, 1964.

GARGI, BALWANT. *Theatre in India*. New York: Theatre Arts Books, 1962.

GETTY, ALICE. *The Gods of Northern Buddhism: Their History, Iconography and Progressive Evolution Through the Northern Buddhist Countries*, trans. J. Deniker. Rutland, Vt.: Charles E. Tuttle, 1962.

178

GILES, HERBERT A. *A History of Chinese Literature.* New York: D. Appleton, 1923.

GORDON, ANTOINETTE K. *The Iconography of Tibetan Lamaism.* Rev. ed.; Rutland, Vt.: Charles E. Tuttle, 1959.

———. *Tibetan Religious Art.* New York: Columbia University Press, 1962.

HAGEN, TONI. *Nepal: The Kingdom in the Himalayas.* Berne, Switzerland: Kummerly and Frey, 1961.

———, Gunter O. Dyhrenfurth, Christoph von Fürer-Haimendorf, and Erwin Schneider. *Mount Everest: Formation, Population and Exploration of the Everest Region,* trans. E. Noel Brown. London: Oxford University Press, 1963.

HAIGH, ARTHUR ELAM. *The Attic Theatre: A Description of the Stage and Theatre of the Athenians and the Dramatic Performances of Athens.* London: Oxford University Press, 1907.

HAMILTON, CLAYTON. *The Theory of the Theatre and Other Principles of Dramatic Criticism.* New York: Henry Holt, 1939.

HARDIE, NORMAN. *In Highest Nepal: Our Life Among the Sherpas.* London: George Allen and Unwin, 1957.

HAVEMEYER, LOOMIS. *The Drama of Savage Peoples.* New Haven: Yale University Press, 1916.

HEDIN, SVEN. *Trans-Himalaya: Discoveries and Adventures in Tibet,* Vol. I. New York: Macmillan, 1909.

HEWITT, BARNARD, J. F. FOSTER, AND MURIEL SIBELL WOLLE. *Play Production: Theory and Practice.* Chicago: J. B. Lippincott, 1959.

HILLARY, EDMUND. *Schoolhouse in the Clouds.* Garden City, N.Y.: Doubleday, 1964.

HOFFMANN, HELMUT. *The Religions of Tibet,* trans. Edward Fitzgerald. New York: Macmillan, 1961.

HOROWITZ, ERNEST PHILLIP. *Indian Theatre: A Brief Survey of the Sanskrit Drama.* London: Blackie, 1912.

HUC, EVARISTE RÉGIS. *Travels in Tartary, Tibet and China during the Years 1844-5-6,* trans. W. Hazlitt. 2 vols. London: Office of the National Illustrated Library, 1852.

HUNNINGHER, BENJAMIN. *The Origin of the Theatre.* New York: Hill and Wang, 1961.

JACQUOT, JEAN (ed.). *Les Théâtres d'Asie.* Paris: Centre National de la Recherche Scientifique, 1961.

KALVADOVA, SIS-VANIS. *The Chinese Theatre,* trans. Iris Urwin. London: Spring Books, 1957.

KEITH, ARTHUR BERRIEDALE. *Sanskrit Drama in Its Origin, Development, Theory and Practice.* London: Oxford University Press, 1924.

KNIGHT, E. F. *Where Three Empires Meet: A Narrative of Recent Travel in Kashmir, Western Tibet, Gilgit, and the Adjoining Countries.* London: Longmans, Green, 1897.

LAUTER, PAUL (ed.). *Theories of Comedy.* Garden City, N.Y.: Doubleday, 1964.

LÉVI, SYLVAIN. *Le Théâtre Indien.* Paris: Champion Press, 1890.

MACDONALD, DAVID. *The Land of the Lama: A Description of a Country of Contrasts and of Its Cheerful, Happy-go-lucky People of Hardy Nature and Curious Customs; Their Religion, Ways of Living, Trade, and Social Life.* London: Seeley, Service, 1929.

MACGOWAN, KENNETH, AND HERMAN ROSSE. *Masks and Demons.* London: M. Hopkin Son, 1924.

MAILLART, ELLA. *The Land of the Sherpas.* London: Hodder and Stoughton, 1955.

MALLA, K. M. *Nepal: A General Geographical Account.* Kathmandu, Nepal: Dharmodaya Sabha, 1956.

MANKAD, D. R. *Ancient Indian Theatre.* Anand, India: R. C. Patel, 1960.

MARAINI, FOSCO. *Secret Tibet,* trans. Eric Mosbacher. London: Hutchinson, 1952.

MARCHAIS, JACQUES. *Objects from the Tibetan Lamaist Collection of Jacques Marchais.* New York: Comet Press, 1941.

MASON, KENNETH. *Abode of Snow: A History of Himalayan Exploration and Mountaineering.* New York: E. P. Dutton, 1955.

MORRISON, MILLICENT H. (ed. and trans.). *Ti-me-kun-dan, Prince of Buddhist Benevolence.* (Wisdom of the East Series, ed. L. Crammer-Bung and S. A. Kapadia.) New York: E. P. Dutton, 1925.

NEBESKY-WOJKOWITZ, RENÉ DE. *Oracles and Demons of Tibet: The Cult and Iconography of the Tibetan Protective Deities.* The Hague: Mouton, 1956.

Nepal: Birth-place of Buddha. Rangoon, Burma: Dharmodaya Sabha, 1954.

NEPALI, GOPAL SINGH. *The Newars: An Ethno-Sociological Study of a Himalayan Community.* Bombay: United Asia Publications, 1965.

NICOLL, ALLARDYCE. *The Theatre and Dramatic Theory.* New York: Barnes and Noble, 1962.

NOEL, J. B. L. *Through Tibet to Everest.* London: Edward Arnold, 1931.

NORBU, THUBTEN JIGME. *Tibet Is My Country: As Told to Heinrich Harrer,* trans. by Edward Fitzgerald. London: Rupert Hart-Davis, 1960.

OLDFIELD, HENRY AMBROSE. *Sketches from Nipal: Historical and Descriptive, with Anecdotes of the Court Life and Wild Sports of the Country in the Time of Maharaja Jung Bahadur, G. C. B., to which Is Added an Essay on Nepalese Buddhism, and Illustrations of Religious Monuments, Architecture, and Scenery from the Author's Own Drawings.* London: W. H. Allen, 1880.

180

PALLIS, MARCO. *Peaks and Lamas*. London: Readers Union, 1948.

PRADHAN, BHAIRAB BAHADUR. *Buddhism in Medieval Nepal*. Kathmandu, Nepal: Dharmodaya Sabha, n.d.

RATNA, KULADHARMA. *Buddhism and Nepal*. Kathmandu, Nepal: Dharmodaya Sabha, 1958.

REGMI, D. R. *Ancient Nepal*. Calcutta: K. L. Mukhopadhyay, 1960.

———. *Modern Nepal: Rise and Growth in the Eighteenth Century*. Calcutta: K. L. Mukhopadhyay, 1961.

REICHELT, KARL LUDWIG. *Truth and Tradition in Chinese Buddhism: A Study of Chinese Buddhism*, ed. H. T. Hidgkin; trans. Kathrina Van Wagenen Bugge. 4th rev. ed.; Shanghai: Commercial Press, 1934.

RICHARDSON, H. E. *A Short History of Tibet*. New York: E. P. Dutton, 1962.

RIDGEWAY, WILLIAM. *The Drama and Dramatic Dances of Non-European Races: In Special Reference to the Origin of Greek Tragedy*. London: Cambridge University Press, 1915.

ROCKHILL, WILLIAM WOODVILLE. *The Land of the Lamas: Notes of a Journey Through China, Mongolia, and Tibet*. New York: The Century Company, 1891.

ROSENTHAL, ETHEL. *The Story of Indian Music and Its Instruments: A Study of the Present and a Record of the Past.* London: William Reeves, n.d.

ROWLAND, BENJAMIN. *The Evolution of the Buddha Image*. New York: Book Craft, 1963.

SARATCHANDRA, E. R. *The Sinhalese Folk Play and the Modern Stage*. Colombo, Ceylon: Daily News Press Lake House, 1953.

SCOTT, A. C. *The Classical Theatre of China*. London: George Allen and Unwin, 1957.

———. *An Introduction to the Chinese Theatre*. New York: Theatre Arts Books, 1959.

SHEN TSUNG-LIEN AND LIU SHEN-CHI. *Tibet and the Tibetans*. Stanford, Calif.: Stanford University Press, 1953.

SHRESTHA, CHANGRA BAHADUR. *Buddhist Geography of Ancient Nepal*. Kathmandu, Nepal: Dharmodaya Sabha, 1956.

SNELLGROVE, DAVID L. *Buddhist Himalaya: Travels and Studies in Quest of the Origins and Nature of Tibetan Religion*. Oxford: Bruno Cassirer, 1957.

———. *Himalayan Pilgrimage: A Study of Tibetan Religion by a Traveller Through Western Nepal*. Oxford: Bruno Cassirer, 1961.

SOUTHERN, RICHARD. *The Seven Ages of the Theatre*. New York: Hill and Wang, 1963.

181

SPATE, O. H. K. *India and Pakistan: A General and Regional Geography.* New York: E. P. Dutton, 1954.

STONOR, CHARLES. *The Sherpa and the Snowman.* London: Hollis and Carter, 1955.

SUZUKI, D. T. (trans.). *Ashvaghosha's Discourse on the Awakening of Faith in the Mahayana.* Chicago: Open Court Publishing Company, 1900.

————. *Outlines of Mahayana Buddhism.* London: Luzac, 1907.

TELANG, KASHINATH TRIMBAK (trans.). *The Bagavadgita with Sanatsugatiya and the Anugita.* Vol. VIII of *The Sacred Books of the East,* ed. F. Max Müller. 2nd ed.; Oxford: Clarendon Press, 1898.

THOMAS, EDWARD J. *The History of Buddhist Thought.* New York: Barnes and Noble, 1951.

TUCCI, GIUSEPPE. *Nepal: The Discovery of the Malla,* trans. Lovett Edwards. London: George Allen and Unwin, 1962.

WADDELL, L. AUSTINE. *The Buddhism of Tibet or Lamaism: With Its Mystic Cults, Symbolism and Mythology, and in Its Relation to Indian Buddhism.* Cambridge: W. Heffner and Sons, 1894.

WINTERNITZ, M. *A General Index to the Names and Subject-Matter of the Sacred Books of the East.* Vol. L of *The Sacred Books of the East,* ed. F. Max Müller. Oxford: Clarendon Press, 1910.

WOOLF, H. I. (trans.). *Three Tibetan Mysteries: Tchrimekunden, Nansal, Djroazanmo: As Performed in the Tibetan Monasteries.* New York: E. P. Dutton, n.d.

WRIGHT, DANIEL (ed.). *History of Nepal,* trans. Mumski Shew Shunker Singh and Pandit Sri Gunanand. Calcutta: Susil Gupta, 1958.

YAJNIK, RAMANLAL KANAIYALAL. *Indian Theatre: Its Origins and Its Later Developments Under European Influences.* New York: E. P. Dutton, 1934.

PERIODICALS AND NEWSPAPERS

BROUGH, JOHN. "Nepalese Buddhist Rituals," *Bulletin of the School of Oriental and African Studies,* XII, Parts 3 and 4 (1948), 688-76.

BROWN, P. "Arts of Nepal," *Asiatic Review,* XXXIV (January, 1938), 1-8.

BULLOUGH, EDWARD. "Psychical Distance as a Factor in Art and an Aesthetic Principle," *British Journal of Psychology,* V (1912), 87-98.

BUSHELL, S. W. "Early History of Tibet from Chinese Sources," *Journal of the Royal Asiatic Society,* XII (1880), 435-541.

CHAMBERS, J. WHEATON. "Devil Dancers of the Black Temple," *Travel,* XXXII, No. 5 (March, 1919), 11-14.

--⊰ Bibliography ⊱--

CHANG KUNG. "On Tibetan Poetry," *Central Asiatic Journal*, II, No. 2 (1956), 129-39.

DELZA, SOPHIA. "The Classic Chinese Theatre," *Journal of Aesthetics and Art Criticism*, XV, No. 2 (December, 1956), 181-96.

———. "The Dance in the Chinese Theatre," *Journal of Aesthetics and Art Criticism*, XVI, No. 4 (June, 1958), 437-52.

DUNCAN, MARION H. "The Tibetan Drama," *China Journal*, XVII, No. 3 (September, 1932), 105-11.

DUTT, NALINAKSHA. "Tantric Buddhism," *Bulletin of Tibetology*, I, No. 2 (October, 1964), 5-16.

EMROCH, EDNA. "Dance of the Orient: A General Survey of the Philosophy and Art of the Dance in the East," *American Dancer*, X (January, 1937), 24-26.

FÜRER-HAIMENDORF, CHRISTOPH VON. "Between the Tree-Line and the Snow: The Hardy Sherpas of the Everest Region," *Illustrated London News*, July 30, 1955, p. 1.

———. "Elements of Newar Social Structure," *Journal of the Royal Anthropological Institute*, LXXXVI, Part 2 (1956), 15-38.

———. "Ethnographic Notes on the Tamangs of Nepal," *Eastern Anthropologist*, IX (March-August, 1956), 166-77.

———. "Hardy Himalayan Highlanders: The Sherpas of Eastern Nepal...," *Illustrated London News*, April 23, 1955, pp. 736-37.

———. "The Interrelations of Caste and Ethnic Groups in Nepal," *Bulletin of the Oriental and African Studies*, XX (1957), 243-60.

———. "Religious Life in a Nursery of Climbers: A Buddhist Revival in the Shadow of Everest," *Illustrated London News*, November 29, 1958, pp. 940-43.

GOVINDA, LAMA AMAGARIKA. "Principles of Buddhist Tantrism," *Bulletin of Tibetology*, II, No. 1 (March, 1956), 9-16.

HAGEN, TONI. "Himalayan Wonderland," *United National Review*, V (January, 1959), 28-31.

HILLARY, EDMUND. "Beyond Everest," *National Geographic Magazine*, CVIII (November, 1955), 579-610.

JERSTAD, LUTHER. "Buddhist Proselytization in the Tibetan Drama, *Drowazangmo*," *Western Speech*, XXXI, No. 4 (Summer, 1967), 199-210.

KOLMAS, J. "Ch'am, the Miming Dances of Tibet," *New Orient*, III (October, 1962), 145.

LIGHTFOOT, LOUISE. "In Search of India's Most Ancient Dance," *Dancing Times* (March, 1939), pp. 742-45.

MENAGH, H. B. "The Question of Primitive Origins," *Educational Theatre Journal*, XV, No. 3 (October, 1963), 236-40.

183

MIGOT, ANDRÉ. "Notes sur le Théâtre Tibetain," *Revue d'Historie du Théâtre*, X, No. 1 (1958), 9-20.

PIERRE, DORATHI BOCK. "Dance Evolution," *Education Dance*, I (February, 1939), 10-12.

REGMI, D. R. "Early Nepal," *The New Review*, XXX (November, 1949), 322-31; XXXI (February, 1950), 85-95.

ROCKHILL, WILLIAM WOODVILLE. "Tibet: A Geographical, Ethnographical, and Historical Sketch, Derived from Chinese Sources," *Journal of the Royal Asiatic Society of Great Britian and Ireland*, No. 4 (1891), pp. 1-291.

"Sherpa Religious Rites," *Illustrated London News*, April 23, 1955, p. 739.

SMYTH, F. S. "Devil Dancers of the Himalaya," *Strand Magazine* (London) (November, 1930), pp. 504-14.

TENDZIN, THUBTEN. "Considerations on Tantric Spirituality," *Bulletin of Tibetology*, II, No. 2 (August, 1965), 17-30.

TOLSTOY, I. "Across Tibet from India to China," *National Geographic Magazine*, XC (August, 1946), 169-222.

WOODCOCK, GEORGE. "The Theocrats of Tibet," *History Today*, XV, No. 2 (February, 1965), 87-98.

WYLIE, TURRELL V. "A Standard System of Tibetan Transcription," *Harvard Journal of Asiatic Studies*, XXII (December, 1959), 261-67.

OTHER SOURCES

ABBOT OF KEROK GOMBA. Thami, Nepal. Personal interview. December 18, 1965.

ABBOT OF TENGPOCHE MONASTERY. Tengpoche, Nepal. Personal interviews. May 27, 1963; December 6-30, 1965.

BALLINGER, THOMAS O. "Drawings by Nepalese Children: Notes on Content, Symbolism, Spatial Concepts and Directional Frequency. A Cross-Cultural Consideration." Unpublished paper, Eugene, Oregon, 1966.

DUNCAN, MARION H. Alexandria, Virginia. Personal interviews with Mr. Duncan, sixteen-year resident in Tibet and author of *Harvest Festival Dramas of Tibet*. December 10-12, 1963.

MONKS AND LAMAS, SWYAMBUNATH SHRINE. Kathmandu, Nepal. Personal interviews. November 20, 1965.

REGENT OF THAMI MONASTERY. Thami, Nepal. Personal interview. December 15, 1965.

SHERPAS AND TIBETAN REFUGEES. Nepal. Personal interviews. February 13–July 1, 1963; September 1, 1965–February 5, 1966.

SURKHANG, RIMSHI L. Seattle, Washington. Personal interviews with Mr. Surkhang, a Tibetan refugee now living in Seattle. Mr. Surkhang was a fourth-rank government official in Lhasa, Tibet, prior to the Chinese takeover. May 22-25, 1966.

TENZING, LAKPA. Tengpoche Monastery, Nepal. Personal interviews with Mr. Tenzing, a monk who resides on the monastic grounds of Tengpoche. December 6-30, 1965.

TENZING, NIMA. Nepal. Personal interviews with Mr. Tenzing, personal companion and interpreter. February 13–July 1, 1963; October 30, 1965–February 10, 1966; November 5, 1967–January 10, 1968.

WYLIE, TURRELL V. Seattle, Washington. Personal interviews with Mr. Wylie, Professor of Asian Languages and Literature at the University of Washington. April 15, 1966; May 22, 1966; June 24, 1966.

185

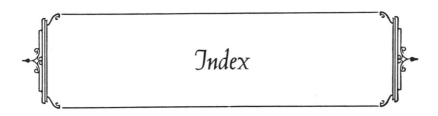

Index

Zhal-'bag: in *Ging-pa,* 120, 121; in *Rdo-rje gro-lod,* 124; in *Mi-tshe-ring,* 130-31; in *Dur-bdag,* 136; in *Chos-skyongs,* 141-46; in *Rtogs-ldan,* 148; of Zur-ra in *Gnas-srung,* 157; in *Lhag-ma Gnyis,* 159; in *Gri-'cham,* 160

Zhi-ba'i sbyin-sreg, 162
Zhwa-nag: Black Hat tantric priests, 116, 118, 120, 159, 161; in *Dur-bdag,* 138, 139, 140
Zor-'cham, 161-62
Zur-ra, 155, 156
Zur-ra Ra-rgyan, 115, 116